DIGITAL HARM AND INTERNATIONAL CRIMINAL LAW

This book examines the promises and perils of pursuing accountability for digital harms under international criminal law (ICL).

Technology can be used as a new method of perpetrating existing international crimes, but it can also inflict novel harms that may only be adequately addressed by the creation of a new offence.

This book analyses how harm has been understood for core international crimes and how digital harms (such as online hate speech and disinformation, sharing footage of crimes online, mass surveillance, and online sexual violence) can be encompassed within definitions of those crimes. It considers theories of criminalisation to determine why digital harms should be criminalised, and explores relevant challenges, such as whether digital harms can meet the gravity threshold under ICL.

Further, obstacles to prosecuting digital harms at international criminal courts and tribunals (ICCTs) are considered, including jurisdiction, digital evidence concerns, and cooperation between ICCTs and States, private companies, and civil society. The book concludes with two case studies—the beheading of American journalist James Foley by ISIS, which was circulated online, and the digital surveillance used against the Uyghur population in Xinjiang, China—to illustrate how digital harms may be criminalised and prosecuted in practice.

Ultimately, the book argues that digital harms are like the harms traditionally encompassed by international crimes, and that these harms should be criminalised to provide justice to victims. As technology will continue to develop and serve as a vehicle for an increasing array of harms, accounting for digital harm should be an issue at the forefront of ICL.

Digital Harm and International Criminal Law

Sarah Zarmsky

• HART •
OXFORD • LONDON • NEW YORK • NEW DELHI • SYDNEY

HART PUBLISHING
Bloomsbury Publishing Plc
Kemp House, Chawley Park, Cumnor Hill, Oxford, OX2 9PH, UK
1385 Broadway, New York, NY 10018, USA
Bloomsbury Publishing Ireland Limited, 29 Earlsfort Terrace, Dublin 2, D02 AY28, Ireland

HART PUBLISHING, the Hart/Stag logo, BLOOMSBURY and the Diana logo are trademarks of Bloomsbury Publishing Plc

First published in Great Britain 2026

1

A catalogue record for this book is available from the British Library.

A catalogue record for this book is available from the Library of Congress.

ISBN: HB: 978-1-50999-773-2
ePDF: 978-1-50999-775-6
ePub: 978-1-50999-774-9

Typeset by Amnet

For product safety related questions contact productsafety@bloomsbury.com

To find out more about our authors and books visit www.hartpublishing.co.uk. Here you will find extracts, author information, details of forthcoming events and the option to sign up for our newsletters.

For my parents, Roxanne and Steven.

ACKNOWLEDGEMENTS

Thank you to all of those who supported the development of this book. In particular, thank you to Carla Ferstman and Daragh Murray for your invaluable guidance throughout my PhD and afterwards – I am so lucky to know and learn from you both. Thank you also to friends, mentors, and colleagues who provided advice, feedback, and encouragement over the last years writing this book, especially (and in no particular order) Emma Irving, Alexa Koenig, Cheryl Lawther, Aoife O'Donoghue, Brianne McGonigle Leyh, Fionnuala Ní Aoláin, Yvonne McDermott Rees, Judy Mionki, Sabina Garahan, Mitchell Lennan, Vanessa Topp, Zuzanna Wojciak, Franka Pues, Stefania di Stefano, Cris van Eijk, Henning Lahmann, Barrie Sander, and Joris van de Riet. There are many others who have shaped my academic and personal journey during this time, including my peers and colleagues at the University of Essex Human Rights Centre and Queen's University Belfast School of Law. Last but not least, thank you to my friends and family for continuing to support me, and to the best boys, Kovu, Jagger, and Bowie.

TABLE OF CONTENTS

1

Introduction

I. Research Background and Questions

Historically, international criminal law (ICL) has been mainly concerned with violent physical crime – the images that come to mind when one imagines an 'international crime' are those of the Holocaust or the genocides in Rwanda and the former Yugoslavia, or more recently the bombing and destruction caused by the Russian invasion of Ukraine or Israeli attacks on Gaza. While these physical harms are undoubtedly important and worthy of attention, other harms, such as psychological suffering or environmental damage, are also significant and cause grave harm to victims. Progressively, ICL has begun to recognise these other types of harms, such as through the mental components of torture and genocide, or the proposed addition of ecocide as a crime under the Rome Statute of the International Criminal Court (ICC).[1] This signifies ICL's capacity to evolve to accommodate novel forms of harm.

However, another novel form of harm has yet to be addressed by ICL frameworks and jurisprudence at international criminal courts and tribunals (ICCTs): digital harm. While the meaning of digital harm and the ways it can manifest will be considered in detail in chapter four, put simply, the term is used in this book to describe harm perpetrated using digital technologies. To date, digital harm has not been explored explicitly in relation to ICL, and the term has not been widely used in legal literature.[2] Digital harm, as used in this book, also encompasses 'online harm', which refers to harms specifically perpetrated through the internet, which has been more widely discussed in relation to the law, and even to international law and human rights.[3] For the purposes of this book, I use the label 'digital harm'

[1] 'Ecocide Definition, Commentary and Core Text' (Stop Ecocide, June 2021) www.stopecocide.earth/expert-drafting-panel.

[2] Dette has considered digital harm that can be caused using technology in humanitarian contexts, and Kelly has considered the legal responses to digital harms relating to public health in New Zealand; R Dette, 'Do No Digital Harm: Mitigating Technology Risks in Humanitarian Contexts' in S Hostettler et al (eds), *Technologies for Development* (Springer, 2018) 11–29; O Kelly, 'New Horizons or Business as Usual? New Zealand's Medico-Legal Response to Digital Harm' (2023) 12 *Laws* 32. To my knowledge, digital harm has not been used in literature pertaining to international law.

[3] For example, 'online harm' has been used to describe harms perpetrated through the internet in domestic legislation, such as the Online Harms White Paper and corresponding Online Safety Act in the United Kingdom; Department for Digital, Culture, Media & Sport, 'Online Harms White Paper' (15 December 2020) www.gov.uk/government/consultations/online-harms-white-paper/online-harms-white-paper; Online Safety Act (2023). Online harms have also been considered in relation

because it allows for consideration not only of online harms, but of those perpetrated through technologies other than the internet.[4]

This book comes following the recent launch of the ICC Office of the Prosecutor (OTP)'s new Policy on Cyber-Enabled Crimes under the Rome Statute (December 2025).[5] This policy will be considered in detail in chapter five, and is a welcome and necessary addition to the existing OTP policies due to the clarifications it will bring during prosecutions of 'cyber-enabled' crimes.[6] However, the Policy does not consider examples of 'cyber-enabled' crimes or the challenges of their criminalisation and prosecution in great detail, and is limited to the ICC. This book is therefore broader in scope (focusing on ICL more generally and other ICCTs besides the ICC), and expands upon the points raised in the Policy (in addition to others).

Digital harms with a nexus to the perpetration of international crimes have increased dramatically in recent years as technology has developed. For instance, terrorist organisations such as ISIL have used social media to spread fear and propaganda to a global audience, such as through sharing videos of public executions.[7] In addition, online 'marketplaces' have been used to facilitate sexual slavery and human trafficking, such as in the context of the Yazidi genocide.[8] Moreover, the development of artificial intelligence (AI) technologies such as facial recognition and other targeting tools has enabled oppressive regimes to maintain power over

---

to social media platform governance and online hate speech, and human rights responses to those harms; see for example RF Jørgensen (ed), *Human Rights in the Age of Platforms* (MIT Press, 2019); T Keipi et al, *Online Hate and Harmful Content* (Routledge, 2017); L Price, 'Platform Responsibility for Online Harms: Towards a Duty of Care for Online Hazards' (2022) 13 *Journal of Media Law* 238–61; A Beduschi, 'Regulatory Approaches to Online Harms and Human Rights: Three Case Studies' (2022) *Geneva Academy Working Papers*. I have previously explored accountability for online harms under ICL: S Zarmsky, 'Is International Criminal Law Ready to Accommodate Online Harm? Challenges and Opportunities' (2024) 22 *Journal of International Criminal Justice* 169–84.

[4] Notably, the terms 'digital harm' and 'online harm' are used instead of digital or online 'acts' because 'harm' is the term colloquially used in legislation and scholarship (see the above footnote). In addition, 'harm' carries the association of the negative consequences of certain activities, which emphasises that the harms considered may not yet be crimes but should be thought of similarly in terms of their wrongness. Further, the term 'harm' allows for a broader scope of activities to be encompassed that goes beyond individual actions.

[5] Office of the Prosecutor, Policy on Cyber-Enabled Crimes Under the Rome Statute (December 2025).

[6] I use the term 'digital harms' as opposed to 'cyber-enabled crimes' for two reasons: (1) the word 'digital', in my view, more clearly encompasses technologies that work both online and offline – although this is clarified in the Policy, the definition of 'cyber' is closely linked to computers and the Internet, and therefore a more narrow term than 'digital' (see for instance the Oxford English Dictionary: 'of, relating to, or involving (the culture of) computers, virtual reality, or the internet' or Merriam-Webster Dictionary: 'of, relating to, or involving computers or computer networks (such as the Internet)'; and (2) 'harm' is the colloquial term used in this area of research to signify the wrongfulness of acts that may not yet legally be crimes.

[7] A Barr and A Herfroy-Mischler, 'ISIL's Execution Videos: Audience Segmentation and Terrorist Communication in the Digital Age' (2017) 41 *Studies in Conflict & Terrorism* 946–67; S Molin Friis, '"Beyond Anything We Have Ever Seen": Beheading Videos and the Visibility of Violence in the War against ISIS' (2015) 91 *International Affairs* 725–46.

[8] A Koenig and U Egan, 'Power and Privilege: Investigating Sexual Violence with Digital Open Source Information' (2021) 19 *Journal of International Criminal Justice* 55–84.

their populations and monitor minorities, leading to arbitrary arrests and detentions, police intimidation, and the overall persecution of marginalised groups.[9]

Yet, although the digital harms like those mentioned above are increasingly common and severe, they are presently not properly addressed by ICL, as they are typically sidelined by 'traditional' (and perhaps arguably outdated) understandings of core international crimes and described as more of an afterthought. In this book, I argue that digital harms have progressed to a level of seriousness that warrant their recognition as international crimes in their own right, whether that be through interpreting the elements of existing offences to encompass digital harms, or through the potential development of an entirely new crime. This book is therefore an innovative, original, and much needed contribution to the field as it questions how ICL may be interpreted and expanded in a way that accommodates novel forms of harm that have come to fruition in a digital era, and will only continue to rapidly evolve with technological developments. In doing so, this book lays the groundwork for 'catching the law up' to modern times and recognising the seriousness of digital harm and its effects on victims, which is critical for ICL to be able to fulfil two of its main goals of providing meaningful justice to victims and establishing a truthful historical record.

Notably, technology has the potential to both progress the international criminal justice project and enable new ways to infringe upon human rights and perpetrate international crimes. Much of the research to date has focused on the former, such as how the digitisation of court documents onto databases can make for more efficient and publicly accessible ICL trials,[10] or how digital information like social media posts and satellite imagery can be used as evidence of international crimes.[11] In terms of the latter, the literature has taken mainly either a rights-based approach (such as by examining how surveillance technology infringes upon the right to privacy or freedom of expression),[12] or one that focuses on the law of armed conflict (such as the legality of cyber-attacks or the use of artificial intelligence in military technologies).[13]

[9] See also K Hao and H Swart, 'South Africa's private surveillance machine is fuelling a digital apartheid' (MIT Technology Review, 19 April 2022) www.technologyreview.com/2022/04/19/1049996/south-africa-ai-surveillance-digital-apartheid/; Amnesty International, 'Automated Apartheid: How Facial Recognition Fragments, Segregates and Controls Palestinians in the OPT' (2 May 2023) www.amnesty.org/en/documents/mde15/6701/2023/en/; O Zahzah, 'Digital apartheid: Palestinians being silenced on social media' (13 May 2021, Aljazeera) www.aljazeera.com/opinions/2021/5/13/social-media-companies-are-trying-to-silence-palestinian-voices.

[10] M Bergsmo, O Bekou and A Jones, 'New Technologies in Criminal Justice for Core International Crimes: The ICC Legal Tools Project' (2010) 10 *Human Rights Law Review* 715–29.

[11] S Dubberley, A Koenig and D Murray (eds), *Digital Witness: Using Open Source Information for Human Rights Investigation, Documentation, and Accountability* (OUP, 2019); see also E Irving, A Koenig, Y McDermott and D Murray (eds), *Special Issue: New Technologies and the Investigations of International Crimes* (2021) 19(1) *Journal of International Criminal Justice.*

[12] See E Watt, 'The Right to Privacy and the Future of Mass Surveillance' (2017) 21 *International Journal of Human Rights* 773–99; D Murray et al, 'The Chilling Effects of Surveillance and Human Rights: Insights from Qualitative Research in Uganda and Zimbabwe' (2023) *Journal of Human Rights Practice* 1–16.

[13] See L Gisel, T Rodenhäuser and K Dörmann, 'Twenty Years On: International Humanitarian

This book is the first of its kind to consider holistically how technology-facilitated 'digital harms' may be accommodated by ICL frameworks. The overall research question is therefore: how can ICL accommodate digital harm? To answer this, the book addresses the following sub-questions:

(1) What is digital harm and how is it similar or different to the types of harm recognised by core international crimes?
(2) What are the reasons digital harm should be criminalised under ICL?
(3) How should digital harm be criminalised (ie as part of an existing offence, or with the creation of an entirely new crime)?
(4) What are the challenges that may arise if digital harms are criminalised and adjudicated at ICCTs, and how might those challenges be overcome?

II. Book Structure and Methods

This book is divided into seven substantive chapters that employ doctrinal, theoretical, and qualitative empirical research methods. Chapter two examines the meaning of 'harm', drawing from both philosophical theories of harm and how harm has been defined in ICL literature and jurisprudence. It surveys theories of harm from several angles, including those that define harm in terms of impact on personal liberty,[14] comparative approaches to harm,[15] and contemporary approaches such as feminist theories of harm.[16] The chapter then explores different types of harm recognised by those theories, including harm to individuals, group harm, and societal or transboundary harm. This analysis is important to understand how digital harms might be similar or different to traditional conceptions of harm, which will inform a consideration of how those harms might fit into existing ICL frameworks in subsequent chapters.

Chapter three explores how harm has been reflected by ICL frameworks and engages in a comparative exercise, evaluating the digital harms alongside similar harms that have been encompassed by core ICL crimes, including genocide,

Law and the Protection of Civilians Against the Effects of Cyber Operations During Armed Conflicts' (2020) *International Review of the Red Cross* 287–334; AL Schuller, 'At the Crossroads of Control: The Intersection of Artificial Intelligence in Autonomous Weapon Systems with International Humanitarian Law' (2017) 8 *Harvard National Security Journal* 379–425; TK Woodcock, 'Human/Machine(-Learning) Interactions, Human Agency and the International Humanitarian Law Proportionality Standard' (2023) 38 *Global Society* 100–21.

[14] See JS Mill, *On Liberty* (1859); J Raz, *The Morality of Freedom* (OUP, 1986); J Feinberg, *Harmless Wrongdoing – The Moral Limits of the Criminal Law* (OUP, 1990).

[15] See EH Morreim, 'The Concept of Harm Reconceived: A Different Look at Wrongful Life' (1988) 7 *Law and Philosophy* 3–33; TS Petersen, *Why Criminalize? New Perspectives on Normative Principles of Criminalization* (Vol 134, Springer Law and Philosophy Library, 2020).

[16] See F Ní Aoláin, 'Exploring a Feminist Theory of Harm in the Context of Conflicted and Post-Conflict Societies' (2009) 35 *Queen's Law Journal* 219; C McGlynn et al, '"It's Torture for the Soul": The Harms of Image-Based Sexual Abuse' (2021) 30 *Social and Legal Studies* 541–62.

crimes against humanity, and war crimes, to assess how digital harms might fit into ICL frameworks in the next chapter (i.e., as an aggravating factor at sentencing, a new mode of commission of an existing crime, or as an entirely new crime). In some cases, where the digital harm has already been prosecuted as an international crime in domestic jurisdictions, those cases are analysed for their relevance to potential future prosecutions at ICCTs. Those cases were found through research using NGO reports and news articles where the cases were mentioned,[17] and through the author's previous familiarity with the ongoing trials after years in the field of digital open source investigations. Embarking on this comparative and analogical exercise with existing international crimes and case law allows for similarities and differences between 'old' and 'new' forms of harm to come to light, which can help to more easily discern where digital harm can be accommodated by existing law or otherwise where the gaps lie.

Chapter four then offers a typology of digital harm, exploring the ways the harms discussed in chapter two may be inflicted through digital technologies. It then identifies four categories of digital harm with potential relevance to the perpetration of international crimes: mass digital surveillance, the spread of hate speech and disinformation, sharing footage of crimes online, and online sexual violence. These categories were chosen because of their similarity to existing international crimes at their root, through factors such as a potential nexus to armed conflict, their known perpetration by non-State and terrorist groups, or their potential to be considered 'grave' enough in nature and scale to constitute international crimes.

Taking the findings of chapter four into account, chapter five then explores how digital harms may be criminalised under ICL. It first presents the different theories of criminalisation common to international law literature, including the harm principle, punishment theories (ie deterrence, retribution), and expressivism, to answer the question of why harms are criminalised. In this regard, the chapter concludes that the reasons for criminalising existing international crimes can be applied to digital harms. For instance, concerning the harm principle, as there are clear parallels between the harm of traditional international crimes recognised by ICL jurisprudence and digital harms, digital harms can (and should) be criminalised to prevent further harms to victims. Regarding punishment, it has been demonstrated through ICL jurisprudence that deterrence and retribution are two well-recognised reasons for international criminalisation, which could be applied to deter or proportionately punish perpetrators of digital harm with a nexus to the perpetration of international crimes. Further, in terms of sending a message, the chapter argues that criminalising digital harm would serve the expressivist

[17] For example, most of the domestic war crimes cases considered in this book can be found in Eurojust, 'Prosecuting war crimes of outrage upon personal dignity based on evidence from open sources - Legal framework and recent developments in the Member States of the European Union' (2018) www.eurojust.europa.eu/sites/default/files/Partners/Genocide/2018-02_Prosecuting-war-crimes-based-on-evidence-from-open-sources_EN.pdf.

function of emphasising that digital harms are severe enough for international prosecution and are worthy of concern from the international community.

Chapter five finishes with a discussion of pathways to criminalisation under international law, including through the development of internal policy documents such as the OTP Policy on Cyber-Enabled Crimes Under the Rome Statute,[18] or amendments to the Rome Statute to include more means of perpetration of existing crimes (such as an additional war crime or crime against humanity), or an entirely new crime. This analysis is particularly important because it explains both *why* and *how* digital harms can be criminalised under ICL, taking into account the obstacles that may be faced by practitioners and providing solutions to overcome them. This elevates this book from a theoretical exercise to one that can provide guidance on real-world applications of its findings, making it a particularly meaningful addition to the wider field of study.

Chapter six explores how the challenges that would be faced by ICCTs should they prosecute digital harm. These include issues with admissibility, including gravity and jurisdiction (given that digital harms may be committed in cyberspace and not on any physical territory), challenges ICCTs will have to address internally (including increasing their technological capacity, security, and expertise), and challenges that will need to be addressed with external parties (namely cooperation with States, private corporations, and civil society). This chapter offers an original analysis of jurisdiction of over acts committed in cyberspace, considering the issue from multiple angles (personal, territorial, and universal jurisdiction) which will be a paramount issue to overcome should digital harms be prosecuted at ICCTs. Further, drawing upon existing literature on issues pertaining to digital evidence, it also provides a comprehensive discussion of how ICCTs can increase their technological capacity and security internally to prepare for prosecutions of digital harms. Last, the chapter addresses the challenges associated with cooperation between ICCTs and States or other external partners, specifically tailoring this analysis to how cooperation can be fostered to prosecute international crimes in a digital era. Holistically, these three sections provide a 'roadmap' for navigating the prosecution of digital harms at ICCTs across a wide range of issues, which will be essential for practitioners to consider should digital harms be criminalised under ICL.

This book cumulates in chapter seven, where the theory developed throughout the book for how digital harms may be accommodated by ICL is applied in two different case studies representing two different types of digital harm – sharing footage of crimes online and mass digital surveillance. The first case study considers the murder of United States journalist James Foley, whose beheading was filmed and shared by ISIS to social media. The second case study analyses the use of digital surveillance methods by the Chinese government against the Uyghur population in Xinjiang. These case studies are based largely on ICC procedure and illustrate how digital harms may be criminalised, investigated, and prosecuted in

[18] Office of the Prosecutor (n 5).

practice. The case study approach used in chapter seven is completely novel for the current field of research, as this comprehensive of an analysis tailored to real-world examples of digital harms has not been conducted previously. Through exploring all relevant issues for each case study – from jurisdiction, to how the harms meet the elements of crimes, to how the harms could be considered of sufficient gravity, amongst other challenges – this chapter provides original and much needed guidance for how two different digital harms can be effectively criminalised and prosecuted at an ICCT.

III. Conclusions

This book concludes that the use of technology often exacerbates traditional forms of violence, and that those digital harms are grave enough to constitute their own crimes under ICL. This is because, in relation to the first research question listed above, the differences between 'digital' and 'traditional' ICL harms can be summarised in two ways: (1) digital harm is less often physical given the nature of the digital space and can be inflicted remotely and/or anonymously; and (2) digital harm can be particularly invasive because perpetrators can access victims at almost any time and place. The findings of this book will demonstrate that as technology has evolved, digital harms have become severe enough to warrant criminalisation under ICL, and that those harms need to be recognised to deliver justice to victims.

However, criminalisation of digital harm will not be an easy process – for instance, some forms of digital harm may be easier to accommodate with existing ICL frameworks than others, which may require the development of new offences. In addition, there will be challenges should digital harm be criminalised and adjudicated at ICCTs. For example, concerning the viability of prosecution of digital harm, factors such as needing to ensure digital evidence is not generated by artificial intelligence, the potential of perpetrators being anonymous online, or technology companies not willing to hand over evidence to international courts may make prosecuting digital harm difficult. Yet, with investing in their own technological capacity and cooperation from States, private companies, and civil society organisations, ICCTs should be able to overcome those obstacles.

Finally, the case studies of digital harms demonstrate that accountability for digital harms under ICL is necessary because at present, digital harms to victims are falling through the cracks – for instance, the family of James Foley did not receive justice for the fact that his death was broadcasted for the world to see, and the scope of the harm to Uyghurs in Xinjiang through digital surveillance cannot be fully recognised without a crime that addresses the scale of the invasiveness and resulting destruction of a group's culture. While there will be challenges to criminalising digital harms, doing so is not impossible, and will be a worthwhile endeavour for the future of ICL.

Overall, this book will equip scholars and practitioners to engage with and adapt ICL so that it recognises and encompasses new forms of harm that result from digital technologies. Recognising and criminalising digital harms can, as eloquently put by McGlynn, help to avoid the 'privileging of existing criminal offences and harms' that can reinforce traditional assumptions and stereotypes behind the law.[19] Further, doing so will allow ICL to embrace the notion of 'kaleidoscopic justice', which emphasises the need to embrace the 'varied, nuanced, ever-changing experience and understandings of justice' in a progressive and modern world.[20]

[19] C McGlynn, 'Challenging Anti-carceral Feminism: Criminalisation, Justice and Continuum Thinking' (2022) 93 *Women's Studies International Forum* 102614, 3.

[20] ibid. See also M Burgis-Kasthala and B Sander, 'Contemporary International Criminal Law after Critique: Towards Decolonial and Abolitionist (Dis-)Engagement in an Era of Anti-impunity' (2024) 22 *Journal of International Criminal Justice* 127–50.

2

What Is Harm?

I. Introduction

The concept of harm is impossible to define in a straightforward manner, as it can encompass a wide range of consequences, from severe pain caused by torture to more minor impairments like a small financial loss caused by petty theft.[1] The purpose of this chapter is not to offer a single definition of harm, but instead to provide an overview of different conceptualisations of harm that may inform an analysis of how harm is reflected in international criminal law (ICL) in subsequent chapters. Further, this understanding will assist in the exploration of how digital harm may be accounted for through criminalisation later in this book.

It is often the case that more time is spent on how exactly to criminalise or redress harm than on the actual analysis of what harm is and how its manifestations should be recognised.[2] The latter analyses are important, as a clear understanding of harm is an essential precondition to establishing the most optimal approach to address harm. In the present book, criminalisation will be explored as one option for how to account for digital harm, but it may not be the most appropriate route for all types of digital harm. To determine the best approach to addressing harm, it is valuable to first discern what the concept of harm (and digital harm) entails and to identify the breadth of harms individuals and groups may experience.

This chapter will engage with philosophical approaches to defining harm before moving on to describe various types of harm at the individual, group, and societal levels. In doing so, this chapter will provide a solid understanding of what harm entails in preparation for an analysis of how harm is accounted for (and how digital harm may be accounted for) by ICL in subsequent chapters.

The importance of understanding harm in the legal context is illustrated using the 'harm principle', or the idea that there is a universal moral duty not to harm

[1] A Linklater, *The Problem of Harm in World Politics: Theoretical Investigations* (CUP, 2011) 43.

[2] F Ní Aoláin, 'Exploring a Feminist Theory of Harm in the Context of Conflicted and Post-Conflict Societies' (2009) 35 *Queen's Law Journal* 219; R West, *Caring For Justice* (New York University Press, 1997) 96.

other people and that personal freedom may be infringed upon by an authority to prevent harm to others.[3] This can be traced back as far as Stoic philosophers, such as Cicero, who argued that the law which governs us ordains 'that no one is justified in harming another for his own advantage'.[4] A core component of modern liberal thought is the defence of this harm principle. For instance, John Stuart Mill stated that the 'moral rules which forbid mankind to hurt one another … are more vital to human well-being than any other maxims … a person may possibly not need the benefits of others; but he always needs that they should not do him hurt'.[5] Other philosophers such as Hart, Kant, and Smith also agreed with Mill that societies must always obligate members not to cause unnecessary harm.[6] The 'harm principle' is thus of extreme importance to theories of criminalisation, which will be discussed in subsequent chapters.

This book focuses on digital harm and the relevance of ICL to address it, and ICL has looked to the harm principle as a basis for criminalisation.[7] For example, Keenan has observed that international law is evolving and moving 'away from a rigid, category-based approach to defining crimes towards a harms-based approach'.[8] To support this claim, Keenan argues that a harms-based approach has been used to 'expand the bounds of international criminal law by defining new crimes or new modes of commission for existing crimes'.[9] He proposes that as evidenced by developments such as the addition of rape as a means of genocide at the International Criminal Tribunal for Rwanda (ICTR) after victims testified to the harms they experienced, or by the decision of the Special Court for Sierra Leone (SCSL) to charge defendants with the novel crime of the crime against humanity of forced marriage under similar circumstances, that ICL has developed mechanisms to account for harms that are not yet fully recognised.[10] Keenan's arguments and critiques of them will be explored further in chapter five, section II.A,[11] but in general, it is clear that preventing and redressing harm to victims is one of the central aims of ICL, and so understanding different types of harm and those that ICL seeks to address is important when considering how those harms may be criminalised.

In addition, May has discussed what he argues is the 'normative principle of international criminal law', the 'international harm principle', which he defines as

[3] JS Mill, *On Liberty* (1859); A Linklater, 'The Harm Principle and Global Ethics' (2006) 20 *Global Society* 329–43, 331. The harm principle will be considered in greater detail as a basis for international criminalisation in ch 5, s II.A of this book.

[4] ibid; Cicero, *On Obligation* (Faber and Faber, 1967) 44.

[5] ibid; JL Mackie, *Ethics: Inventing Right and Wrong* (Penguin, 1977) 135.

[6] ibid 332.

[7] Of course, the harm principle is not the only basis for international criminalisation. Other theories, such as retributivism and expressivism, will be considered in ch 5.

[8] PJ Keenan, 'Doctrinal Innovation in International Criminal Law: Harms, Victims, and the Evolution of the Law' (2020) 42 *University of Pennsylvania Journal of International Law* 407–44.

[9] ibid 415.

[10] ibid 419–21.

[11] See ch 5, s II.D of this book.

> only when there is serious harm to the international community, should international prosecutions against individual perpetrators be conducted, where normally this will require a showing of harm to the victims that is based on non-individualized characteristics of the individual, such as the individual's group membership, *or* is perpetrated by, or involves, a State or other collective entity.[12]

This illustrates the distinction between May and Keenan's perspectives – while Keenan focuses on harm to direct victims, May requires a larger harm 'to the international community'. Both conceptions are important to ICL and have strengths and weaknesses. For instance, Keenan's approach is important for accounting for harms to victims, and would likely allow for a more flexible approach to encompass novel forms of harm within ICL frameworks because the focus would be on the direct harm to victims as opposed to having a requirement of a broader societal harm. However, May's approach seems to better consider the difference between international and domestic criminal law, specifically concerning the gravity threshold for international crimes.[13] This is because the requirement that there also be a 'serious harm to the international community' emphasises that harms should be considered international crimes only when they are grave enough to affect global society, which Keenan's theory does not address. Yet, May's 'international harm principle' may be inadequate in the sense that it implies that ICL should only be concerned with group-based harms as opposed to individual harms, which can also be grave and are worthy of prosecuting to achieve justice for victims.[14] The application of the harm principle to ICL will be explored further in chapter five as a basis for criminalising digital harms, but overall and regardless of the exact approach to defining it, it remains an important theory of criminalisation under international law.

Further, the inclusion and evolution of harm itself (as opposed to the harm *principle*) as encompassed by definitions of international crimes will be discussed in detail in chapter three. Ultimately, though, as eloquently put by Petersen, if we believe harm matters in the justification of legal sanctions, we must clarify what it means to be harmed – otherwise, 'we cannot hope to characterize fully the acts which we have reason to criminalize'.[15] Therefore, if this book ultimately aims to discuss whether digital harm may be criminalised under ICL, drawing from the harm principle in its analysis, then it is necessary to define what is meant by both 'harm' and 'digital harm'.

[12] L May, 'The International Harm Principle' in L May, *Crimes Against Humanity: A Normative Account* (CUP, 2004) 83.

[13] The gravity threshold will be explained later in ch 6 but is roughly synonymous with the notion that international crimes should have a certain degree of grossness or seriousness.

[14] For a more comprehensive critique of May's 'international harm principle', see M Rinzo, 'A Criticism of the International Harm Principle' (2010) 4 *Criminal Law and Philosophy* 267–82.

[15] TS Petersen, *Why Criminalize? New Perspectives on Normative Principles of Criminalization* (Vol 134, Springer Law and Philosophy Library, 2020) 21–22.

II. Theories of Harm

There are many theories for what constitutes harm across multiple disciplines. This section will first consider general theories of harm that are relevant to understanding harm as it is accounted for by criminal law frameworks. These theories are categorised by three common ways in which they define harm: harm in terms of impacts on freedom and liberty, comparative theories of harm, and contemporary theories of harm. Following this, this section will explore more specific types of harm on different levels – harm to individuals, harm to groups, and harm to society – that may be experienced in the context of international crimes.

A. General Approaches to Defining Harm

Moral and legal philosophers have provided different definitions for the concept of harm, and these definitions encompass a few key themes. These include harm defined in terms of impact on freedom and liberty, comparative approaches to harm, and contemporary approaches, which will be explained further in the following sections.

i. Impacts on Freedom and Liberty

To begin, harm is defined by some in terms of the impact on freedoms or liberties. Arguably the most well-known of these accounts is John Stuart Mill's *On Liberty*, in which he argues that 'the only purpose for which power can be rightfully exercised over any member of a civilized community, against his will, is to prevent harm to others'.[16] Here, Mill does not state precisely what harm is, but alludes to the concept of harm as being wrongful enough for the State to intervene to prevent it. Mill illustrates this by stating that 'no person is an entirely isolated being', and that harming someone's property, for instance, harms those who derive support from it and diminishes the general resource of the community.[17] Moreover, if someone's physical or mental state is harmed, the harm-doer negatively affects all those who depended on the victim and detracts from the 'general sum of good'.[18] Mill then goes so far as to say that even if an individual does no direct harm to others through their vices, they are 'injurious by [their] example' and could mislead or corrupt the wider community.[19]

Thus, in Mill's view, harm can manifest in many ways – whether it be to someone's person (physical and/or mental), or to someone's property, or on either an individual or collective level. Still, the concept of harm is never actually defined.

[16] Mill (n 3) 13.
[17] ibid 74.
[18] ibid.
[19] ibid.

Mill's failure to characterise harm has been criticised, with some arguing that it caused the harm principle to 'collapse' without an accepted definition.[20] This has led numerous scholars to propose their own definitions of harm,[21] which Gibney and Wyatt argue to be 'watered down and relativistic',[22] asserting that definitions of harm are 'effectively useless for anyone wishing to make decisions from among competing claims that invoke the harm principle for either liberty or social authority'.[23] This is a valid point, as no matter how restrictively it is defined, harm will never be a completely objective concept because what one considers harmful will differ from person to person. Especially in the context of criminalisation, where it is equally as important that defendants are not harmed by wrongful prosecutions and have the right to a fair trial,[24] it is essential that there be a consistent way of approaching the harm that is criminalised. This is because while judges and others making decisions should be capable of dealing with concepts like harm that include some subjective elements, the way decisions are taken should be non-arbitrary and transparent and should recognise subjective elements of the decision.

In contrast, Turner argues that Mill's critics have wasted time trying to propose more restrictive definitions of harm because Mill uses harm as a 'general term for bad consequences, requiring no further specification'.[25] Turner argues in favour of Mill's expansive approach to defining harm by pointing out the flaws in other common definitions. For example, one view of harm is the 'rights-violation' definition, which classifies harm as 'threatening someone else's rights'.[26] The 'rights-violation' rests on the assumption that if harm is not restricted to a violation of a person's rights, then the harm principle cannot fulfil its purpose.[27] This rights-violation definition of harm may vary in the sense that not every society has the same view of what individual 'rights' are, and thus the idea of what constitutes harm would differ depending on the society. This is not necessarily a problem depending on why one is trying to define harm, but for the purposes of addressing the harm, whether by criminalisation or by any other means, and the reasoning stated in the previous paragraph, it is preferable to have a clear, more objective

[20] E Gibney and T Wyatt, 'Rebuilding the Harm Principle: Using an Evolutionary Perspective to Provide a New Foundation for Justice' (2020) 9 *International Journal for Crime, Justice and Social Democracy* 100.

[21] As summarised by Turner, most proposals severely restrict the concept of harm to rights violations or damage to vital interests; PN Turner, '"Harm" and Mill's Harm Principle' (2014) 124 *Ethics* 299–326, 300.

[22] Gibney and Wyatt (n 20) 103. Some of these definitions include 'a setback to human interests that community norms have deemed to be significant', AC Lin, 'The Unifying Role of Harm in Environmental Law' (2006) 3 *Wisconsin Law Review* 898–985; and 'a wide range of immoral, wrongful and injurious acts that may or may not be deemed illegal', E McLaughlin and J Muncie, *Criminological Perspectives: Essential Readings* (3rd edn, SAGE, 2013).

[23] ibid.

[24] In fact, one of the only clear distinctions Mill makes regarding harm in *On Liberty* is that a form of harm is that which would be inflicted on an individual whose rights are unduly interfered with by the social authority; Mill (n 3) and Turner (n 21) 326.

[25] Turner (n 21) 301.

[26] ibid 302.

[27] ibid 303.

definition of harm – especially in the context of international criminal justice, where our understanding of harm needs to encompass what society collectively considers it to be.

A second view of harm is Riley's definition, which is less restrictive than the 'rights-violation' view because it encompasses more harms than those that could be seen as violations of rights. Riley defines harm as 'perceptible damage suffered against one's wishes … including physical injury (not excepting death), forcible confinement, financial loss, damage to reputation, broken promises (contractual or otherwise) and so on'.[28] Riley excludes 'mere dislike', or emotional effects on people's feelings, from the concept of harm – in this view, consistent with the harm principle, the State cannot interfere with even very offensive actions if the only result of those actions is emotional distress (and not harm).[29] Most of Turner's critique of Riley's definition surrounds his disagreement over the interpretation of Mill's *On Liberty*, which is outside the scope of this book. However, Turner does also point out that this definition is too restrictive, as it does not even allow for some basic formulations of the harm principle, such as 'conduct which concerns others' or 'cases in which an individual makes himself a nuisance to other people'.[30] Turner argues that it is difficult to say how 'emotional distress in others does not concern those others or does not regard the external relations of the individual',[31] and therefore that excluding it from the definition of harm does not allow for the full use of the harm principle. In addition, and of more relevance to this book, Riley's definition which rejects emotional distress excludes a wide range of digital harms (in addition to existing international crimes like serious mental suffering as an element of torture) which will be discussed later in this chapter, as most of them are entirely non-physical and involve mental or emotional harm.

Moving on from Mill's conception of harm and definitions which have spawned from it, other philosophers, such as Raz, have provided views also encompassing a general theme of freedoms and liberties. For instance, Raz proposes that harm is a principle which impacts freedom, and that to harm a person is to diminish their prospects or to adversely affect their possibilities.[32] Thus, this could happen physically, but harm could also manifest in less tangible or even less direct ways – in Raz's view, harm is a setback to autonomy. Raz also states that 'one harms another when one's action makes the other person worse off than he was, or is entitled to be, in a way which affects his future well-being'.[33] In this view, harm does not really depend on the way it manifests (ie physically, mentally, financially, etc), but is defined as harm when an individual is negatively impacted in some way.

[28] ibid 310; J Riley, *Mill on Liberty* (Routledge, 1998) 98.
[29] ibid 310.
[30] ibid 313.
[31] ibid.
[32] J Raz, *The Morality of Freedom* (OUP, 1986) 413.
[33] ibid 414.

In contrast with Raz, Feinberg defines harm not as a setback to autonomy, but as a setback to interest ('an action that makes the harmed party "worse off"').[34] He draws a distinction between this sense of harm as a 'setback to interest'[35] and the 'normative' sense of harm as a 'wrong' or a 'violation of an individual's rights'.[36] Feinberg argues that in the legal context, the proper form of harm to be criminalised is an overlap of both these senses – 'wrongful harm', that is, something that sets back someone else's interests *and* is wrongful.[37] In this view, something can be harmful to someone but not necessarily wrong; for instance, Feinberg argues that if an individual has consented to harm or voluntarily inflicts it upon himself, then the harm is not a 'wrongful harm'.[38] This distinction is important in terms of addressing harm, especially pertaining to digital harm and how direct the connection between the digital act and the harm must be to result in liability or criminality, which will be discussed in later chapters.[39]

ii. *Comparative Approaches*

Aside from definitions which focus on harm as infringements upon freedoms or liberties, other scholars have proposed definitions that take a comparative approach that understands harm as resulting in a negative change or difference from an original state. For instance, harm has been defined using the 'otherwise-condition', meaning that harm occurs when a certain event causes an individual's condition to be 'adversely different from that condition in which [they] would otherwise have been' had the event not occurred.[40] Morreim has argued that harm encompasses several key features – the first being that fact must be separated from fantasy, meaning that there must be specifically identifiable states which would have happened to the individual had some precise event not occurred.[41] She emphasises that to identify a harm, we must be able to pinpoint the event that caused it narrowly.[42] As Morreim notes, the 'otherwise-condition' method of defining harm requires harm to be thought of in terms of change – '[s]imply an unfortunate condition cannot of itself constitute a harm'.[43] Therefore, using this definition would require a solid understanding of the individual's state before and after the event which caused the impairment in order to determine the harm and a strong link between cause

[34] N Peršak, *Criminalising Harmful Conduct: The Harm Principle, its Limits and Continental Counterparts* (Springer 2007) 13–14; J Feinberg, *Harmless Wrongdoing – The Moral Limits of the Criminal Law* (OUP, 1990).

[35] Feinberg defines 'interest' as something 'in which one has a stake'; J Feinberg, *The Moral Limits of Criminal Law Volume 1: Harm to Others* (OUP, 2003) 34.

[36] Peršak (n 34).

[37] ibid.

[38] Feinberg (n 35) 35.

[39] See chs 4 and 5 of this book.

[40] EH Morreim, 'The Concept of Harm Reconceived: A Different Look at Wrongful Life' (1988) 7 *Law and Philosophy* 3–33, 10.

[41] ibid 11.

[42] ibid.

[43] ibid; Feinberg (n 35) 101.

and effect. Further, Morreim argues that this definition requires the possibility of placing value on the individual's current condition and on their 'otherwise-condition' in order to ascertain which is 'worse than' the other.[44] Finally, she stresses that all the causal results of the event (not merely some of them) must be considered, because in some cases an event can have positive consequences that outweigh the adverse ones (ie the harm).[45]

Morreim's analysis of harm coincides with the distinction made by Petersen between 'comparative' and 'non-comparative' accounts of harm.[46] In this sense, 'comparative' accounts of harm define harm in a similar way to Morreim, as the person would need to be worse off than they were previously in order to have experienced harm.[47] Petersen describes different baselines for determining harm using a comparative approach – temporal baselines ('A person P1 is harmed by another person P2 doing C if and only if P1's well-being, because of C, is lower than it was *prior* to C'), mankind baselines ('A person P1 is harmed by another person P2 doing C if and only if P1's well-being, because of C, is *lower than the well-being for mankind*'), and counterfactual baselines (A person P1 is harmed by another person P2 doing C if and only if P1's well-being, because of C, is worse, compared to the closest world *where P2 did not do C*').[48] Petersen argues that the counterfactual baseline is the least problematic way of defining harm, because considering temporal and mankind baselines, there can be situations in which an individual is harmed by another's action even though they are no worse off after the action, as well as situations in which a person is harmed even though they are actually better off after the action.[49] However, a critique of the counterfactual comparative account of harm is that it cannot adequately address the harm of death, because a person who dies is not necessarily 'worse off' than they would have been because after death, they would not have a state of well-being to compare to.[50] I argue that this could be challenged with the assertion that not having a state of well-being (ie being deceased) is still comparable to a person's individual state while alive if one assumes that having zero state of well-being is always worse off than having one. If a comparative approach to harm assesses harm based on a decrease in well-being, then death, by this logic, would always constitute a harm.

On the other hand, 'non-comparative' accounts of harm define harm such as when an action 'causes a person to be in a bad state'.[51] 'Bad states' can be understood 'as states that are in themselves bad, not bad because they are worse than the state the person would otherwise have been in'.[52] Yet, similar to comparative accounts,

[44] ibid 12.
[45] ibid.
[46] Petersen (n 15) 24.
[47] ibid.
[48] ibid 25–34.
[49] ibid 30.
[50] D Purves, 'Accounting for the Harm of Death' (2014) 97 *Pacific Philosophical Quarterly* 89–112, 89.
[51] Petersen (n 15) 24.
[52] ibid; E Harman, 'Harming as Causing Harm' in MA Roberts and DT Wasserman (eds), *Harming Future Persons: Ethics, Genetics and the Non-identity Problem* (Springer, 2009) 137–54.

the way non-comparative accounts of harm are able (or not able) to account for death has also been criticised. In the view of Petersen and Bradley, the main issue with non-comparative definitions of harm is that 'although they can recognize that dying can be harmful, they cannot account for the view that death can be harmful for a person, because death or being dead is not something a person can experience'.[53] This argument presents a narrow view of harm which seems to require an individual to feel or endure pain or loss in a tangible way,[54] rather than merely suffering a wrong without any obvious consequences to the person that can lead to harm. This raises question as to how some harms which may not be as tangibly felt or that could be foreseeably experienced after death (such as harm to one's reputation or dignity) can or should be classified – a question which will have particular relevance in coming chapters when the potential criminalisation of harms relating to international crimes is discussed.[55] Further, outside the question of proof (ie whether something is sufficiently tangible to show or constitute a certain element or crime), this argument could potentially impede understandings of or marginalise certain kinds of moral harm where tangibility may never be possible.

Yet, as noted by Shiffrin, comparative accounts are not without faults, as they can both under- and overidentify harm in certain cases.[56] In terms of under-identifying harms, comparative accounts place the effects of actions as being 'harms' or 'benefits' but never both – as Shiffrin describes it, one can either move up the scale, down the scale, or stay put.[57] However, this does not take into account more complex events that frequently occur, such as when a lesser harm is inflicted in order to avert a greater harm.[58] When a comparative approach is used in this case, it will only take into account that someone has been harmed, even if the net result is positive.[59] An example of this could perhaps be if someone's leg must be amputated in an emergency in order to stop a potential infection from spreading to the rest of the body – in this instance, using a comparative approach, a person would be 'harmed' as they are technically in a worse off state than before after losing a limb. However, using a non-comparative approach to harm, the overall picture could be taken into account – that is, the person was not actually harmed by the amputation because it eliminated the risk of a fatal infection.

Moreover, Shiffrin also argues that harm can be overidentified when comparative approaches are used. For instance, if harm is only defined comparatively

[53] ibid; B Bradley, 'Doing Away with Harm' (2012) 85 *Philos Phenomenol Res* 390–412.

[54] The term 'tangible' in this book is used in the common sense, referring to things that can be touched, felt, or easily perceived. In this respect, a physical injury or emotional distress are harms that may be more tangible than more 'abstract' harms like moral or reputational injury, depending on their severity.

[55] For instance, assaults on personal dignity and desecration of the deceased are classified as war crimes under international humanitarian law (IHL) under the Geneva Conventions and criminalised under ICL under Article 8 of the Rome Statute. This will be revisited in ch 3 of this book.

[56] SV Shiffrin, 'Harm and its Moral Significance' (2012) 18 *Legal Theory* 357–98.

[57] ibid 370.

[58] ibid.

[59] ibid.

without other context, something very minor – such as if a billionaire loses a thousand dollars – can be classified as harm even if no damage or loss is tangibly felt.[60] Further, she notes that for counterfactual accounts of harm, a missed opportunity for a billionaire to earn a thousand dollars would also count as a harm, even if it is not a loss or even non-negligible.[61]

While Shiffrin's arguments are compelling, they are very subjective in nature and rely upon what one considers to be serious enough to be a harm. This subjectivity is not necessarily problematic in all contexts, but as this book focuses on digital harms in relation to international crimes, which will likely be more serious than Shiffrin's 'billionaire' example, it is worth noting that this subjectivity could be a 'slippery slope' if used for purposes of criminalisation in a courtroom. This is because harms that should not be considered severe enough to constitute international crimes could be encompassed. It is also important to consider that the strong relative component of Shiffrin's arguments could be problematic with regards to consistency, which is important if harms are criminalised. For example, returning to the example of the billionaire who loses a small amount of money, context may seem very important in determining whether harm was actually caused (as Shiffrin argues). However, if this same logic were to be applied to victims of a crime like torture, it would also be a 'slippery slope' to conclude, for instance, that a victim who was more resilient to the effects of the crime suffered less harm than others who were not as resilient. Thus, Shiffrin's argument about counterfactual accounts of harm and their need to take into account context may not always be best in the context of criminalisation.

Overall, comparative theories of harm can be useful, especially when the response is criminal law, since they are able to account for death as a harm which is important when considering crimes involving death. However, it is also possible that comparative theories can exclude some harms that are worthy of criminalisation or, conversely, include harms that are less severe, depending on the approach.

iii. Contemporary Theories

Apart from more traditional freedom/liberty-based approaches and comparative accounts of harm, present-day scholars have developed more contemporary, gendered theories of harm that may better account for all victims' experiences.[62] As noted by Ní Aoláin, a 'gender-infused theory of harm' is important in order to allow women to 'reconceptualize how and what they experience on their own

[60] ibid 371.
[61] ibid.
[62] In this book, 'gender' can encompass a range of identities, including male, female, and other identities that do not correspond within that binary; and is generally understood with reference to the social and cultural differences of males and females. Consequently, 'gendered theories of harm' are those that take into account aspects relating to gender, such as special considerations for those identifying as women as opposed to men. See also J Santos de Carvalho, 'The Powers of Silence: Making Sense of the Non-definition of Gender in International Criminal Law' (2022) 35(4) *Leiden Journal of International Law* 963–85.

terms and then to translate this into a legal form'.[63] One type of feminist approach to defining harm is that which is utilised by McGlynn et al. in their study of image-based sexual abuse through interviews with 75 victim-survivors in the United Kingdom, Australia, and New Zealand – a feminist phenomenological method of describing harm.[64] McGlynn et al. emphasise the importance of detailing the harms experienced by victims of sexual violence (which will be discussed in detail in chapter four, section III.A)[65] in a more holistic way that can capture experiences that traditionally medicalised trauma frameworks may not account for.[66] In their view, assessing harms using the medicalised trauma framework may be inadequate because (1) harms may become defined in too narrow ways that do not capture the wide array of complex ways sexual abuse may impact victim-survivors, and (2) medical trauma conceptions can end up inadvertently colluding with the gendered status quo to decontextualise and depoliticise the harms of sexual violence.[67]

Outside of sexual violence, feminist harm theory has been applied in the context of conflict and post-conflict societies.[68] Ní Aoláin has discussed how in societies affected by conflict, it is especially important to identify which harms are 'precisely directed at women' because perpetrators seek group effects that follow from individual harm.[69] She argues that women's experiences of group and communal harms are 'qualitatively different from those of men', and that legal mechanisms fail to capture the nature of this in times of war.[70] Ní Aoláin engages with Catherine MacKinnon's discussion of the harms women experience by the pornography industry, which rejects the idea that harm is 'singular, atomistic and individuated' – in her view, the concept of harm can only effectively address women's experiences 'when it fully encompasses the social and group effects of certain acts'.[71] The distinction between discussing harm to women both at the individual and collective levels will be considered further in section II.B.ii.[72]

Contemporary theories of harm (especially feminist harm theory) can be especially valuable for understanding harm because they place particular emphasis on ensuring that all forms of harm to all categories of victims are adequately recognised. This is important in relation to international crimes, especially sexual and gender based crimes that will be considered in later chapters,[73] because traditional understandings of harm (that can translate into definitions of crimes) may be insufficient to fully account for effects on certain victims. In this sense, contemporary

[63] Ní Aoláin (n 2).
[64] C McGlynn et al, '"It's Torture for the Soul": The Harms of Image-Based Sexual Abuse' (2021) 30 *Social and Legal Studies* 541–62, 543.
[65] See ch 4, s III.A of this book.
[66] ibid.
[67] ibid 544–45.
[68] Ní Aoláin (n 2).
[69] ibid.
[70] ibid 226.
[71] ibid 224; C MacKinnon, 'Sexual Harassment: Its First Decade in Court' in *Feminism Unmodified* (Harvard University Press, 1987) 103–16.
[72] See ch 2, s II.D of this book.
[73] See chs 3 and 4 of this book.

theories of harm can be useful to apply to novel harms, such as digital harms, because they allow for more modern and progressive interpretations of harm.

B. Harm and the Law

The theories mentioned in the previous section provide a philosophical basis for our understanding of harm, which is reflected in how harm has been theorised in the legal sphere and codified into the law. As described by Linklater, these 'harm conventions' are implemented (either formally or informally) in every society (domestic and international) to maintain order and limit avoidable suffering.[74] While theories specific to the criminalisation of harm will be discussed in detail in chapter five,[75] this section provides a general overview of how philosophical theories of harm have made their way into various legal systems.

Harm has been incorporated into both civil and criminal law – for civil law, harm is important in determining the damage or wrong that has been caused that an individual or group is liable for.[76] In addition, theories of harm have been used for the purposes of consumer and competition law in order to devise tools that may repair harm after it is caused and to help deter harmful conduct in the first place.[77] On the other hand, in penal matters, acts are criminalised (at least in part) because they cause harm.[78] Theories which assist us in understanding different types of harm help to answer the question of who has standing as a victim in criminal cases and how the harm suffered can be linked to wrongdoing.

In both civil and criminal matters, a critical element once harm is brought into the equation is how to identify the causal link between the act (tort or crime) and the harm, and how direct this link needs to be, so that the law may be applied fairly and consistently. This is likely more or less difficult depending on the nature of the harm – for instance, it could be harder to establish that viewing a violent image posted by someone on the internet directly caused mental harm to an individual than to determine if a physical assault caused harm to the victim. These different types of harm will be discussed in the subsequent sections.

i. Harm to Individuals

In the present book, which focuses on digital harm, while physical harms may be relevant (perhaps, for example, if information posted online directly leads to

[74] Linklater (n 1) 29.

[75] See ch 5, s II.A of this book.

[76] The maxim of *sic utere tuo ut alienum non laedas* ('use your own so as not to harm another') has been commonly described as the fundamental proposition of tort law; RA Epstein, 'The Harm Principle and How It Grew' (1995) 45 *University of Toronto Law Journal* 369.

[77] P Siciliani, C Riefa, and H Gamper, *Consumer Theories of Harm: An Economic Approach to Consumer Law Enforcement and Policy Making* (Hart Publishing, 2019).

[78] Harm as a basis for criminalisation will be discussed in more depth in subsequent chapters. For a detailed analysis of this, see also Feinberg (n 35) Volumes 1–4.

a physical harm inflicted on an individual), most of the direct harms experienced by individuals will likely be of a non-physical nature. For this reason, this section will focus on the 'less obvious' harms experienced by individuals aside from direct physical harm or a loss of property.

A large school of research focuses on mental or emotional harm.[79] Teff notes that '[a]lthough "personal harm", as generally understood, extends well beyond bodily injury, no single term fully captures the sheer range of suffering which is not manifestly physical.'[80] Further, Teff argues that in the context of criminal law and legal redress for harm, it is 'neither desirable nor necessary for a "recognisable *psychiatric* illness" to constitute the threshold' for injury under the law.[81] In his view, this is because there can be severe emotional harm without an identifiable psychiatric illness.[82] In addition, aside from psychiatric illness or mental distress, non-physical individual harm may also include a sense of indignity associated with a deprivation of liberty, injury to reputation, interference with privacy, and other ways in which personal well-being may be diminished.[83] Teff thus raises question as to whether there should even be a threshold for causing non-physical harm under the law, and emphasises that should it be deemed necessary, a flexible and inclusive requirement would be most desirable.[84] On this note, it is worth recognising that there will also likely not always be such a clear dividing line between physical and non-physical harm, as physical harm will likely have mental repercussions at times and vice-versa – therefore flexible requirements under the law would useful for this reason as well.

Further, literature concerned with mental suffering experienced by torture victims is especially relevant in the context of ICL. Twiss makes the distinction between 'primary' and 'secondary' victims of torture – 'primary victims' being those who directly experience the torture, and 'secondary victims' being those who experience trauma as a result of the torture to the primary victims.[85] For primary victims of torture, harms are known to include not only physical injuries, but also 'less visible' harm such as chronic anxiety, inability to trust others, subsequent deliberate self-injury, violent behaviour towards others, substance abuse, depression (often leading to suicide), paranoia, severe insomnia, uncontrollable nightmares and flashbacks, self-loathing, psychosomatic illness, shortened lifespan, permanent alterations of brain patterns, and more.[86]

[79] See H Teff, *Causing Psychiatric and Emotional Harm: Reshaping the Boundaries of Legal Liability* (Hart Publishing, 2009); BJ Grey, 'The Future of Emotional Harm' (2015) 83 *Fordham Law Review* 2605; DW Shuman, 'How We Should Address Mental and Emotional Harm' (2007) 90 *Judicature* 248.

[80] Teff (n 79) 4.

[81] ibid 9.

[82] ibid.

[83] ibid 5.

[84] ibid 9.

[85] SB Twiss, 'Torture, Justification, and Human Rights: Toward an Absolute Proscription' (2007) 29 *Human Rights Quarterly* 346, 358–59.

[86] ibid; JK Harbury, *Truth, Torture, and the American Way: The History and Consequences of US Involvement in Torture* (Beacon Press, 2005); J Conroy, *Unspeakable Acts, Ordinary People: The Dynamics of Torture* (University of California Press, 2001); E Peters, *Torture (New Perspectives on the Past)* (Blackwell, 1985).

However, while Twiss does note that those close to the 'primary victims' of torture can experience 'extreme hardship and trauma',[87] it is very well possible that indirect victims of torture (and crimes in general) may experience the same types of harms as direct victims by being exposed to stories or footage of the abuse. It is for this reason that, in contrast with Twiss' labelling of those who witness torture of their family members as 'secondary' as opposed to 'primary' victims, it has been determined by some international criminal courts and tribunals (ICCTs) and human rights bodies that the 'mental suffering of relatives that are forced to watch severe mistreatment' can amount to the level of gravity required to be a torture offence in itself.[88] For instance, in the *Fofana and Kondewa* case at the SCSL, the Chamber considered

> that a third party could suffer serious mental harm by witnessing acts committed against others, particularly against family or friends … the Accused may be held liable for causing serious mental harm to a third party who witnesses acts committed against others.[89]

Moreover, in the *Kvočka et al.* case at the International Criminal Tribunal for the Former Yugoslavia (ICTY), the Trial Chamber found that 'the mental suffering caused to an individual who is forced to watch severe mistreatment inflicted on a relative would rise to the level of gravity required under the crime of torture'.[90] In addition, in *Furundžija*, the Trial Chamber found that being forced to watch a female acquaintance be raped constituted torture for the observer.[91] These cases will be analysed in further detail in chapter three.

Empirical studies have also demonstrated that torture inflicts extreme trauma on the victim's family members.[92] For instance, a study conducted in Denmark on the families of Chilean torture survivors found that of 84 children of survivors, 34 had insomnia and nightmares, five had tics, 12 had chronic stomach pains, 13 suffered from headaches, 15 experienced bed wetting, 13 had anorexia, four had memory problems, and 16 demonstrated behavioural problems.[93] This illustrates

[87] Twiss (n 85) 359.

[88] OHCHR, 'Interpretation of Torture in the Light of the Practice and Jurisprudence of International Bodies' (2010) www.ohchr.org/sites/default/files/Documents/Issues/Torture/UNVFVT/Interpretation_torture_2011_EN.pdf, 23.

[89] *Prosecutor v Fofana and Kondewa* (Judgment) SCSL-04-14-T, Trial Chamber I (2 August 2007) ('*Fofana and Kondewa* Trial Judgment') [153]. This case concerned charges of crimes against humanity and war crimes against two high-ranking members of the Civil Defense Forces in Sierra Leone.

[90] *Prosecutor v Kvočka et al* (Judgment) IT-98-30/1-T, Trial Chamber (2 November 2001) ('*Kvočka et al* Trial Judgment') [149]. This case concerned charges of crimes against humanity and war crimes against five individuals involved with the police for events that took place at the Omarska, Keraterm, and Trnoplje camps in Bosnia and Herzegovina.

[91] *Prosecutor v Furundžija* (Judgment) IT-95-17/1-T, Trial Chamber (10 December 1998) ('*Furundžija* Trial Judgment') [267]. This case concerned charges of crimes against humanity and war crimes against the commander of the 'Jokers', a unit of the Croatian Defence Council, for events in Bosnia and Herzegovina.

[92] Twiss (n 85); Harbury (n 86).

[93] Harbury (n 86).

the harm that can be caused to individuals who hear about brutal acts experienced by their loved ones. In addition, families of those who are tortured or disappeared experience the extreme difficulty of endlessly waiting for their relatives to be found, which can cause severe mental anguish.[94] This study indicates that harms to individuals extend past those physically harmed and can affect their friends and family members in nearly equally as traumatic ways.

Aside from mental or emotional types of harm, individuals may also experience harm to non-tangible entities, such as personal autonomy or privacy (although overlap between the two harms may well occur, as harm to personal autonomy will likely result in mental ramifications). In Raz's *The Morality of Freedom*, he discusses how depriving someone of the ability to use opportunities is a form of harm.[95] In other words, an individual can be harmed if their personal liberty and freedom of choice is somehow inhibited. Moreover, as discussed by Petersen, an individual can experience harm to morality, or 'moral harm'.[96] Moral harm is a type of harm that an individual can experience if their character is somehow injured in a moral way, such as through watching pornography (which some may consider to be immoral and detrimental to the 'purity' of the individual).[97] However, this type of harm which rests on one's subjective moral compass is more difficult to discern and analyse in the context of criminalisation, since morality can differ greatly from person to person. Yet, subjective analyses or value judgements can still be important as while they may not necessarily on their own determine whether a crime has been committed for instance, they can potentially come into play during sentencing hearings or reparations proceedings.[98]

ii. Harm to Groups

Aside from harm to individuals, harm may also be experienced as a collective group or by a whole community. For instance, as also noted by Twiss, the torture of one person can cause damage to the wider community through 'fomenting hatred and spirals of violence … resulting in the breakdown of civilian institutions amounting to a kind of collective trauma'.[99] In addition, research on communities affected by war crimes, crimes against humanity, and genocide, such as those affected by the Holocaust or the conflict in Kosovo, has also demonstrated the effects of collective

[94] ibid 150.

[95] Raz (n 32) 413.

[96] Petersen (n 15) 22.

[97] ibid; W Sumner, *The Hateful and the Obscene: Studies in the Limits of Free Expression* (University of Toronto Press, 2004).

[98] For example, there are multiple elements listed in the International Criminal Court (ICC) Rules of Procedure and Evidence that the Chamber may consider in determining a sentence or awarding reparations which would require some level of subjective analysis, such as the scope of the harm to victims, or the conduct of the accused after the crime; International Criminal Court Rules of Procedure and Evidence (2nd edn 2013) ICC-PIDS-LT-02-002/13_Eng ('ICC RPE'), Rules 97 and 145.

[99] Twiss (n 85) 359.

suffering even when crimes are against individuals.[100] Thus, it is possible that some acts can cause both individual and collective harms.

May distinguishes between organised and disorganised groups, which has implications for the harm the group can experience.[101] In the context of corporate law, May argues that harm to 'unorganised groups' (those without distinct roles or hierarchies within them, such as gendered or ethnic groups) should be given higher standing because it entails harm to all members of the group, whereas harm to organised groups (such as corporations) does not necessarily affect all members of the group.[102] This is because a company is highly organised and therefore harm would be experienced in greater amounts depending (presumably) on factors like rank or role.[103] May also notes that harm to individual members of organised groups like corporations can be mitigated or eliminated once they cease to work at the company, whereas those in unorganised groups cannot easily distance themselves from the group to avoid harm.[104]

Further, May discusses how one of the most common forms of harm to unorganised groups is negative stereotyping, which he defines as when all members of a group are indiscriminately perceived in terms of a model (regardless of whether they fit it) and the model unjustifiably incorporates unfavourable characteristics.[105] The impact of these stereotypes can be felt by every member of the group – a key example is of women, who because (in part) of stereotypes of the group as a whole, are subjected to sexual harassment and discrimination in their individual lives.[106] In this sense, a harm inflicted upon a group as a whole or on a subset of that group (such as a stereotype) can have a cascading effect and branch off to affect many individuals associated with the group. As May writes, 'the direct harms to some women lead to indirect harms to many other women, with no evident limit to the total number who are affected'.[107]

It has also been argued that such harms would be better understood if conceptualised as 'social injuries', or 'injuries endured by virtue of membership of a minority status social group'.[108] As stated by Cain and Howe, this is because harms to women are not sporadic, but endemic.[109] They cite the example of how criminal courts continue to 'indulge the lame excuses of homicidal men', who plead not guilty to murdering their wives on the ground of provocation – in this situation,

[100] See for instance R Eyerman, JC Alexander, and EB Breese (eds), *Narrating Trauma: On the Impact of Collective Suffering* (Routledge, 2011).

[101] L May, *The Morality of Groups: Collective Responsibility, Group-Based Harm, and Corporate Rights* (University of Notre Dame Press, 1987) 135.

[102] ibid.

[103] ibid 136.

[104] ibid.

[105] ibid.

[106] ibid 139.

[107] ibid.

[108] M Cain and A Howe, 'Introduction' in M Cain and A Howe (eds), *Women, Crime and Social Harm: Towards a Criminology for the Global Era* (Hart Publishing, 2008) 3.

[109] ibid.

as courts continue to allow victim-blaming arguments for femicide on behalf of possessive men, they perpetuate 'a social injury' against all women.[110]

Considering both May's and Cain and Howe's analyses, there seems to be a link between group harm and individual harm. Group harms, such as stereotypes or prejudice, can negatively impact all members of a group by subjecting them to hate or limiting opportunities in educational or employment sectors. However, group harms can easily translate into individual harms – for instance, if a group is labelled with a stereotype and a member of the group participated in a behaviour that went against that stereotype, the individual could suffer ostracism on behalf of those who are not members of the same group.[111] The individual harm of ostracism or exclusion, which was caused by the group harm of a stereotype in this case, could result in a wide range of other inflictions to the individual, such as emotional distress or a feeling of a loss of identity. Moreover, as in the case described by Cain and Howe, a court culture which continues to entertain victim-blaming excuses for femicide can perpetuate a social mindset that can both harm the group as a whole and enable more crimes against individuals.

iii. Harm to Society and Transboundary Harm

At the largest level, harm can be experienced by national societies or the global community. Torture is a clear example of this – for example, as observed by Harbury, the systematic use of torture by a government 'foments public terror and paralysis' which can lead to the breakdown of institutions such as courts and legislatures.[112] The harm in this instance is therefore that of public fear and the collapse of civilian institutions. In addition, practices like torture by governments may have a chilling effect on public debate and dissent, and could prevent judges or lawmakers from properly exercising their functions if they are afraid of punishment.[113] Further, this chilling effect and the inability for public institutions to work properly could lead to a decline in economic and social growth,[114] which could set off a cascade of other harms to society (ie mass loss of jobs, poverty, hunger, increased crime, etc). Harbury uses Guatemala as an illustrative example of this, whose economy was 'once favored … as a showcase for capitalism and democracy' and is now in 'shambles' due to (in part) torture becoming systematically used by the government.[115]

The point of society being 'paralysed by terror' was raised by investigators in an unofficial truth commission in Uruguay, who noted that 'torture is not directed at the body of the prisoner alone, but at the social body'.[116] Further, '[t]orture is

[110] ibid.
[111] ibid 140.
[112] Harbury (n 86) 158.
[113] ibid.
[114] ibid.
[115] ibid.
[116] TS Coonan, 'Rescuing History: Legal and Theological Reflections on the Task of Making Former Torturers Accountable' (1996) 20 *Fordham International Law Journal* 512.

transformed from the method to make a few talk, to a silencer of everyone'.[117] On this note, the ideas of societal harm which stem from literature on torture may also be extended to other international crimes, such as terrorism. Just as torture can breed public fear that cripples a society, terrorist acts are, by definition, committed to elicit the same type of harm.

At the broadest level, aside from social harm, research has also focused on transboundary harm, which is typically discussed in relation to environmental harm. As established by international cases such as the Advisory Opinion on the *Legality of the Threat or Use of Nuclear Weapons* at the International Court of Justice (ICJ) or the *Trail Smelter* Arbitration,[118] transboundary harm is typically thought of as hazardous or environmental damage caused by a State that crosses into the border of and affects another State. However, Dupuy and Hoss suggest that international terrorism is similar to environmental pollution in its effect of transboundary harm due to the fact that the harm is cross-border, is many times caused by non-State actors, and cannot be left to domestic legal orders alone to respond effectively.[119] Nevertheless, the concept of transboundary harm as opposed to broader societal harm seems to be most relevant from a legal perspective, as it implies that harm caused within one border transcended into another territory, which is significant when considering liability avenues. Outside of the legal realm, this distinction is likely less relevant, as acts associated with transboundary harm such as environmental damage or terrorism could be considered wider societal harms as well.

C. Conclusion

Section II provided an overview of how harm has been defined both generally and in a legal context and explored some of the main types of harm on the individual, group, and societal levels. The purpose of this discussion was to prepare for a later analysis of how harm is reflected in ICL in chapter three, and subsequently what the best solutions are for addressing digital harms. This is because understanding how harm is conceptualised and defined, and the different ways it can manifest, is necessary to evaluate the types of harms that are addressed by ICL. The next section will take the information considered previously and reflect upon the differences in nature between 'traditional' and digital harms, which will be applied in later chapters to analyse how ICL can account for those discrepancies.

[117] ibid.

[118] ILC, 'Draft articles on Prevention of Transboundary Harm for Hazardous Activities, with commentaries' (2001) UN Doc A/56/10; *Legality of the Threat or Use of Nuclear Weapons* (Advisory Opinion) ICJ Rep 1996 (8 July 1996); *Trail Smelter Arbitration (United States v Canada)* (Decision) (16 April 1938).

[119] P Dupuy and C Hoss, '*Trail Smelter* and Terrorism: International Mechanisms to Combat Transboundary Harm' in RM Bratspies and RA Miller (eds), *Transboundary Harm in International Law: Lessons from the Trail Smelter Arbitration* (CUP, 2006) 225.

III. Conclusion

From this chapter, two key takeaways emerge. First, there are many different approaches to defining harm, all with their own strengths and weaknesses. This chapter does not settle on one specific definition of harm, but instead explores the benefits and detriments of each approach and the contexts in which one definition might be more useful over another. Moreover, regardless of whether it is difficult (or even impossible) to concretely define harm, this does not mean theories of harm do not have value or cannot be used. Ever since Mill first coined the harm principle, it has been used and evolved into different subtypes of harm principles that have been applied in domestic and international legal orders, even without a clear consensus as to what harm actually means. Going forward to subsequent chapters, this overview of theories of harm will be useful to keep in mind and factor into the analysis of how harm has been incorporated into international criminal law frameworks, and how new harms may be accounted for in the future.

Second, from the analysis of different types of harm, it becomes apparent that the various levels of harm (individual, group, and societal) are interconnected in many ways. It is seemingly impossible to identify an act which occurs at the individual level (such as a murder) that will not, at least in some way, affect surrounding groups, communities, and broader society. Conversely, 'larger' societal harms, such as the spread of disinformation in the context of election meddling, can start off cascades of 'smaller' harms. Thus, it is evident that harm is not a concept which can be completely isolated at an individual or collective level, but needs to be thought of holistically, which will have implications for how harm is (or should be) accounted for in terms of criminalisation.

Moving forwards, the following chapter will discuss the concept of harm specifically in relation to ICL, in order to discern how harms are accounted for by ICL frameworks and by ICCTs. Later in this book, the best solutions for accommodating digital harm in the context of international crimes, and the challenges that come with their criminalisation and adjudication, will be assessed.

3

Harm and International Criminal Law

I. Introduction

This chapter will explore how harm generally has been understood in international criminal law (ICL) jurisprudence to develop a theory as to how digital harms with foreseeable relevance to the perpetration of international crimes may be accommodated by ICL frameworks.[1] As explained in the previous chapter, there is no universal definition for harm, but harm is a basis for one of the main theories of criminalisation: the harm principle. This principle, first articulated by Mill, provides that 'the only purpose for which power can be rightfully exercised over any member of a civilized community, against his will, is to prevent harm to others'.[2] As described by Linklater, 'harm conventions' which aim to prevent harm to others are implemented (either formally or informally) in every society (domestic and international) to maintain order and limit avoidable suffering.[3]

This is also the case for ICL, as the harm to victims is considered in multiple stages of ICL procedure – for instance, harm is a main consideration when determining whether the gravity requirement of a crime has been met, which is assessed by various factors including scale, nature, manner of commission, and impact.[4] The Office of the Prosecutor (OTP) of the International Criminal Court (ICC)'s Policy Paper on Preliminary Examinations states that

> [t]he scale of the crimes may be assessed in light of, *inter alia*, the number of direct and indirect victims, the extent of the damage caused by the crimes, in particular the bodily or psychological harm caused to the victims and their families.[5]

Further, the harm caused to victims also plays an important role in determining whether they can indeed be recognised as such for the purposes of participating

[1] See also S Zarmsky, 'Is International Criminal Law Ready to Accommodate Online Harm? Challenges and Opportunities' (2024) 22 *Journal of International Criminal Justice* 169–84.

[2] JS Mill, *On Liberty* (1859) 13.

[3] A Linklater, *The Problem of Harm in World Politics: Theoretical Investigations* (CUP, 2011) 29.

[4] Regulations of the Office of the Prosecutor (entered into force 23 April 2009) ICC-BD/05-01-09, 29.

[5] Office of the Prosecutor, Policy Paper on Preliminary Examinations (November 2013) www.icc-cpi.int/sites/default/files/iccdocs/otp/OTP-Policy_Paper_Preliminary_Examinations_2013-ENG.pdf [62].

in proceedings,[6] and at the sentencing and reparations phases – in accordance with the ICC Rules of Procedure and Evidence (RPE), in determining a sentence, the Court shall consider 'the extent of the damage caused, in particular the harm caused to the victims and their families'.[7] Moreover, on a broader level, some scholars have argued that the purpose of ICL as a whole is to provide accountability for conflict-related harms that would not have been addressed otherwise.[8]

Historically, ICL has been primarily concerned with direct physical violent crime.[9] While ICL has recognised the importance of psychological forms of suffering (such as for mental elements of torture and genocide), this has typically been done as part of cases that have focused on physical harm at their root. Until recently, ICL did not recognise any offences concerning other forms of harm, such as serious economic or environmental harm.[10] Yet, the proposed addition of new crimes such as ecocide under the Rome Statute demonstrates the capacity of ICL to change and accommodate novel (or at least previously unrepresented) types of harm.[11]

This chapter is broken up into sections, the first analysing how harm has been understood for each category of crime under ICL frameworks and jurisprudence, including genocide, crimes against humanity, and war crimes.[12] In particular, only crimes that encompass harms that could foreseeably be linked to the digital harms to be explored in this book, given current trends in how technology is used to inflict harm and the fact that those harms may often not be physical, will be considered.

II. Harm in International Crimes

This section will explore how harm has been understood in relation to three main categories of crime under ICL: genocide, crimes against humanity, and war crimes. For crimes against humanity and war crimes, specific crimes falling under each

[6] International Criminal Court Rules of Procedure and Evidence (2nd edn, 2013) ICC-PIDS-LT-02-002/13_Eng ('ICC RPE') Rule 85.

[7] ibid Rule 145(1)(c).

[8] J Ramji-Nogales, 'Questioning Hierarchies of Harm: Women, Forced Migration, and International Criminal Law' (2011) 11 *International Criminal Law Review* 463–76, 465.

[9] J Werle and F Jeßberger, *Principles of International Criminal Law* (4th edn, OUP, 2020) 155.

[10] ibid.

[11] 'Ecocide Definition, Commentary and Core Text' (Stop Ecocide, June 2021) www.stopecocide.earth/expert-drafting-panel.

[12] This book does not focus on the fourth type of crime under the Rome Statute, the crime of aggression, which requires the use of armed force against another state. While scholars have argued that certain types of cyber-attacks can constitute armed force, this book is not concerned with cyber warfare. For more information about cyber-aggression, see JA Ophardt, 'Cyber Warfare and the Crime of Aggression: The Need for Individual Accountability on Tomorrow's Battlefield' (2010) 3 *Duke Law & Technology Review* 1–28; KL Miller, 'The Kampala Compromise and Cyberattacks: Can There Be an International Crime of Cyber-Aggression?' (2014) 23 *Southern California Interdisciplinary Law Journal* 217–60; or K Ambos, 'International Criminal Responsibility in Cyberspace' in N Tsagourias and R Buchan (eds), *Research Handbook on International Law and Terrorism* (Elgar, 2015) 118, 137–41.

umbrella category are chosen for analysis based on their foreseeable link to the digital harms considered (ie, mass surveillance, hate speech and disinformation, sharing footage of crimes online, and online sexual violence). These crimes, such as torture, other inhumane acts, sexual violence, and outrages upon personal dignity, are those which often include or encompass elements related to psychological, emotional, and cultural harms (which are more common in cases of digital harms than physical harms given the nature of the digital environment).

A. Genocide

As provided by the Convention on the Prevention and Punishment of the Crime of Genocide (the 'Genocide Convention'), genocide means any of the listed acts[13] committed with the intent to destroy, in whole or in part, a national, ethnical, racial, or religious group.[14] This same definition was included under Article 2 of the International Criminal Tribunal for Rwanda (ICTR) Statute, Article 4 of the International Criminal Tribunal for the former Yugoslavia (ICTY) Statute, and Article 6 of the Rome Statute.[15]

In its nature, genocide more obviously represents a collective harm as it is directed at destroying a particular group (though this group must fall under the specific categories listed in the definition of genocide in the Genocide Convention and subsequent ICL statutes). Although, the term 'genocide' was coined by Lemkin, who originally thought of genocide as a crime against humanity more focused on individuals.[16] In this sense, Lemkin argued that the goal of prohibiting genocide 'was not to make the right of groups to exist inviolate but to prohibit people from attempting to destroy entire ways of life and ethnic traditions, which caused real suffering for individuals'.[17] Nevertheless, scholars have interpreted the harm of genocide to be both collective and individual. Concerning collective harms, as argued by Stahn, genocide is 'essentially an attack upon human diversity',[18] which implies that the collective harm of genocide can be viewed as not only harm to the targeted group, but one to broader humanity. This perspective has been argued

[13] Article II of the Genocide Convention provides the following acts: (a) killing members of the group, (b) causing serious bodily or mental harm to members of the group, (c) deliberately inflicting on the group conditions of life calculated to bring about its physical destruction in whole or in part, (d) imposing measures intended to prevent births within the group, or (e) forcibly transferring children of the group to another group; Convention on the Prevention and Punishment of the Crime of Genocide (adopted 12 January 1951) ('Genocide Convention).

[14] ibid art II.

[15] Statute of the International Tribunal for Rwanda (adopted 8 November 1994 by S/RES/955) ('ICTR Statute') art 2; Updated Statute of the International Criminal Tribunal for the Former Yugoslavia (adopted 25 May 1993 by Resolution 827, as amended 7 July 2009 by Resolution 1877) ('ICTY Statute') art 4; Rome Statute art 6.

[16] D Irvin-Erickson, *Raphael Lemkin and the Concept of Genocide* (University of Pennsylvania Press, 2017) 3.

[17] ibid.

[18] C Stahn, *A Critical Introduction to International Criminal Law* (CUP, 2018) 15.

by scholars such as Hannah Arendt, who characterised the nature of the harm of genocide as such:

> If a people or nation, or even just some specific human group, which offers a unique view of the world arising from its particular position in the world – a position that, however it came about, cannot readily be duplicated – is annihilated, it is not merely that a people or a nation or a given number of individuals perishes, but rather that a portion of our common world is destroyed, an aspect of the world that has revealed itself to us until now but can never reveal itself again.[19]

As observed by Lederman, Arendt argues that the distinctive harm of genocide is 'the loss to humanity of the richness of our understanding of the world we share', and that this is not a moral loss, but an existential loss – or the 'loss of the possibilities of thoughts, points of view and ways of life open to us'.[20] Lederman argues that it is clear from Arendt's writings that the harm caused by genocide is different than simply the mass murder of individuals due to the fact that in addition to loss of life, the world loses a significant cultural faction of society.[21] Lederman emphasises that Arendt's overall conception of the harm of genocide as an existential loss to humanity is unique and valuable so that understandings of such harm are not limited to strictly moral considerations or 'exhaustive categories of individualism versus collectivism'.[22]

The views of Arendt and Lederman are in contrast with those of May, who contends that groups have no value in themselves, so the destruction of a group cannot be the harm of genocide.[23] Instead, May argues that the unique harm of genocide is 'the loss of an essential status for the individual members of the group, one that is crucial to the protection of their individual rights'.[24] Lederman argues that the problem with individual accounts of the harm of genocide such as May's is that it does not capture the richness of the meaning of genocide, which lies in the destruction of a group along with their way of life, collective historical memories, and cultural artefacts.[25] Of course, individuals will be directly affected by the acts which in sum, constitute genocide, but the gravity of genocide and its importance to ICL stems from its harm not only to individuals or the victim groups, but to humanity itself.

As stated in ICL jurisprudence, such as the Appeals Chamber of the ICTY in *Krstić*:

> Those who devise and implement genocide seek to deprive humanity of the manifold richness its nationalities, races, ethnicities and religions provide. This is a crime against

[19] H Arendt, *The Promise of Politics* (Schocken Books, 2005) 175; S Lederman, 'A Nation Destroyed: An Existential Approach to the Distinctive Harm of Genocide' (2017) 19 *Journal of Genocide Research* 112–32, 117.

[20] Lederman (n 19) 126.

[21] ibid.

[22] ibid 128.

[23] ibid; L May, *Genocide: A Normative Account* (CUP, 2010) 7.

[24] ibid.

[25] ibid 116.

all of humankind, its harm being felt not only by the group targeted for destruction, but by all of humanity.[26]

This idea of a 'harm to humanity' has value in the context of addressing digital harm, as it demonstrates that ICL (in part) seeks to account for these existential losses to society, such as a loss of a culture. This argument will be expanded upon in a later section of this chapter.[27]

A key element of genocide, as provided in both the Genocide Convention and the statutes of international criminal courts and tribunals (ICCTs), is 'serious bodily or mental harm' to members of the group.[28] The inclusion of 'serious bodily or mental harm' allows for a broad interpretation of the type of harm associated with genocide, as it is not limited to strictly physical harms. However, as noted by Milaninia, what constitutes 'serious bodily or mental harm' is not defined further in any treaty which includes genocide, rendering it 'inherently vague and inherently broad'.[29] Milaninia has explored the historical and jurisprudential development of 'serious bodily or mental harm', starting from the deliberations for the Genocide Convention, in which he reports that 'neither the specific acts leading to, nor the harms encompassing, "bodily harm" were discussed'.[30] Although there is no information available about why these acts were not discussed,[31] it could be speculated that in the aftermath of the Holocaust at the time the Convention was drafted, the acts that constituted 'bodily harm' in relation to genocide were seemingly obvious. Thus, defining 'bodily harm' has been left to ICCTs. In the case of *Kayishema and Ruzindana* at the ICTR, the Trial Chamber noted that 'serious bodily harm should be determined on a case-by-case basis, using a common sense approach'.[32] Further, the Chamber held that it agreed with the findings in the *Akayesu* judgment that 'serious bodily harm' could include 'acts of sexual violence, rape, mutilations, and interrogations combined with beatings, and/or threats of death'.[33]

[26] *Prosecutor v Krstić* (Judgment) IT-98-33-A, Appeals Chamber (19 April 2004) 36. This case concerned charges of genocide, crimes against humanity, and war crimes against the former Chief of Staff and Deputy Commander of the Drina Corps of the Bosnian Serb Army.

[27] See s III.A.

[28] Genocide Convention art II(b); Rome Statute art 6(b); ICTY Statute art 4; ICTR Statute art 2.

[29] N Milaninia, 'Understanding Serious Bodily or Mental Harm as an Act of Genocide' (2018) 51 *Vanderbilt Journal of Transnational Law* 1383.

[30] ibid 1387.

[31] See also H Abtahi and P Webb (eds), *The Genocide Convention: The Travaux Préparatoires* (Brill, 2008).

[32] Milaninia (n 29); *Prosecutor v Kayishema and Ruzindana* (Judgment) ICTR-95-1-T, Trial Chamber II (1 May 1999) ('*Kayishema and Ruzindana* Trial Judgment') [108]. This case concerned charges of genocide, crimes against humanity, and war crimes against two senior officials in Kibuye in relation to multiple massacres in Rwanda.

[33] ibid; Concerning 'serious mental harm', the Chamber wrote that the Prosecution suggested that serious mental harm could include 'inflicting of strong fear or terror, intimidation or threat', but unlike with 'serious bodily harm', the Chamber did not state whether it agreed with this argument of the Prosecution.

Multiple chambers in the ad-hoc tribunals put forth their own interpretations of what constitutes 'serious *bodily* harm',[34] though what is most relevant to digital harms, for which direct bodily harm is not as common given the space between the perpetrator and the victim(s), is how 'serious *mental* harm' has been interpreted.

During the drafting of the Genocide Convention, the inclusion of mental harm as an act of genocide was the subject of some disputes between State delegates.[35] It was first proposed by China, who wanted to capture Japan's use of narcotics against the Chinese during the Second World War as an act of genocide, arguing that these harms were not any less destructive to the population than killings in gas chambers.[36] China's delegate proposed that the text under Article II be 'impairing the physical integrity or mental capacity of members of the group' or 'impairing the health of members of the group' to ensure that the use of narcotics against a group would be covered.[37] China's argument failed until a broader concept was introduced by India and adopted by the Sixth Committee, which proposed what ended up being the final wording in the Convention ('causing serious bodily or mental harm to members of the group').[38]

Later on, during the negotiations leading to the adoption of the Rome Statute of the ICC, the Preparatory Committee rejected the idea that 'mental harm' as an act of genocide should be limited to the effects of narcotics, as propositions that 'mental harm' be defined as 'permanent impairment of mental faculties through drugs, torture, or similar techniques' were not adopted.[39] Instead, during the drafting of Article 6 (on genocide), the Preparatory Committee added a footnote stating that 'the reference to "mental harm" is understood to mean more than the minor or temporary impairment of mental facilities'.[40]

This broader view of mental harm is consistent with case law from the ICTY, in which the *Krstić* and *Tolimir* Trial Chambers both have disagreed with a restrictive view of serious mental harm as an act of genocide.[41] For instance, in *Krstić*, the

[34] For instance, the *Kayishema and Ruzindana* Trial Chamber defined bodily harm as 'harm that seriously injures the health, causes disfigurement or causes any serious injury to the external, internal organs or senses'. In addition, the *Seromba* Appeals Chamber defined bodily harm as the 'quintessential examples' of 'torture, rape, and non-fatal physical violence that [cause] disfigurement or serious injury to the external or internal organs'. As determined in the cases of *Akayesu* (ICTR), *Blagojević and Jokić* (ICTY), *Popović* (ICTY), *Rutaganda* (ICTR), *Brđanin* (ICTY), *Stakić* (ICTY), *Karadžić* (ICTY), *Musema* (ICTR), and the case against Eichmann in the District Court of Jerusalem, 'bodily harm' has also been determined to include inhumane and degrading treatment, deportation, enslavement, starvation, persecution, and interrogations combined with beatings; ibid 1387–88.

[35] ibid 1390; UN ESCOR Ad Hoc Committee on Genocide 28th mtg, (9 June 1948) UN Doc E /AC.25/SR.28, 6–7.

[36] ibid; UN GAOR 6th Committee 81st mtg, (22 October 1948) UN Doc A/C.6/SR.81.

[37] UN ESCOR (n 35); Abtahi and Webb (n 31) 1125.

[38] Milaninia (n 29) 1420.

[39] ibid fns 47 and 48.

[40] W Schabas, *The International Criminal Court: A Commentary on the Rome Statute* (2nd edn, OUP, 2016) 139.

[41] Milaninia (n 29) 1391–92; *Prosecutor v Krstić* (Judgment) IT-98-33-T, Trial Chamber (2 August 2001) ('*Krstić* Trial Judgment') [510]; *Prosecutor v Tolimir* (Judgment) IT-05-88/2-A, Appeals Chamber (8 April 2015) ('*Tolimir* Appeal Judgment') [204].

Trial Chamber noted that 'serious mental harm' appeared 'to have been restricted originally to the injection of pharmacological substances occasioning the serious impairment of mental faculties' in the context of the Genocide Convention, but stated in its opinion that serious mental harm 'need not cause permanent and irremediable harm, but it must involve harm that goes beyond temporary unhappiness, embarrassment or humiliation'.[42] In this case, the Chamber found that the trauma suffered by those who managed to survive the mass executions constitute serious mental harm within the meaning of Article 4 of the ICTY Statute.[43] Further, the Chamber stated that mental harm 'results in a grave and long-term disadvantage to a person's ability to lead a normal and constructive life', and that 'inhuman treatment, torture, rape, sexual abuse and deportation are among the acts which may cause serious bodily or mental injury'.[44] Finally, in the context of the genocide allegations against *Krstić*, the Chamber wrote that it was 'fully satisfied that the wounds and trauma suffered by those few individuals who managed to survive the mass executions do constitute serious bodily and mental harm'.[45]

The *Krstić* Trial Chamber also provided that the list of acts which can constitute 'serious mental harm' for an act of genocide is non-exhaustive and must be determined on a 'case by case basis'.[46] Though the Chamber did not provide detailed reasoning as to why this act should be determined on a case by case basis, it can be assumed that this was decided in order to allow for a progressive understanding of the crime.[47] In addition, as observed by Milaninia, the breadth of the 'case by case basis' approach means that acts rejected or left out by drafters are still acts of genocide if they result in serious bodily or mental harm.[48] He argues that this breadth allowed for the Trial Chamber in *Akayesu* to become the first to recognise rape and other acts of sexual violence as acts of genocide and the Appeals Chamber in *Krstić* to do so in terms of forcible transfer (both in terms of serious bodily and mental harm).[49] These examples illustrate the benefit of the 'case by case basis' approach to defining 'serious bodily and mental harm' – that the law is able to accommodate previously underrepresented types of harm to provide better protection of targeted groups.

The definition of 'serious mental harm' was also a key issue in the *Tolimir* appeal. In the Trial Judgement, the Trial Chamber found that in the context of killings of the Bosnian Muslim population, the requirement of 'causing serious bodily

[42] *Krstić* Trial Judgment (n 41) [513]; *Prosecutor v Akayesu* (Judgment) ICTR-96-4-T, Trial Chamber I (2 September 1998) ('*Akayesu* Trial Judgment') [502]. On this note, in *Kayishema and Ruzindana*, the Prosecutor suggested that 'serious mental harm' could include 'inflicting of strong fear or terror, intimidation or threat', but in its judgment, the Trial Chamber did not state whether it agreed with this definition.

[43] ibid 514.

[44] *Krstić* Trial Judgment (n 41) [513].

[45] ibid [514].

[46] ibid [513]; Milaninia (n 29) 1394. The findings of the *Krstić* Trial Chamber were later reaffirmed in *Blagojević and Jokić* and in *Tolimir*.

[47] Milaninia (n 29) 1389.

[48] ibid.

[49] ibid.

or mental harm' for genocide had been met.[50] This was in reference to the forced separation of men and women, the horrific conditions the Bosnian men were subjected to while detained in temporary facilities, the awareness that the men had 'that they would ultimately meet their death at the hands of Bosnian Serb Forces who were detaining them', and the forced transfer of members of the group.[51] The Trial Chamber found that all of these acts constituted 'serious bodily or mental harm' within the meaning of the Statute because 'their suffering prevented these members of the group from leading a normal and constructive life'.[52]

However, in its appeal, the Defence argued (amongst other points) that the Trial Chamber erred in law and fact in its analysis of the actus reus of genocide, in part, by misinterpreting 'serious mental harm'.[53] In the Defence's view, the Trial Chamber 'adopted and applied a much broader definition of mental harm' than that adopted in the Genocide Convention, and further, 'serious mental harm' must 'involve permanent impairment to mental faculties that is sufficiently serious so as to contribute or tend to contribute to the destruction of the group'.[54] The Defence argued that the victims did not experience 'serious mental harm' within the meaning of the Statute because they experienced harms as individuals, and thus the harm could not have contributed to the destruction of the group, and also because the mental harm was not permanent enough to contribute to the destruction of the group.[55]

The Appeals Chamber recalled that 'it [did] not directly [address] what constitutes serious mental harm as an act of genocide', but that 'it [was] satisfied that the definition of serious mental harm adopted in the Trial Judgment [was] consistent with the case law of the ICTY and the ICTR and aligns with the letter and spirit of the Genocide Convention'.[56] It therefore rejected the Defence's arguments, and held that as was found in previous jurisprudence, 'serious mental harm must be lasting but need not be permanent and irremediable'.[57] However, the Appeals Chamber provided no further explanation as to the meaning of 'serious mental harm'.

The nature of the 'mental harm' associated with an act of genocide therefore is seemingly vague but encompasses two components stemming from ICL jurisprudence – first, the harm must be more than a minor or temporary impairment of mental facilities, and second, this harm does not need to be permanent and irremediable. Although this definition does not reveal much about what 'serious mental harm' should mean, it does allow for a wide range of harms, including

[50] *Prosecutor v Tolimir* (Judgment) IT-05-88/2-T, Trial Chamber II (12 December 2012) ('*Tolimir* Trial Judgment') [750-782]; *Tolimir* Appeal Judgment (n 41) [175]. This case was concerned with charges of genocide, crimes against humanity, and war crimes against the Assistant Commander for Intelligence and Security of the Bosnian Serb Army.

[51] *Tolimir* Trial Judgment (n 50) [738], [754]–[755].

[52] ibid [755].

[53] *Tolimir* (Appeal Judgment) (n 41) [176].

[54] ibid [193].

[55] ibid [194]–[195].

[56] ibid [202].

[57] ibid [203], footnotes omitted.

potential novel acts, to be accounted for. As will be considered in chapter four,[58] there are various digital harms which could be captured by this definition.

B. Crimes Against Humanity

Crimes against humanity were first prohibited in international law by Article 6(c) of the Charter of the International Military Tribunal of Nuremberg in 1945, which was established to prosecute leaders of the Nazi party after World War II.[59] The use of the term 'crimes against humanity' was famously proposed for inclusion in the Nuremberg Charter by Lauterpacht in the wake of the horrors of the Holocaust, although it had been used previously in other contexts to describe the violence of the French Revolution and colonial violence in the Belgian Congo.[60] As observed by Cassese, the crimes against humanity set out in Article 6(c) 'clearly envisaged the prosecution and punishment of atrocities and persecutions which are so abhorrent that they shock our sense of human dignity'.[61] Crimes against humanity may cause a wide range of harms, including both physical and mental harms.[62] Yet, what distinguishes this category of crimes from its domestic counterparts, such as 'murder' under a domestic criminal code, is the fact that the acts are so atrocious that they offend 'humanity' as a whole. This is illustrated well by the following excerpt from the judgment of the *P.* case of the Supreme Court in the British Occupied Zone in 1948:

> The action [against humanity] must objectively manifest the idea that a human being in his entire value or in one of these values is a nonentity, for instance that he is subhuman and to be treated accordingly, or that, for the person who gained power over him, he is a piece of machinery that one uses, exploits and then throws away, or even that thanks to one's own power, one can do with a human being what he pleases or make use of him only for a particular goal. The harm to the victim must therefore express a total or partial degradation of a human being.[63]

Considering the above, Cassese identified two common features of crimes against humanity: (1) that they are 'particularly odious offences in that they constitute a

[58] See ch 4 of this book.

[59] A Cassese, 'Chapter 11.2 Crimes Against Humanity' in A Cassese, P Gaeta, and J Jones (eds), *The Rome Statute of the International Criminal Court* (OUP, 2002) 353.

[60] P Sands, 'Introduction (on the Occasion if its Republication)' in H Lauterpacht, *An International Bill of the Rights of Man* (OUP, 2013); D Irvin-Erickson, 'Hersch Lauterpacht and Early Formulations of Crimes Against Humanity' in O Grech, *Crimes Against Humanity: Towards a More Comprehensive Approach?* (Centre for the Study and Practice of Conflict Resolution, University of Malta, 2021) 7.

[61] Cassese (n 59) 354.

[62] For example, under the Rome Statute of the ICC, crimes against humanity include violent physical acts such as murder and extermination, and those that could also result in severe mental suffering, such as torture or deportation.

[63] Cassese (n 59) 355; *P. case* (Judgment) Entscheidungen des Obersten Gerichtshofes für die Britische Zone in Strafsachen Vol I (20 May 1948) 14–15.

serious attack on human dignity or a grave humiliation or degradation of one or more human beings', and (2) that 'they are not isolated or sporadic events, but are part either of a governmental policy … or of a widespread practice of atrocities tolerated or condoned by a Government or a de facto authority'.[64] These features are in line with the two chapeau Elements of Crimes against humanity derived from customary international law, namely that there was an attack directed against a civilian population and that the attack was widespread or systematic.[65] These two chapeau elements encompass different types of harm.

The first chapeau element of crimes against humanity is that there was an attack against a civilian population. There are two key components of this element to consider in an analysis of harm – first, what constitutes an 'attack', and second, whether that attack could be considered directed against a civilian population.

The way 'attack' has been interpreted has implications for the type of harm that may result from a crime against humanity. An 'attack' can include acts resulting in more physical harms, such as murder, rape, or physical torture, but can also encompass acts not involving immediate physical violence.[66] For example, in the *Akayesu* Trial Judgment, the ICTR Trial Chamber implied this notion, finding that an 'attack' could be an act that is 'violent in nature, like imposing a system of apartheid'.[67] Second, the phrase of 'directed against' requires that the civilian population was the primary object of the attack and not just an incidental victim.[68] Drawing from this, it can be inferred that the harm of a crime against humanity would need to be one that manifests as a broader societal harm and not a single person or a small group of victims.

The second chapeau element of a crime against humanity is that it must be widespread or systematic. Generally, 'widespread' relates to the large-scale nature of an attack and the number of victims, while 'systematic' refers to the organised nature of the acts and the 'improbability of their random occurrence'.[69] Though either of these can meet the threshold for the chapeau element, they can foreseeably encompass different classifications of harm. For instance, if an attack is 'widespread', it would likely amount in harm to a large number of victims, as ICCTs tend to consider (in part) the number of victims in their assessment.[70] On the other hand, harms resulting from 'systematic' attacks could be conceived as more targeted, as they typically involve a plan or policy to commit crimes against

[64] ibid 360.

[65] G Mettraux, *International Crimes: Law and Practice: Volume II: Crimes Against Humanity* (OUP, 2020) 194.

[66] ibid 210.

[67] ibid; *Akayesu* Trial Judgment (n 42) [581]. This case concerned charges of genocide, crimes against humanity, and war crimes against the former mayor of Taba in the context of the Rwandan genocide.

[68] ibid 233; *Prosecutor v Kunarac et al* (Judgment) IT-96-23/1-A, Appeals Chamber (12 June 2001) [90]–[92]; *Prosecutor v Naletilić & Martinović* (Judgment) IT-98-34-T, Trial Chamber (31 March 2003) [235]; *Prosecutor v Kunarac et al* (Judgment) IT-96-23-7 & IT-96-23/1-T, Trial Chamber (22 February 2001) ('*Kunarac et al* Trial Judgment') [421].

[69] ibid 276.

[70] C Stahn, *A Critical Introduction to International Criminal Law* (CUP, 2018) 57.

a certain group.[71] However, the two elements are not necessarily distinct and may overlap.

Regardless of whether an attack is widespread or systematic, this element demonstrates the notion that crimes against humanity go beyond one instance with one individual. This notion was summarised well by the Trial Chamber of the ICTY in the *Erdemović* case:

> Crimes against humanity are serious acts of violence which harm human beings by striking what is most essential to them: their life, liberty, physical welfare, health, and/or dignity. They are inhumane acts that by their extent and gravity go beyond the limits tolerable to the international community, which must perforce demand their punishment. But crimes against humanity also transcend the individual because when the individual is assaulted, humanity comes under attack and is negated. It is therefore the concept of humanity as victim which essentially characterizes crimes against humanity.[72]

In its decision, the Trial Chamber makes clear that the harm of a crime against humanity can constitute both physical and mental impairments ('life, liberty, physical welfare, health and/or dignity').[73] Moreover, the Trial Chamber illustrates that the specific harm of a crime against humanity is one which extends beyond the individual victim and 'attacks' humanity as a whole,[74] emphasising the collective aspects of the harm as well as the individual.

Turning to the specific acts which can constitute crimes against humanity, four have particular relevance to digital harm due to the nature of the harm they encompass, which is often not only physical – torture, sexual violence, persecution, and other inhumane acts. These will be considered in the following sections.

i. *Torture*

As provided by the Convention against Torture and Other Cruel, Inhuman or Degrading Treatment or Punishment (hereafter referred to as the Torture Convention), 'torture' means

> any act by which severe pain or suffering, whether physical or mental, is intentionally

[71] In *Blaškić,* the Trial Chamber held that 'systematic' refers to: (i) the existence of a political objective, a plan pursuant to which the attack is perpetrated or an ideology, in the broad sense of the word, to destroy, persecute, or weaken a community; (ii) the perpetration of a criminal act on a very large scale against a group of civilians or the repeated and continuous commission of inhumane acts linked to one another; (iii) the preparation and use of significant public or private resources, whether military or other; and (iv) the implication of high-level political and/or military authorities in the definition and establishment of the methodical plan; *Prosecutor v Blaškić* (Judgment) IT-95-14-T, Trial Chamber (3 March 2000) [263]. The *Blaškić* case concerned charges of war crimes and crimes against humanity against a General and Commander of the Croatian Defence Council.

[72] *Prosecutor v Erdemović* (Sentencing Judgment) IT-96-22-T, Trial Chamber (29 November 1996) [28]. This case concerned crimes against humanity and war crimes charges against a soldier in the 10th Sabotage Detachment of the Bosnian Serb Army.

[73] ibid.

[74] ibid.

> inflicted on a person for such purposes as obtaining from him or a third person information or a confession, punishing him for an act he or a third person has committed or is suspected of having committed, or intimidating or coercing him or a third person, or for any reason based on discrimination of any kind, when such pain or suffering is inflicted by or at the instigation of or with the consent or acquiescence of a public official or other person acting in an official capacity.[75]

Under Article 7 of the Rome Statute, it is defined instead as 'the intentional infliction of severe pain or suffering, whether physical or mental, upon a person in the custody or under the control of the accused'.[76] Therefore, in the context of crimes against humanity at the ICC, there is no requirement for a particular purpose as there had been in the Torture Convention, which leaves a broader scope for the acts that could be prosecuted as torture under the Rome Statute.[77]

There are many physical harms that can be classified as torture or cruel, inhuman or degrading treatment (eg pulling teeth, waterboarding, or withholding food), but also psychological harms, such as threats of physical injury or sleep deprivation.[78] In general, torture causes shame and stigma in its victims, and in additional to physical harms, victims typically experience long-term and often lifelong psychological consequences.[79]

Acts of torture that satisfy all parts of the definition are criminalised under the Rome Statute as both a crime against humanity (Article 7(1)(f)) and a war crime (Article 8(2)(a)). Apart from the crime against humanity of torture needing to be a widespread or systematic attack against the population and the war crime of torture requiring a nexus to armed conflict, the rest of the elements of the crimes are the same.[80] Notably, torture is constituted when the perpetrator inflicts 'severe physical or mental pain or suffering' upon the victims.[81] Thus, similar to the previously discussed crime of genocide, the harm of torture can be either physical, mental, or both.

A crucial aspect of torture is its link to indignity, which continues to influence jurisprudence on the crimes of torture and inhuman or degrading treatment.[82] Further, as noted by the UN Special Rapporteur on Torture, 'the decisive criteria for distinguishing torture from [cruel, inhuman, or degrading treatment] may best be understood to the purpose of the conduct and the powerlessness of the victim,

[75] Convention against Torture and Other Cruel, Inhuman or Degrading Treatment or Punishment (adopted 10 December 1984) ('Torture Convention') art 1.
[76] Rome Statute art 7(2)(e).
[77] However, torture does have a purpose requirement when charged as a war crime under Article 8, which will be addressed later in this book. See Rome Statute Elements of Crimes arts 8(2)(a)(ii)-1 and 8(2)(c)(i)-4.
[78] J Werle and F Jeßberger, *Principles of International Criminal Law* (4th edn, OUP, 2020) 1071; Stahn (n 70) 61.
[79] ibid.
[80] Rome Statute arts 7(1)(f) and 8(2)(a)(ii).
[81] ibid.
[82] C Ferstman, 'Integrity of the Person' in D Moeckli, S Shah, and S Sivakumaran (eds), *International Human Rights Law* (4th edn, OUP, 2022) 169.

rather than the intensity of the pain or suffering inflicted'.[83] Thus, this demonstrates that a primary harm of torture is the way its victims are degraded and humiliated, and not treated as human beings. This understanding of the harm of torture is particularly relevant for the digital harms to be analysed in chapter four, section IV, especially sharing footage of crimes online and online sexual violence, which can be (in part) characterised by the degradation and dehumanisation of the victims.[84]

The humiliation component of torture has been considered multiple times throughout ICL jurisprudence. For instance, in *Furundžija* at the ICTY, the Trial Chamber considered 'that among the possible purposes of torture one must also include that of humiliating the victim'.[85] The Chamber wrote that this proposition was 'warranted by the general spirit of international humanitarian law', and that the 'primary purpose of this body of law is to safeguard human dignity'.[86] Further, the Chamber referenced provisions of the Geneva Conventions and Additional Protocols, and noted that 'the notion of humiliation is, in any event close to the notion of intimidation, which is explicitly referred to in the Torture Convention's definition of torture'.[87]

In addition to direct victims of physical or mental acts of torture, their family members or witnesses to these acts have also been considered victims of the crime, which demonstrates an understanding of the harm of torture as also encompassing the pain caused to individuals who view cruel acts being inflicted on other people. For example, in the *Furundžija* case, the ICTY Trial Chamber found that being forced to watch sexual attacks on a female acquaintance constituted the severe mental suffering threshold needed to be considered an act of torture.[88] In this case, the Chamber also noted the humiliation element of the torture, but for both the woman being raped and the observer: 'He was made to watch rape and sexual assault perpetrated upon a woman whom he knew, in order to force him to admit allegations made against her. In this regard, both witnesses were humiliated'.[89]

Additionally, in the *Fofana and Kondewa* case at the Special Court for Sierra Leone (SCSL), the Chamber considered 'that a third party could suffer serious mental harm by witnessing acts committed against others, particularly against family or friends' and that 'the Accused may be held liable for causing serious mental harm to a third party who witnesses acts committed against others'.[90] In this case, a witness testified that he was forced to watch the defendants' group cut

[83] ibid; UN HRC, 'Report of the Special Rapporteur on torture and other cruel, inhuman or degrading treatment or punishment' (5 January 2016) UN Doc A/HRC/31/57 [39].

[84] See ch 4 of this book.

[85] *Prosecutor v Furundžija* (Judgment) IT-95-17/1-T, Trial Chamber (10 December 1998) ('*Furundžija* Trial Judgment') [162].

[86] ibid.

[87] ibid.

[88] ibid [267(ii)].

[89] ibid [127].

[90] *Prosecutor v Fofana and Kondewa* (Judgment) SCSL-04-14-T, Trial Chamber I (2 August 2007) ('*Fofana and Kondewa* Trial Judgment') [153].

off his brother's head.[91] Although the Chamber did not provide reasoning for its finding that the accused could be held liable for the harm suffered to persons as a result of watching acts committed against others, it could be linked to the fact that it was forced – as stated by the witness,

> I tried to turn my face so that I could not see how they were slashing my brother's throat, but they had to slap me, they forced me, you know. They used to bang me with the butt of the gun to make me look at what was happening. So I had to look at how my brother was being killed.[92]

In this instance, it could be reasonably inferred that the fact that the accused intentionally forced the witness to watch the murder of his brother likely contributed to the Chamber's assessment that the accused could be held liable for the serious mental harm to the witness.

Further, in the case of *Kvočka et al*, the ICTY Trial Chamber found that 'the mental suffering caused to an individual who is forced to watch severe mistreatment inflicted on a relative would rise to the level of gravity required under the crime of torture'.[93] This was in relation to torture that took place against detainees at a prison camp, and the Chamber relied upon the aforementioned findings in *Furundžija* in its decision.[94]

In summary, the harm of torture can be understood as both one which affects the direct victims, physically or mentally, or both, inflicting a sense of degradation and humiliation, and one which affects those who view and/or are close to the person being tortured, knowing the intense suffering that the individual endured. These two harms will be relevant in considering digital harms that could possibly constitute torture, which will be considered later in this book.[95]

ii. Sexual Violence

Sexual violence is criminalised both as a crime against humanity and a war crime under Articles 7(1)(g), 8(2)(b), and 8(2)(e) of the Rome Statute.[96] As stated in the Elements of Crimes, sexual violence can occur either when a perpetrator commits an act of a sexual nature against a victim, or when the perpetrator causes another person to engage in an act of a sexual nature 'by force, or by threat of force or coercion, such as that caused by fear of violence, duress, detention, psychological oppression or abuse of power', or 'by taking advantage of a coercive environment

[91] *Prosecutor v Fofana and Kondewa* (Transcript of 15 June 2004) SCSL-04-14-T, Trial Chamber I (15 June 2004) 31.
[92] ibid.
[93] *Prosecutor v Kvočka et al* (Judgment) IT-98-30/1-T, Trial Chamber (2 November 2001) ('*Kvočka et al* Trial Judgment') [149].
[94] ibid.
[95] See ch 4 of this book.
[96] Rome Statute arts 7(1)(g), 8(2)(b), and 8(2)(e).

or … [the] incapacity to give genuine consent'.[97] As noted by the ICC OTP in its Policy on Sexual and Gender-Based Crimes, 'an act of a sexual nature is not limited to physical violence, and may not involve any physical contact – for example, forced nudity'.[98] Thus, sexual violence crimes encompass a wide range of offences and are not limited to rape or other physical violence.

Historically, the act of sexual violence was viewed as harming the victim's 'honour' (and particularly the honour of the family and community) rather than as a violent crime.[99] This was problematic, as it implied that a woman's honour was something 'lent to women by men', and that a women who is raped is thereby without any honour or personal dignity.[100] While sexual violence can of course harm an individual's sense of honour or dignity, considering this as the *only* harm resulting from it is a sexist and limited view which can trivialise other harms experienced by victims of violent crimes that violate bodily integrity.[101] Contemporary interpretations of sexual violence understand that its harm can take many forms, ranging from rape, to enforced prostitution, to forced pregnancy or enforced sterilisation,[102] and this harm is committed to intimidate or punish the victim or to inflict a sense of humiliation.[103] In addition, in the context of conflict, sexual violence is often part of an ongoing situation of gender-based violence,[104] and thus may harm certain groups more than others depending on the targeted gender.

As humiliation has been a recognised component of torture, it has also been for sexual violence. For instance, the UN Special Rapporteur on Torture and Other Cruel, Inhuman or Degrading Treatment or Punishment published a report specifically focusing on women and girls and the LGBTQ+ community, in which humiliation frequently arises as a form of sexual violence or torture.[105] This can be the case whether the sexual violence is of a violent physical nature or encompasses no physical contact at all. For example, invasive body searches from prison staff can constitute a form of humiliating sexual violence, in addition to when male guards watch female prisoners undressing or showering, or when women and girls are denied safe abortions and subjected to judgemental attitudes for inquiring about sexual healthcare.[106] The humiliation component of sexual violence is one that can directly connect to harms perpetrated through digital means, such as

[97] Rome Statute Elements of Crimes art 7(1)(g)–6(1).

[98] Office of the Prosecutor, Policy Paper on Sexual and Gender Based Crimes (June 2014) 3.

[99] Stahn (n 70) 62.

[100] United Nations Division for the Advancement of Women, 'Women2000: Sexual Violence and Armed Conflict: United Nations Response' (2000) 6.

[101] ibid.

[102] Stahn (n 70) 63.

[103] Werle and Jeßberger (n 78) 1082.

[104] ibid.

[105] Though sexual violence and torture are separate crimes under ICL statutes, it has been found in ICL jurisprudence that sexual violence can also constitute torture. The report of the UN Special Rapporteur focuses on torture and inhuman treatment (not necessarily the crime of sexual violence) but may be applicable to illustrate the harm of sexual violence as the crimes described in the report are those of a sexual nature; UN HRC (n 83).

[106] ibid.

non-consensual image distribution, which will be considered in chapter four, section IV.[107]

Further, the harms of sexual violence are not restricted to one gender, as men and boys have also been recognised as victims of sexual crimes in ICL jurisprudence. Oosterveld argues that ICCTs have been very inconsistent in their consideration of male victims of sexual violence, both in the charging (or failure to charge) rape and other forms of sexual violence against men and boys and in the way in which courts address secondary victimisation as a result of sexual violence.[108] In some instances, sexual violence against men and boys has been charged as rape,[109] whereas other instances have been charged as inhuman and cruel treatment as a violation of the laws and customs of war,[110] torture and persecution.[111] This inconsistency signifies an uncertainty of ICCTs regarding the type of harm caused by sexual violence towards men and boys, whether it differs from the harm caused to women in similar situations, and how it should best be criminalised under the law. This is a relevant consideration for this book because it demonstrates that (whether it is problematic or not given the gender differences in the approaches) ICCT Chambers have charged instances of sexual violence in a variety of ways and therefore have some degree of flexibility when approaching digital harms like online sexual violence.

Like the crime of torture, ICL jurisprudence has also recognised secondary victimisation in connection with sexual violence. Oosterveld notes that ICCTs appear unsure as to whether to address it as sexual violence or as something else, such as a form of psychological torture.[112] As was discussed in the previous section, in *Furundžija*, it was found that forcing a man to watch the rape of a female friend constituted torture.[113] However, at the SCSL in the *RUF* case, the Trial Chamber recognised the harm caused to a man being forced to watch the rape and death of his wife as 'fomenting terror by sexual means'.[114] In this case, the man and his children were forced to watch as eight men raped his wife, and was ordered to count each man as they went along while the others laughed and mocked him.[115] Following

[107] See ch 4, s IV of this book.

[108] V Oosterveld, 'Sexual Violence Directed against Men and Boys in Armed Conflict or Mass Atrocity: Addressing a Gendered Harm in International Criminal Tribunals' (2014) 10 *Journal of International Law & International Relations* 110.

[109] ibid; *Prosecutor v Bemba* (Decision Pursuant to Article 61(7)(a) and (b) of the Rome Statute on the Charges of the Prosecutor Against Jean-Pierre Bemba Gombo) ICC-01/05-01/08, PTC II (15 June 2009) [159]; *Prosecutor v Češić* (Sentencing Judgment) IT-95-10/1-S, Trial Chamber (11 March 2004) [13]–[14], [33].

[110] Oosterveld (n 108); *Prosecutor v Mucić et al* (Judgment) IT-96-21-T, Trial Chamber (16 November 1998) [1060].

[111] Oosterveld (n 108); *Prosecutor v Simić et al* (Judgment) IT-95-9-T, Trial Chamber II (17 October 2003) [728], [772].

[112] Oosterveld (n 108) 114.

[113] *Furundžija* Trial Judgment (n 85).

[114] Oosterveld (n 108) 114; *Prosecutor v Sesay, Kallon, and Gbao* (Judgment) SCSL-04-15-T, Trial Chamber I (2 March 2009) ('*RUF* case') [1347].

[115] ibid [1347]–[1352].

this, his wife was stabbed in front of her entire family.[116] The Trial Chamber found that this type of psychological harm had a 'direct effect of instilling fear on entire communities', which it classified as an act of terror, but still referred to the harm as being caused by 'sexual violence'.[117] This signifies that while certain acts may constitute offences other than sexual and gender-based crimes, Chambers can still recognise their harms as sexual in nature.

As noted by Grey, there has been increased attention paid to sexual violence by ICCTs over time.[118] However, other forms of gender-based violence, such as reproductive harms, have been slower to come to the forefront of international criminal jurisprudence.[119] In 2016, the *Ongwen* case at the ICC became the first case in any ICCT to include charges of forced pregnancy and to 'expressly consider the reproductive autonomy of individual women and girls'.[120] Though 'forced pregnancy' is explicitly provided as a crime against humanity and a war crime under the Rome Statute,[121] the development of case law concerning reproductive harm demonstrates that ICL Chambers are able to progressively recognise crimes that have been previously overlooked. It is therefore possible that similarly, ICL Chambers may be able to use their discretion and flexibility to recognise digital harms that meet the elements of existing crimes.

iii. Persecution

Dating back to the Nuremberg Charter,[122] crimes against humanity were broken up into two categories – (1) the 'murder types', including inhumane acts such as murder, extermination, enslavement, and deportation, and (2) the 'persecution types' based on persecution on political, racial, or religious grounds.[123] This definition of persecution was reflected in the statutes of the ad-hoc tribunals, such as the ICTY, which provided that the discrimination must be on 'specific grounds, namely race, religion, or politics'.[124] At present, the crime against humanity of persecution is defined under the Rome Statute as 'the intentional and severe deprivation of fundamental rights contrary to international law by reason of the identity of the group or collectivity'.[125] As provided by the Elements of Crimes, the

[116] ibid.
[117] ibid.
[118] R Grey, 'The ICC's First "Forced Pregnancy" Case in Historical Perspective' (2017) 15 *Journal of International Criminal Justice* 905–30, 906.
[119] ibid.
[120] ibid 909.
[121] Rome Statute Elements of Crimes arts 7(1)(g-4), 8(2)(b)(xxii-4) and 8(2)(e)(vi-4).
[122] Agreement for the prosecution and punishment of the major war criminals of the European Axis, Signed at London, 8 August 1945 (The Charter of the International Military Tribunal or 'Nuremberg Charter').
[123] *Prosecutor v Tadić* (Judgment) IT-94-1, Trial Chamber II (7 May 1997) ('*Tadić* Trial Judgment') [651] and [694]; O Swaak-Goldman, 'Case Analysis: The Crime of Persecution in International Criminal Law' (1998) 11 *Leiden Journal of International Law* 145, 147.
[124] ICTY Statute art 5(h).
[125] Rome Statute art 7(2)(g).

list of targeted groups for persecution is broader than that of genocide – it includes targeting 'based on political, racial, national, ethnic, cultural, religious, gender … or other grounds that are universally recognised as impermissible under international law'.[126]

From the definition of the crime itself, the harm of persecution is not necessarily physical or mental, but a deprivation of one's fundamental rights. The deprivation of rights can, of course, lead to various physical and mental harms, but these harms all stem from the 'umbrella' harm of being denied core human rights, such as those of liberty, privacy, or freedom of expression.

The acts which constitute persecution are also not limited to physical violence. For example, the Nuremberg Judgment considered that persecution consists of acts such as discriminatory laws limiting the offices and professions available to Jewish people, restrictions placed upon Jewish family life and rights of citizenship, the creation of ghettos, and the imposition of collective fines.[127] At the ICTY, the Trial Chamber in the *Tadić* case noted that persecution 'can take numerous forms, so long as the common element of discrimination in regard to the enjoyment of a basic or fundamental right is present', and that it does 'not necessarily require a physical element'.[128] In addition the Chamber found that persecution 'encompasses a variety of acts, including, *inter alia*, those of a physical, economic, or judicial nature, that violate an individual's right to the equal enjoyment of his basic rights'.[129]

In *Tadic*, the Chamber made reference to the International Law Commission (ILC) 1991 Report, which provided that persecution could also include prohibitions on practicing certain kinds of religious worship, prolonged and systematic detention of individuals belonging to a certain group, prohibitions on the use of a national language (even in private), and systematic destruction of monuments or buildings representative of a particular group.[130] Holistically, the harm of these acts seems to stem from the inability to exercise one's rights due to being identified as part of a certain targeted group, which could undoubtedly lead to mental or emotional distress. Moreover, similarly to what was discussed previously in relation to genocide,[131] there may also be collective harms that come with persecution, such as group trauma or the loss of cultural richness to society.

iv. Other Inhumane Acts

The crime against humanity of 'other inhumane acts' encompasses other forms of inhumane treatment which are not expressly prohibited.[132] As provided by the

[126] Rome Statute Elements of Crimes art 7(1)(h)(3).

[127] *Tadić* Trial Judgment (n 123) [704]; *The Trial of Major German War Criminals (Göring et al.)* (Judgment) (1 October 1946). The *Tadić* case concerned charges of crimes against humanity and war crimes against the president of the Local Board of the Serb Democratic Party in Kozarac.

[128] *Tadić* Trial Judgment (n 123) [707].

[129] ibid [710].

[130] ibid [703].

[131] See s II.A of this book.

[132] Stahn (n 70) 72.

Elements of Crimes under Article 7(1)(k) of the ICC Statute, the crime against humanity of other inhumane acts occurs when '[t]he perpetrator inflicted great suffering, or serious injury to body or to mental or physical health, by means of an inhumane act'.[133] As quoted by the ICTY Trial Chamber in *Kupreškić et al.*, the International Committee of the Red Cross (ICRC) Commentary on the Fourth Geneva Convention stated that 'other inhumane acts' is purposely broad, resting on the notion 'that however great the care taken in drawing up a list of all the various forms of infliction, it would never be possible to catch up with the imagination of future torturers who wished to satisfy their bestial instincts; and the more specific and complete a list tries to be, the more restrictive it becomes'.[134] The flexibility of the crime of other inhumane acts supports a critical takeaway of this book: that ICL is a body of law that is able to adapt to accommodate novel harms, including digital harms.

At the ICC, Pre-Trial Chamber I in the *Katanga* case interpreted 'other inhumane acts' as 'serious violations of international customary law and the basic rights pertaining to human beings, drawn from the norms of international human rights law, which are of a similar nature and gravity to the acts referred to in article 7(1) of the Statute'.[135] From this, it can be inferred that the harm of 'other inhumane acts' should be (1) those which inflict upon established human rights and (2) those of a similar nature and severity to the harms of other crimes against humanity. This has potential implications for accommodating digital harms under ICL, as human rights such as the right to privacy and freedom of expression are key at the intersection of technology and human rights law, but not necessarily always thought of as immediately in relation to international crimes. Although the law is vague and case law is not as developed regarding 'other inhumane acts', its room to encompass a variety of harms not recognised as explicitly by other crimes is something to keep in consideration in potential future prosecutions of digital harms. This is discussed further in chapter four, section IV.[136]

C. War Crimes

War crimes consist of grave breaches of the Geneva Conventions of 12 August 1949 (the list of which can also be found under Article 8(2)(a) of the Rome

[133] Rome Statute Elements of Crimes art 7(1)(k)(1).

[134] 'Convention (IV) relative to the Protection of Civilian Persons in Time of War, Geneva, 12 August 1949, Commentary of 1958' (ICRC IHL Treaties Database) ihl-databases.icrc.org/en/ihl-treaties/gciv-1949/article-3/commentary/1958?activeTab=, 39; *Prosecutor v Kupreškić et al* (Judgement) IT-95-16-T, Trial Chamber (14 January 2000) ('*Kupreškić et al* Trial Judgment') [563]. This case concerned charges of crimes against humanity and war crimes against six members of the Bosnian Croatian forces.

[135] *Prosecutor v Katanga et al* (Decision on the Confirmation of the Charges) ICC-01/04-01/07, PTC I (30 September 2008) ('*Katanga et al* Confirmation of Charges') [448]. This case concerned charges of crimes against humanity and war crimes against two military leaders in the Democratic Republic of the Congo.

[136] See ch 4, s IV of this book.

Statute), and other serious violations of the laws and customs applicable in armed conflict.[137] Though there are chapeau elements for war crimes, such as a nexus to armed conflict (international or non-international), these elements do not necessarily have significant implications for the actual harms inflicted by war crimes (for example, the harm of killing a civilian is generally the same whether the conflict is international or non-international). Overall, war crimes can be classified into violations of certain fundamental principles of international humanitarian law (IHL) grounded in the protection of persons and property, including (a) the protection of non-combatants, (b) the principle of distinction between civilians and combatants, (c) the principle of proportionality, and (d) the prohibition of employing restricted means and methods of warfare that can result in unnecessary suffering.[138] The digital harms that will be analysed in this book generally relate to the first principle (the protection of non-combatants and persons hors de combat), which refers to the notion that parties to an armed conflict must treat civilians, prisoners of war, and wounded or sick former combatants humanely.[139]

Generally, victims of international (IAC) and non-international armed conflicts (NIAC) are protected by most of the same rules under customary IHL,[140] and the lists of war crimes for each under the Rome Statute are very similar.[141] Moreover, aside from physical forms of violence which are criminalised as war crimes, some crimes incorporate non-physical harms and therefore may have more relevance to a later analysis of digital harm. These crimes, namely 'inhuman treatment', 'wilfully causing great suffering', and 'outrages upon personal dignity', will be discussed in subsequent sections.[142]

i. *Inhuman or Cruel Treatment*

Although inhuman or cruel treatment is closely linked to torture and considered the same under international human rights law,[143] the Rome Statute distinguishes

[137] Rome Statute art 8.

[138] Stahn (n 70) 81–93.

[139] ibid 81.

[140] For instance, the ICRC Study on Customary IHL found that based upon State practice and opinio juris, 141 out of 161 rules of customary IHL that apply to IACs also apply to NIACs; 'Non-international armed conflict' (ICRC) casebook.icrc.org/law/non-international-armed-conflict#footnote5_u5cbgoi. However, some commentators consider the scope of protections for NIACs to be significantly less than that for IACs under the Rome Statute; see D Willmott, 'Removing the Distinction Between International and Non-International Armed Conflict in the Rome Statute of the International Criminal Court' (2004) 5 *Melbourne Journal of International Law* 196.

[141] Rome Statute art 8. Of particular relevance to the digital harms considered in this book are the war crimes concerned with inhuman, cruel, and degrading treatment, which appear in both sections of the Statute dedicated to IACs and NIACs.

[142] It should be noted that torture and sexual violence also constitute war crimes, but the analysis of the actual harm of the acts is not dependent upon whether they are classified as crimes against humanity or war crimes. Thus, this analysis will not be repeated in the present section.

[143] For instance, Article 5 of the Universal Declaration of Human Rights (UDHR) provides that 'no one shall be subject to torture or to cruel, inhuman or degrading treatment or punishment'; UDHR art 5. Similarly, Article 3 of the European Convention on Human Rights (ECHR) provides that 'no one

between the two in the Elements of Crimes. While Article 8(2)(a)(ii) and 8(2)(c)(i) list 'torture or inhuman treatment' and 'torture and cruel treatment' as the same offence (respectively), the Elements of Crimes differ slightly and are separated as 8(2)(a)(ii)-1 (torture) and -2 (inhuman treatment), and 8(2)(c)(i)-3 (cruel treatment) and -4 (torture).[144] Further, while torture is also criminalised as a crime against humanity under Article 7, inhuman and cruel treatment are only listed under Article 8.[145] 'Degrading treatment' is not listed as a crime under the Rome Statute in relation to torture, but is instead mentioned with the war crime of outrages upon personal dignity.[146]

Article 8(2)(a)(ii)-2 defines 'inhuman treatment' as when '[t]he perpetrator inflicted severe physical or mental pain or suffering upon one or more persons'.[147] As established by the ICTY Trial Chamber in *Delalić et al* (known also as the *Čelebići* case), the degree of physical or mental harm necessary to constitute cruel or inhuman treatment is of a lower threshold than for torture.[148] In addition, for an act to constitute inhuman treatment, it must violate basic respect for human dignity.[149] However, as noted by the ICRC, although a violation of human dignity is encompassed within inhuman treatment under customary IHL and implied given the meaning of 'inhuman' (ie cruel and barbaric, treating someone as though they lack human qualities, without compassion for suffering),[150] 'a serious attack on human dignity' was ultimately not included in the Rome Statute because the drafters felt that 'outrages upon personal dignity' would better cover this element.[151]

In ICL jurisprudence, inhuman or cruel treatment has been used to encompass a variety of different harms. For example, at the ICTY, inhuman treatment has been found to consist of injuries and mistreatment of detainees, and the use of persons as human shields.[152] At the ICC, acts classified as inhuman treatment have included tying or restraining civilians, forcing civilians, under threat of death, to carry plundered property, forcing them to march under armed guard and threat of

shall be subject to torture or to inhuman or degrading treatment or punishment'; ECHR art 3. The Torture Convention also addresses the offences together as the 'Convention against Torture and Other Cruel, Inhuman or Degrading Treatment or Punishment'; Torture Convention (n 289).

[144] Rome Statute Elements of Crimes arts 8(2)(a)(ii) and 8(2)(c)(i).

[145] Rome Statute arts 7 and 8.

[146] Rome Statute arts 8(2)(b)(xxi) and 8(2)(c)(ii).

[147] Rome Statute Elements of Crimes art 8(2)(a)(ii-2)(1).

[148] *Prosecutor v Delalić et al* (Judgment) IT-96-21-T, Trial Chamber (16 November 1998) ('*Delalić et al* Trial Judgment') [542]; *Kvočka et al* Trial Judgment (n 93) [161].

[149] Schabas (n 40) 245; *Delalić et al* Trial Judgment (n 148) [442]. This case concerned charges of crimes against humanity and war crimes against four militants at the Čelebići camp.

[150] 'Convention (III) relative to the Treatment of Prisoners of War, Geneva, 12 August 1949, Commentary of 2020: Article 130 (Grave Breaches)' (ICRC IHL Treaties Database) ('ICRC 2020 Commentary') ihl-databases.icrc.org/en/ihl-treaties/gciii-1949/article-130/commentary/2020?activeTab=#_Toc42767226 5243.

[151] ibid 5245.

[152] ibid; *Prosecutor v Kordic and Čerkez* (Judgment) IT-95-14/2-T, Trial Chamber (26 February 2001) ('*Kordic and Čerkez* Trial Judgment') [256]; *Kvočka et al* Trial Judgment (n 93) [161]. This case concerned charges of crimes against humanity and war crimes against two military leaders of the Bosnian Croat forces.

death, and beating and abducting civilians.[153] Thus, the harm of inhuman treatment can generally be physical or mental, and is flexible in what it can accommodate.

ii. Wilfully Causing Great Suffering

'Wilfully causing great suffering' is defined by Article 8(2)(a) as when '[t]he perpetrator caused great physical or mental pain or suffering to, or serious injury to body or health of, one or more persons', and is only applicable in cases of international armed conflict.[154] It includes acts that do not meet the definition or threshold of torture, and though there must be a showing of serious mental or physical harm, this harm need not be permanent.[155] In addition, the ICRC has stated that grave breaches of inhuman treatment and wilfully causing great suffering are defined very similarly with 'certain overlap' – the main difference between the two crimes is that inhuman treatment also extends to constituting an attack on human dignity, which is not covered by wilfully causing great suffering.[156]

Examples of wilfully causing great suffering could therefore consist of many forms of serious injury to body or health, including the mutilation of the wounded, exposure to useless and unnecessary suffering, severe beatings, or other severe forms of mistreatment.[157] At the ICTY in *Delalić*, the accused was found guilty of wilfully causing great suffering for having tied a victim to a roof beam, beaten him with a baseball bat, and setting his trousers on fire using gasoline.[158] Although these examples are mainly physical which may differ in the case of digital harms, there is no requirement listed in the Rome Statute or in any previous ICL jurisprudence that the acts prosecuted as 'wilfully causing great suffering' only be instances of physical violence. Therefore, like the crime against humanity of 'other inhumane acts', 'wilfully causing great suffering' is a crime that is flexible and could potentially encompass types of digital harm that will be discussed later in this book,[159] and further represents an area where ICL was meant to and can expand to account for new harms.

iii. Outrages Upon Personal Dignity

'Outrages upon personal dignity' are defined under Article 8(2)(b) and 8(2)(c) as when '[t]he perpetrator humiliated, degraded or otherwise violated the dignity

[153] ibid; *Prosecutor v Kony* (Arrest Warrant) ICC-02/04, PTC II (8 July 2005) 13; *Prosecutor v Lukwaya* (Arrest Warrant) ICC-02/04, PTC II (8 July 2005) 9; *Prosecutor v Otti* (Arrest Warrant) ICC-02/04, PTC II (8 July 2005) 14; *Prosecutor v Mudacumara* (Decision on the Prosecutor's Application under Article 58) ICC-01/04-01/12, PTC II (13 July 2011) [44]–[45].

[154] Rome Statute Elements of Crimes art 8(2)(a)(iii)(1).

[155] Schabas (n 40) 251.

[156] ICRC 2020 Commentary (n 150) 5248.

[157] ibid 5264.

[158] ibid, *Delalić et al* Trial Judgment (n 148) [1012]–[1018].

[159] See ch 4 of this book.

of one or more persons'.[160] The Elements of Crimes also state that 'the severity of the humiliation, degradation or other violation was of such degree as to be generally recognized as an outrage upon personal dignity'.[161] This definition makes it explicitly clear that the harm of an outrage upon personal dignity is, in essence, the humiliation and absence or dignity felt by the victim, regardless of how the act was perpetrated.

Outrages upon personal dignity can be perpetrated through both physical and mental suffering, so long as the humiliation of the victim is 'real and serious', and 'so intense that any reasonable person would be outraged'.[162] For example, at the ICC, the Pre-Trial Chamber held in the case of *Katanga et al.* that being forced to hang naked from handcuffs or to stay in a certain position for a long period of time constituted extremely humiliating treatment of female prisoners.[163] Further, in its report on the preliminary examination in the Gaza Flotilla situation, the ICC OTP listed a wide range of acts as sufficiently serious to constitute outrages upon personal dignity, including (but not limited to) overly tight handcuffing for extended periods, beatings, being denied access to a toilet or watched while using the toilet, denial of medication, and physical and verbal harassment.[164] It is therefore clear that outrages upon personal dignity can come in many forms, all constituting the same underlying harm of severe humiliation and shame.

Notably, victims need not be living to suffer the harm of an outrage upon personal dignity. The Rome Statute also lists a footnote after the definition of 'outrages upon personal dignity', which states that 'persons' can include dead persons.[165] This expands the harm of the crime not just to humiliation and degradation to surviving victims, but to the dignity and reputation of victims after they have died. This aspect will have particular importance for certain digital harms in which images of the dead are shared on the internet, which will be discussed in the next chapter.

III. Conclusion

This section explored how harm has been understood for core ICL crimes with potential relevance to a theory of addressing digital harm. Generally, there are some commonalities among the different harms discussed. Regarding their similarities,

[160] Rome Statute Elements of Crimes arts 8(2)(b)(xxi) and 8(2)(c)(ii).

[161] ibid.

[162] Schabas (n 40) 250.

[163] *Katanga et al* Confirmation of Charges (n 135) [370].

[164] Office of the Prosecutor, Situation on Registered Vessels of Comoros, Greece and Cambodia Article 53(1) Report (6 November 2014) www.icc-cpi.int/sites/default/files/iccdocs/otp/OTP-COM-Article_53(1)-Report-06Nov2014Eng.pdf, [71]–[72]; *Situation on Registered Vessels of the Comoros, the Hellenic Republic of Greece and the Kingdom of Cambodia* (Application for Review pursuant to Article 53(3)(a) of the Prosecutor's Decision of 6 November 2014 not to initiate an investigation in the Situation) ICC-01/13 (29 January 2015) Annex A, [64].

[165] ibid.

all the international crimes encompass multiple forms of harm, including both physical and mental harms. This demonstrates the focus of ICL in accounting for not only violent bodily harms, but also severe forms of psychological or emotional suffering.

Further, a major challenge of conducting an analysis of the harm of international crimes is that the harm is not always explained in the law itself, and throughout ICL jurisprudence, chambers generally have not provided clear interpretations as to what the harm of each crime actually is. For instance, the definitions of genocide in ICL statutes do not explain what is meant by 'serious bodily or mental harm', and when discussing this element in judgments, chambers have provided limited guidance as to what acts can constitute this harm, especially for 'serious mental harm'. In addition, relating to crimes such as torture or inhuman treatment, no concrete definition exists as to what constitutes severe physical or mental suffering.

A possible and plausible explanation for the lack of clear guidance as to what constitutes harm for certain international crimes is that the drafters of provisions and judges at ICCTs simply view the harm as obvious and thus not needing further explanation. This was explicitly stated in *Kayishema and Ruzindana*, where the Trial Chamber stated that '[i]t is the view of the Trial Chamber that, to large extent, "causing serious bodily harm" is self-explanatory'.[166] This view of the harms of international crimes being 'obvious' and not needing much explanation can of course result in uncertainty about the law, but the benefit of not having an exhaustive list outlined in ICL frameworks for what can constitute the harms of these crimes is that the law may evolve to accommodate different types of harm.

[166] *Kayishema and Ruzindana* Trial Judgment (n 32) [109].

4

Digital Harm and International Criminal Law

I. Introduction

'Digital harm' encompasses a variety of harms inflicted through digital technologies. This chapter will explore how digital harms differ in nature from more traditional forms of harm. In addition, it will consider some key categories of digital harm that have relevance to international criminal law (ICL), including online sexual violence, online hate speech and genocidal denial, online terrorist or violent content, and digital threats to democracy. Following this, four specific examples of digital harms will be identified and explained to demonstrate how digital harms may fit in with existing ICL frameworks. These include mass surveillance, online hate speech, sharing footage of crimes online, and online sexual violence.

II. What Makes 'Digital Harm' Different?

In contrast with general harm to individuals, digital harm is notably different in multiple ways. First, the harm is less often directly physical, simply because of the nature of the digital space. Digital harm can still manifest in physical ways, if for instance an individual is driven to self-harm, but the direct physical contact between the harm-doer and the person who is harmed is mostly removed. It is possible to argue that a direct linkage between a digital act and a physical harm that follows it could constitute a physical digital harm – for example, in cases where a murderer finds his victims and locates them using a social media website.[1] However, this can be arbitrary, as it is difficult to discern what constitutes a 'direct link' and exactly how direct (ie how long after the online act the physical harm took place, any other factors that could have led to the harm aside from the digital element, etc) it should be.

Second, paradoxically, while the fact that harm is digital does provide a physical distance between perpetrators and their victims, it also enables perpetrators

[1] MR McGuire, *Technology, Crime and Justice: The Question Concerning Technomia* (Routledge, 2012) 59.

to access victims at almost any time and place through their devices. With widespread internet and mobile technology now around the globe, it is much easier for individuals to encounter harmful content, or to be harassed, humiliated, or stalked no matter where they are. This is well illustrated by research on cyberstalking, in which the perpetrator 'utilizes remote forms of pursuit to stalk the victim, including communications technologies such as texts, instant messages, and emails; and monitoring tools, such as spyware, GPS devices, and audio/video recording devices'.[2] In recent times, it has only become easier for perpetrators of crimes like stalking to be able to use digital environments to reach their victims, which heightens the importance of the question of whether digital harm may be of a different nature to individuals than other types of harm.

On this note, the 'online disinhibition effect' has been confirmed in research on cyber-harassment, cyberbullying, and cyberstalking.[3] As explained by Suler, the 'online disinhibition effect' refers to when people act differently in cyberspace than they do in the real, face-to-face world.[4] In this sense, it has been found that perpetrators perceive online environments as 'arena[s] where real-world rules and norms do not apply', and that the minimisation of the seriousness of digital threats by legal systems only further validate this believe and perpetuate hostile environments where victims of digital violence have limited recourse and agency.[5] An analysis of how digital harms might differ and require different means of addressing them is thus of extreme importance to victims of international crimes and to potentially prevent future digital harm.

Sandberg and Ugelvik argue that the addition of technology to a traditional offence would change the nature of the harm associated with the crime. They explored why offenders record and share footage of their crimes at the domestic level, ranging from a desire to distribute amateur and rape pornography to a need to further degrade a victim in a 'new online culture of humiliation'.[6] In these instances, they argue that it is clear that 'the recording of the act in some ways changed the offence', and that it would be 'difficult to know whether [the] crime would not have happened at all without readily available image recording technology'.[7] The authors note that 'smartphones were used to make victims suffer more' in the cases that they discussed.[8]

Sandberg and Ugelvik also analysed how recording a crime has influenced the way in which the case was handled in the courtroom.[9] For example, in their study of 51 Norwegian higher court decisions describing the use of a camera as an

[2] HC Chan and L Sheridan (eds), *Psycho-Criminological Approaches to Stalking Behavior: An International Perspective* (Wiley, 2020) 15.

[3] ibid 302.

[4] J Suler, 'The Online Disinhibition Effect' (2004) 7 *Cyberpsychology & Behavior* 321.

[5] Chan and Sheridan (n 2) 302.

[6] S Sandberg and T Ugelvik, 'Why Do Offenders Tape Their Crimes? Crime and Punishment in the Age of the Selfie' (2017) 57 *British Journal of Criminology* 1023–40.

[7] ibid 1035.

[8] ibid 1036.

[9] ibid.

'integrated part of an offence', Sandberg and Ugelvik found that the act of recording images 'explicitly led the courts to increase the sentence' in 24 cases, while for the remaining 27 cases, the footage was solely presented as evidence.[10] In the cases where the use of the camera did increase the sentence, the courts paid attention to details such as how the 'recording seemed itself to have been part of the salacious attraction of the abuse' and how recording victims adds to the violence suffered because they have no control over the future dissemination of the images.[11] Thus, when a crime is filmed, victims must not only cope with the harm inflicted by the physical crime, but also then must deal with the fear and humiliation of knowing the footage may be circulated to a wider audience.

Further, victims depicted in violent footage of crimes could foreseeably suffer forms of harm besides that of fear or humiliation if the footage is shared online. This harm could come in the form of what Tran et al describe as discrimination harm (suffering from discrimination actions and attitudes from others), connection harm (suffering from interrupted social connections with family, friends or working partners), or isolation harm (suffering due to social isolation from the community).[12] Additionally, financial harm could also result if the emotional trauma experienced by the victims from the sharing of the footage renders them unable to fulfil their work duties, or if an employer is reluctant to hire someone after viewing the content or after knowing it has gone 'viral'.

In cases where the international crime in the footage resulted in the deaths of victims, an added form of harm can be done to the victims' dignity and reputation, which could also negatively impact the well-being of their families and friends. This notion is expressed in ICL, where the mutilation of dead bodies is covered by the war crime of committing outrages upon personal dignity in the Rome Statute of the International Criminal Court (ICC),[13] and in international humanitarian law (IHL), where the obligation to respect the remains of the dead and prevent their despoilation, and to protect individuals from 'public curiosity', is codified in the Geneva Conventions.[14] These laws demonstrate the emphasis placed upon respecting persons after they are deceased, and implies that one's reputation or dignity could still be harmed even after they are no longer living.

In addition, individuals can experience digital harms (particularly those inflicted online) uniquely in that generally threats can seem particularly invasive and chilling when made over the internet. For example, a perpetrator's perceived

[10] ibid 1027.

[11] ibid 1029–30.

[12] T Tran, R Valecha, P Rad, and HR Rao, 'An Investigation of Misinformation Harms Related to Social Media during Two Humanitarian Crises' (2020) 23 *Information Systems Frontiers* 931–39.

[13] Rome Statute Elements of Crimes art 8(2)(b)(xxi)) fn 49.

[14] See Protocol Additional to the Geneva Conventions of 12 August 1949 and relating to the Protection of Victims of International Armed Conflicts (Protocol I) (8 June 1977) art 34(1); 'Rule 113. Treatment of the Dead' (ICRC Customary IHL Database) ihl-databases.icrc.org/en/customary-ihl/v1/rule113; Convention (III) relative to the Treatment of Prisoners of War, Geneva (12 August 1949) art 13; Convention (IV) relative to the Protection of Civilian Persons in Time of War, Geneva (12 August 1949) art 27.

(or actual) power can be heightened by factors such as victims feeling a lack of control over the dissemination of content, the threatener's anonymity, and the victims having limited capacity to defend themselves against a 'potentially infinite online audience and the bandwagon effect of additional aggressors from the online audience joining the persecution'.[15] Adding to this, in the context of a poll about online sexual harassment, participants noted that online harassment was 'most distressing precisely because "the absence of cues about attackers led participants to fear the worst"'.[16] Thus, the element of the unknown in digital harms – both in terms of not knowing who the perpetrator is and who the content about the victim might reach – is particularly distressing for victims and is distinct from what is experienced from non-digital harms. Moreover, it is also possible that feelings of unease and insecurity are heightened by the fact that the legal frameworks to address these digital harms are often vague and can leave victims feeling as if they have less options for help or justice.

III. A Typology of Digital Harm

This section will provide an overview of the emerging literature on different categories of digital harms with relevance to international law, including online sexual violence, mass surveillance, online hate speech and genocidal denial, online terrorist content, and digital threats to democracy (including mis- and disinformation).

A. Online Sexual Violence

One unique form of harm caused by digital means is that which arises from online sexual violence, such as online sexual harassment and 'image-based sexual abuse'. 'Image-based sexual abuse' refers to non-consensual taking and/or sharing of nude or sexual images, which includes what is commonly described as 'revenge pornography'.[17] McGlynn et al studied the types of harms caused by image-based sexual abuse, including when images were shared online via pornographic websites, chat rooms, and social media platforms without consent, and found there to be five holistic harms amongst victim-survivors: social rupture, constancy, isolation, existential threat, and constrained liberty,[18] all of which may be applied to the concept of digital harm. 'Social rupture' refers to the 'marked and overwhelming breach

[15] Chan and Sheriden (n 2) 304; Colette Langos, 'Cyberbullying: The Challenge to Define' (2012) 15 *Cyberpsychology, Behavior and Social Networking* 285.

[16] ibid; JK Biber, D Doverspike, D Baznik, A Cober and BA Ritter, 'Sexual Harassment in Online Communications: Effects of Gender and Discourse Medium' (2002) 5 *Cyberpsychology & Behavior* 33–42.

[17] C McGlynn et al, '"It's Torture for the Soul": The Harms of Image-Based Sexual Abuse' (2021) 30 *Social and Legal Studies* 541, 543.

[18] ibid 550.

– or rupture – that radically disrupted [victims'] lives, altering their sense of self, their identity and their relationships with their bodies and others' – in essence, the experience of image-based sexual abuse divided victims' lives into clear 'before' and 'after' periods around the abuse.[19] The harm of 'social rupture' can foreseeably come into play for digital harm, as if, for example, a video of a crime is shared on social media, the victim depicted in the footage could likely see their life as divided between 'before' and 'after' the video was posted and when they had to start worrying about the humiliation of others seeing the crime that was done to them.

McGlynn et al also discuss the notion of 'constancy', which refers to the 'level of permanence' of the harms experienced that 'affects everything' for victims (in other words, the ability of the harms to constantly and permanently affect all areas of life).[20] 'Constancy' also applies well to the general concept of digital harm, as once information about or footage of an individual is posted online, it is extremely difficult to get rid of it completely, and it thus could affect victims throughout their lives – with harms ranging from humiliation of the post being available, the fear of not knowing where it may spread, or damage to one's reputation that could prevent them from future career opportunities. Relating to this, the authors discuss 'existential threat', which is used to describe the constant threat that images could be re-shared or re-emerge online, and the consequential fear that never goes away.[21] Finally, McGlynn et al describe the harms of 'isolation' (meaning that image-based sexual abuse can cause victims to isolate themselves from family and friends) and 'constrained liberty' (a sense of vulnerability and distrust in others).[22]

As stated previously, the authors highlight the importance of characterising these harms in a feminist phenomenological way instead of a more traditional medicalised trauma-based understanding of sexual abuse.[23] The authors note that this characterisation is extremely important given the online dimension of image-based sexual abuse, as technology-facilitated violence 'intersects physical and digital realities, as well as individuals' "online" and "offline" worlds'.[24] The feminist phenomenological approach is thus relevant for this book, as it provides a way to more holistically account for harms experienced by victims instead of limiting harm to medical frameworks.

B. Online Hate Speech and Genocidal Denial

Digital harm can also be experienced by groups, such as that which comes as a result of online hate speech. Hate speech, such as racist, homophobic, or misogynistic speech, can cause a number of impairments, including psychological

[19] ibid.
[20] ibid 552.
[21] ibid 553.
[22] ibid 554–55.
[23] ibid.
[24] ibid 546.

damage to members of the targeted group, a breakdown in community relations, or a threat to law and order.[25] On this note, Waldron emphasises the concept of hate speech as a 'social harm' which undermines the 'public good', which he defines as 'a sense of security in the space we all inhabit'.[26] Waldron argues that at the group level, hate speech serves as an assault on group reputation, which can then harm one's dignity or social standing at the individual level.[27] Further, he argues that harms to group reputation can diminish educational or career opportunities for members of the group, and infringes upon the dignity of group members.[28]

On the other hand, Peršak argues that hate speech constitutes a psychological harm, as it 'goes to the heart' of a person's group identity, 'negates their individuality, and derives their identity from stereotypes and prejudices'.[29] Further, it is also worth noting that hate speech is often a precursor to other crimes such as persecution, genocide, or other mass violence, which can add to its dehumanising nature.[30] She observes that the 'residue of hate speech is its impact on identity, which is a particularly insidious and long-lasting consequence, since its victim cannot do anything to change their race, sexual orientation, ethnicity etc'.[31] Thus, the psychological harm, including known effects on the health of minorities,[32] is many times inescapable.

While Waldron's and Peršak's focus is on hate speech in general and not necessarily hate speech that is circulated digitally, the harms they describe may also apply to online hate speech. As recognised by the European Court of Human Rights in several cases, including in *Ahmet Yıldırım v Turkey*,[33] *Times Newspapers Ltd (nos. 1 and 2) v the United Kingdom*,[34] and *Delfi AS v Estonia*,[35] the internet 'provides an unprecedented platform for the exercise of freedom of expression',[36] which can easily be abused. In *Delfi AS v Estonia*, the Court noted that in particular, hate speech on the internet may be 'disseminated like never before, worldwide, in a matter of seconds, and sometimes remain persistently available online'.[37]

[25] E Barendt, 'What is the Harm of Hate Speech?' (2019) 22 *Ethical Theory and Moral Practice* 539–53, 540.

[26] J Waldron, *The Harm in Hate Speech* (Harvard University Press, 2012) 4, 95.

[27] ibid 5, 56.

[28] ibid 56–59.

[29] N Peršak, 'Pathways to the Criminalization of Emotional Distress: An Offence- and Harm-Based Typology' (2020) 63 *International Journal of Law, Crime and Justice* 7.

[30] W Timmermann, 'Counteracting Hate Speech as a Way of Preventing Genocidal Violence' (2008) 3 *Genocide Studies and Prevention* 353. See also M Williams, P Burnap, A Javed, H Liu, and S Ozalp, 'Hate in the Machine: Anti-Black and Anti-Muslim Social Media Posts as Predictors of Offline Racially and Religiously Aggravated Crime' (2019) 60 *The British Journal of Criminology* 93–117, for a study of how hate speech against Black and Muslim communities directly led to racially motivated crimes in London.

[31] ibid.

[32] ibid.

[33] *Ahmet Yıldırım v Turkey* (2012) 3111/10.

[34] *Times Newspapers Ltd (nos. 1 and 2) v the United Kingdom* (2009) 3002/03 and 23676/03.

[35] *Delfi AS v Estonia* (2015) 64569/09.

[36] ibid [110].

[37] ibid.

On this note, it is possible that the harm caused by online hate speech could be even more severe than that would be caused by hateful speech in the offline world, since it would be much easier for the harmful speech to reach a wide audience in a shorter amount of time. This is, in part, because the online environment now has low entry barriers, as it is no longer necessary to negotiate one's way through traditional media avenues to share one's message with the masses.[38] In addition, online hate speech has extra potential to be amplified due to the ability for online users to filter the content they see or to join certain pages on platforms where users can reinforce each other's views, acting as a sort of 'online echo chamber'.[39] This is especially important considering the findings of Perry and Alvi, which demonstrate that simply an awareness of violence directed toward a target group 'yields strikingly similar patterns of emotional and behavioural responses among vicarious victims' in the same community.[40] In an online environment, it is much easier for individuals even outside of an individual's or a group's immediate community to bear witness to hate speech towards a targeted group, and thus it is likely also easier for more to be harmed vicariously.

Like online hate speech, another form of harm to groups which is incurred through digital means is that of genocidal or Holocaust denial. For example, in 2021, Twitter and YouTube (owned by Google) announced a new effort to remove content that denies the Srebrenica genocide due to the fact that those denying or minimising the genocide on said platforms were humiliating victims and inflicting further pain and suffering on survivors.[41] In addition to pain felt by victims and survivors, content posted online that denies or even glorifies genocide can encourage more behaviour of this kind,[42] and potentially incite crimes against the survivors' groups. The harms caused by genocidal and Holocaust denial alone have been argued to amount to the level of gravity necessary to be criminalised under international law,[43] which were considered in chapter three.[44]

[38] T McGonagle, 'The Council of Europe Against Online Hate Speech: Conundrums and Challenges' (2013) Expert Paper. See also R Wilson and M Gillett, 'The Hartford Guidelines on Speech Crimes in International Criminal Law' (Peace and Justice Initiative, 2018).

[39] ibid 34.

[40] B Perry and S Alvi, '"We Are All Vulnerable": The *In Terrorem* Effects of Hate Crimes' (2012) 18 *International Review of Victimology* 1.

[41] 'Twitter, Google to ban content denying Srebrenica genocide: RFE' (Aljazeera, 11 August 2021) www.aljazeera.com/news/2021/8/11/twitter-google-to-ban-content-denying-srebrenica-genocide-rfe.

[42] ibid.

[43] W Timmermann, 'The Relationship between Hate Propaganda and Incitement to Genocide: A New Trend in International Law Towards Criminalization of Hate Propaganda?' (2005) 18 *Leiden Journal of International Law* 257–82.

[44] See ch 3, s II of this book.

C. Online Terrorist or Violent Content

Considering the general harms to society discussed in chapter two,[45] it is relatively easy to see how the harms of widespread terror or chilling effects on speech could come into play through a digital environment. On the subject of terrorism, Barr and Herfroy-Mischler discuss the motives for the Islamic State of Iraq and the Levant's (ISIL) dissemination of hostage execution videos online, which mainly include desires to spread political messages, incite fear, and facilitate audience segmentation.[46] The ongoing conflict in Syria and the rise of ISIL has been referred to as the 'first YouTube war' based on how critical of a role social media has played in the situation.[47] This is due to the fact that modern terrorist organisations are 'very much aware' of the standards governing social media coverage and 'exploit these norms to accomplish their objectives'.[48] Groups such as ISIL not just use social media websites, but *rely* on them to spread their agendas.[49]

Barr and Herfroy-Mischler studied ISIL execution videos which were shared online and found a strategy of audience segmentation.[50] This means that the group used a range of variables, including the way in which executions were depicted, the garments worn by victims and perpetrators in the videos, and the languages spoken in the footage, to spread different messages to different audiences within larger society.[51] Through this, terrorist groups are able to use tailored videos posted online to appeal to more people in a more efficient manner. Thus, the addition of the 'digital' element enables terrorist messages to spread more quickly and to penetrate groups that they otherwise may not have been able to before social media became widely used. The overall societal harm in this is (1) that terrorist propaganda is more widespread and can lead to other crimes associated with terrorism and (2) that terrorism can become more visible and instil more fear in the public.

In addition to terrorist content posted online, other violent footage is frequently posted to social media, especially in the context of armed conflict. For instance, photos and videos from the current war between Russia and the Ukraine began circulating on platforms such as Twitter, Facebook, Instagram, and Tik Tok almost immediately after the Russian invasion.[52] This also has occurred previously in

[45] See ch 2, s II.E of this book.

[46] A Barr and A Herfroy-Mischler, 'ISIL's Execution Videos: Audience Segmentation and Terrorist Communication in the Digital Age' (2018) 41 *Studies in Conflict & Terrorism* 946–67.

[47] ibid 946.

[48] ibid 946–47.

[49] ibid 947.

[50] ibid.

[51] ibid.

[52] See, eg J York, '"World's first TikTok war": Ukraine's social media campaign 'a question of survival' (France 24, 24 February 2023) www.france24.com/en/europe/20230224-world-s-first-tiktok-war-ukraine-s-social-media-campaign-a-question-of-survival.

relation to conflicts in Syria,[53] Myanmar,[54] and Cameroon,[55] amongst others. The posting of violent content online in relation to armed conflicts is especially relevant to my focus on accountability for digital harm in relation to ICL and will be explored more in-depth later in this book.[56] For now, strictly in terms of identifying the types of digital harm associated with this phenomenon, two main kinds of harm arise – one being the harm to the victims depicted in the footage (and their families or loved ones) akin to that discussed previously regarding Sandberg and Ugelvik's study,[57] and the second being the harm to those who come across the footage.

The harm to those who come across the footage may manifest in what is known as 'vicarious trauma', which has been studied previously in the context of open-source investigations, in which investigators review images of crimes posted online.[58] Notably, in a study conducted by Eyewitness Media Hub on staff working for news, human rights, and humanitarian organisations, unexpected or surprising exposure to distressing video content was 'almost universally cited by interviewees as having a more traumatic impact upon them in comparison to distressing images and video that the individual was prepared to view'.[59] Placing these findings in a more general context, it can be reasonably assumed that innocent internet users who view violent propaganda or content online will not always be searching for it or prepared to see it, which can lead to a wide range of psychological harms. This element of surprise is likely more critical in a digital environment, where windows can simply pop up in front of the user's face without warning, as opposed to if a trained police officer were physically attending a crime scene and had some knowledge of what they were about to see and could approach it at their own pace.

D. Digital Threats to Democracy and Freedom of Expression

Aside from terrorism and violent extremism, political threats have also been on the rise in the digital sphere, such as through cyber and web-based attacks that threaten national security or result in 'election meddling', which may undermine

[53] See, eg Top of FormBottom of FormA Varghese, 'Social Media Reporting and the Syrian Civil War' (United States Institute of Peace Brief 151, 7 June 2013) www.usip.org/sites/default/files/PB-151.pdf.

[54] See, eg P Brody, 'Myanmar Witness verifies citizens' photos and videos to document human rights concerns' (France 24, 12 November 2021) observers.france24.com/en/tv-shows/the-observers/20211112-myanmar-witness-citizen-photos-videos-human-rights-verification-osint.

[55] See, eg N Turse, 'Cameroon Is a Close US Ally – and Its Soldiers Carried Out a Shocking Execution of Women and Children' (The Intercept, 26 July 2018) theintercept.com/2018/07/26/cameroon-executions-us-ally/.

[56] See ch 4, s IV and ch 7, s II of this text.

[57] Sandberg and Ugelvik (n 6).

[58] S Dubberley, E Griffin, and HM Bal, 'Making Secondary Trauma a Primary Issue: A Study of Eyewitness Media and Vicarious Trauma on the Digital Frontline' (Eyewitness Media Hub Report, 2015) firstdraftnews.org/wp-content/uploads/2018/03/trauma_report.pdf.

[59] ibid 6.

democracy and the right to self-determination. These online threats can be perpetrated by States – for example, the Russian government is known to have used a variety of tactics, ranging from hacking personal email accounts of American political figures, to distributing material online and to media outlets, in order to influence the outcome of the 2016 United States Presidential Election and the 2019 United Kingdom General Election.[60] This form of election meddling simply would not have been possible to this extent without the use of technology. For example, in the case of the US, Russia was able to spread information and pro-Trump propaganda easily to millions of online users. The harm caused in this instance was not only an infringement upon democracy and the right to self-determination, but also an increased polarisation amongst the American public.[61] This political polarisation could lead, and likely already has led, to a variety of other individual and group harms such as through discrimination or hate crimes.

On a similar note, digital harm to society can be caused through mis- or disinformation. Misinformation refers to false information that is spread without the intent of doing so, whereas disinformation concerns false information that is purposely circulated with the intention of causing harm. However, both misinformation and disinformation may be harmful on both individual and collective levels. On the individual level, the spread of mis- or disinformation about a person could cause them undue reputational or financial harm and could likely result in their emotional distress. On the collective level, mis- and disinformation can cause extremely severe harms to global society – a key example being the effects of false information spread on social media during the COVID-19 pandemic, in which misinformation has been shown to be closely linked to a decline in vaccination intent,[62] which could then harm greater society by perpetuating the spread of the virus.

Further, McKay and Tenove studied the harms caused by online disinformation in relation to the 2016 United States election, and found that in addition to the aforementioned harms, disinformation campaigns advanced 'corrosive falsehoods' which led citizens to sometimes become hostile or indifferent to processes with higher epistemic demands (which they label 'epistemic cynicism').[63] In turn, individuals may feel overwhelmed with not knowing who or what to believe, and may reduce their information-seeking and consume less news overall,[64] leading to a

[60] MN Schmitt, '"Virtual" Disenfranchisement: Cyber Election Meddling in the Grey Zones of International Law' (2018) 19 *Chicago Journal of International Law* 34; F Seatzu and N Carrillo-Santarelli, 'Towards a Strengthening of Non-Interference, Sovereignty, and Human Rights from Foreign Cyber Meddling in Democratic Electoral Processes' (2023) 48 *Brooklyn Journal of International Law* 579, 581.

[61] P Barrett, J Hendrix, and G Sims, 'How tech platforms fuel US political polarization and what government can do about it' (Brookings, 27 September 2021) www.brookings.edu/blog/techtank/2021/09/27/how-tech-platforms-fuel-u-s-political-polarization-and-what-government-can-do-about-it/.

[62] S Loomba, A de Figueiredo, SJ Piatek, K de Graaf, and HJ Larson, 'Measuring the Impact of COVID-19 Vaccine Misinformation on Vaccination Intent in the UK and USA' (2021) 5 *Nature Human Behaviour* 337–48.

[63] S McKay and C Tenove, 'Disinformation as a Threat to Deliberative Democracy' (2021) 74 *Political Research Quarterly* 703–17.

[64] ibid.

less-informed public. McKay and Tenove also observed that 'unjustified inclusion' (such as foreign interference, in which actors 'who lack normative entitlements to participate may insert themselves in democratic discussions') may produce a systemic harm of 'pervasive inauthenticity', where the 'democratic discourse is corrupted by the belief that a significant number of interlocutors hold problematic identities, such as fake accounts, foreign agents, and bots'.[65] Thus, in the case of online election meddling, significant portions of the public can become overly sceptical of certain actors and, in turn, devalue contributions of legitimate actors within political and government spheres.[66]

Aside from harms stemming from online speech, other digital technologies such as those used for surveillance can pose threats to privacy, freedom of expression, and democracy. This is because, generally, in addition to being an infringement on the right to privacy, digital surveillance (which can be particularly invasive as individuals can be monitored on their personal devices as well as cameras in public and private spaces) can cause individuals to limit their expression due to a fear of being watched and the consequences that may be associated with doing something 'wrong'. For example, as argued by Murray in the context of facial recognition technologies, there is an immediate impact on the individual's right to privacy due to the recording of their movements and biometric processing, but also a 'compound human rights harm' that results in chilling effects.[67] Concerning the latter, Murray emphasises that the suppression of behaviour individuals may resort to when they are aware of surveillance also can limit the free exchange of ideas and the development of one's personal identity (including political opinions).[68]

Due to the fact that the free exchange of ideas and the development of individuals' political beliefs are central components of a democratic society, digital surveillance can also result in harms to democracy, in addition to infringements upon the rights to identity and freedom of expression.[69] Similarly, in the context of telecommunications interceptions, Parsons argues that such pervasive surveillance 'erodes essential boundaries' between public and private spaces by compromising individuals' ability to communicate freely, which leads to the erosion of integrity of democratic processes and institutions.[70] The harms of digital surveillance technologies will be explored further in sections IV and VII.C.[71]

Overall, the spread of mis- and disinformation online and harms upon freedom of expression, privacy, and democracy resulting from other digital technologies demonstrate that these acts have the potential to create a cascade of harms on

[65] ibid.
[66] ibid.
[67] D Murray, 'Police Use of Retrospective Facial Recognition Technology: A Step Change in Surveillance Capability Necessitating an Evolution of the Human Rights Law Framework' (2024) 87 *Modern Law Review* 833–63, 840.
[68] ibid 843.
[69] ibid.
[70] C Parsons, 'Beyond Privacy: Articulating the Broader Harms of Pervasive Mass Surveillance' (2015) 3(3) *Media and Communication* 1–11, 1.
[71] See s IV of this chapter and ch 7, s III.

individual, group, and societal levels. These harms will be especially relevant to the analyses of online hate speech and disinformation,[72] mass surveillance,[73] and their potential abilities to constitute core international crimes that will be considered later in this chapter.

This section demonstrated that there are critical differences between harm in general and digital harm. In summary, digital harms can consist both of new ways of perpetrating 'traditional' harms, and of novel forms of harm that could not come to fruition without the development of digital technologies. Digital harms on an individual level tend to be more easily and quickly inflicted than their non-digital counterparts, and can reach more victims regardless of physical distance from the perpetrator. At the level of hate speech directed towards groups, racist, misogynistic, homophobic, and other problematic attitudes can be easily spread and amplified through 'online echo chambers' and can many times act as precursors to violence against members of those groups. Finally, at the societal level, online terrorist or violent content can quickly and easily instil fear in a population, and mis/disinformation and cyber-meddling can pose harms to democracy and self-determination in an efficient manner.

IV. Digital Harms Relevant to ICL

This section will explore examples of digital harms which could conceivably be linked to the core crimes discussed earlier, which will continue to form the basis of the analysis throughout the book: mass surveillance, the spread of hate speech and disinformation, sharing footage of crimes online, and online sexual abuse. These specific digital harms were chosen because they are already being discussed in relation to international crimes in the public sphere and are similar to harms previously criminalised under ICL in relation to their seriousness and context. As noted previously, other digital harms that are already comprehensively addressed by domestic or transnational law (such as online child sexual abuse or online human trafficking) or that would likely not be considered grave enough to constitute international crimes (such as cyberbullying) are not considered in this book.

A. Mass Surveillance

The use of mass surveillance against a targeted minority group is not new. For instance, the Nazis gathered extensive amounts of data in occupied territories during World War II in order to keep track of the Jewish population.[74] In some

[72] See s IV.B.
[73] See s IV.A.
[74] Z Rahman, 'Dangerous Data: the role of data collection in genocides' (Responsible Data, 21 November 2016) responsibledata.io/2016/11/21/dangerous-data-the-role-of-data-collection-in-genocides/.

countries, such as The Netherlands, population registration systems which were already in place by the government were taken over by the Nazis and adapted to create special registration systems covering Jewish and Roma populations. Further, even this long ago, technology was used to facilitate surveillance of targeted groups – the tech company known today as IBM worked closely with the Nazi command, developing punch cards and tabulating technology to speed up the collection of data of the Jewish people.[75] Although some forms of mass surveillance, such as population registration systems, may not be particularly egregious when used for a legitimate and necessary purpose, mass surveillance can become worthy of consideration as an international crime when it is weaponised against a population (such as when the above population registration systems were used to collect data to aid in the persecution and genocide of a particular group). The digital mass surveillance considered in this book will therefore be focused on when such surveillance is used maliciously and/or in excess (as opposed to, for example, legitimate electronic voter registrations, medical, or census information systems).

The trend of using surveillance technology continued during the Cold War, where the United States and Russia used new technologies, particularly those that could be used for 'electronic eavesdropping', to gather information about the other's capabilities and on any individuals who were labelled as suspicious.[76] Some examples of these technologies include portable transmitters that could be easily hidden under furniture, typewriters that were equipped with motors that could determine what keys were being pressed, and black boxes that could attach to power lines and hunt for radio signals.[77] Digital surveillance carried on after the 9/11 terrorist attacks, when the United States began heavily tracking the American Muslim population.[78] In addition to non-digital means of surveillance, such as the use of undercover police to monitor certain groups, the National Security Agency (NSA) also began analysing phone records and collecting user information from internet service providers.[79]

Further, the US government began using several electronic surveillance programs to monitor those suspected of terrorist activity's internet use, including Carnivore ('a computer program that can read a suspect's email and other electronic data on a real-time basis and print, or store the information for FBI agents to view or save as electronic evidence for prosecution') and Echelon ('a "global eavesdropping system" that links supercomputers throughout the world to "automatically search

[75] E Black, 'How IBM Technology Jump Started the Holocaust' (Gizmodo, 16 June 2011) gizmodo.com/how-ibm-technology-jump-started-the-holocaust-5812025.

[76] 'Listening In: Electronic Eavesdropping in the Cold War Era' (US Department of State, July 2008) www.state.gov/wp-content/uploads/2019/05/107507_listeningInColdwar.pdf.

[77] ibid.

[78] S Khan and V Ramachandran, 'Post-9/11 surveillance has left a generation of Muslim Americans in a shadow of distrust and fear' (PBS News Hour, 16 September 2021) www.pbs.org/newshour/nation/post-9-11-surveillance-has-left-a-generation-of-muslim-americans-in-a-shadow-of-distrust-and-fear; D Lyon, 'Technology vs "Terrorism": Circuits of City Surveillance since September 11th' (2003) 27 *International Journal of Urban and Regional Research* 666-678.

[79] ibid.

through the millions of intercepted messages for ones containing preprogrammed keywords or fax, telex and email addresses'").[80] Since then, the technology used for 'counterterrorism' purposes by the United States (and other countries, such as the United Kingdom) has become even more advanced – for example, cameras using AI facial recognition technology have been implemented in spaces such as airports and adopted by law enforcement.[81]

The harms caused by the disproportionate mass surveillance used against Muslim populations post-9/11 significantly violate members of the group's fundamental rights to privacy and freedom of expression,[82] and therefore could potentially be addressed by the crime against humanity of persecution. As explained in chapter three,[83] persecution involves the infringement upon fundamental rights of members of a group, in addition to the chapeau elements of crimes against humanity and a connection to another crime under the Rome Statute (in the case of the ICC). As a result of this surveillance upon personal devices, Muslim communities have suffered invasions upon their rights to privacy and family life, as enshrined in Article 12 of the Universal Declaration of Human Rights (UDHR) and Article 17 of the International Covenant on Civil and Political Rights (ICCPR).[84] In addition, their right to freedom of expression provided by Article 19 of both the UDHR and ICCPR is infringed upon, as surveillance has been found to cause a chilling effect on the speech of Muslim individuals online.[85] The surveillance inflicted seemingly arbitrarily upon Muslim groups post-9/11 directly contributes to a loss of their fundamental rights and is done so on the basis of their religion, which could fit the definition of persecution provided the chapeau elements for the crime against humanity (widespread or systematic attack against a civilian population) were met.

However, at the ICC, the crime of persecution requires a connection to another alleged crime under the Rome Statute.[86] For the above example pertaining to Muslim groups post-9/11, it would not be possible to proceed with a case at the ICC unless evidence of another crime under Article 7(1) came to light, which demonstrates a potential weakness of the ICC framework regarding its suitability for persecution in a digital age, since surveillance alone likely cannot satisfy all the requirements for the offence even if it meets the level of severity required. In the *Al Hassan* judgment, the Trial Chamber clarified that the acts of persecution themselves need not equate to an act under Article 7(1) or any other crime under the

[80] DS Sidhu, 'The Chilling Effect of Government Surveillance Programs on the Use of the Internet by Muslim-Americans' (2007) 7 *University of Maryland Law Journal of Race, Religion, Gender and Class* 375–92, 388 (footnotes omitted).

[81] K McKendrick, 'Artificial Intelligence Prediction and Counterterrorism' (August 2019) Chatham House view.ckcest.cn/AllFiles/ZKBG/Pages/875/2019-08-07-AICounterterrorism.pdf.

[82] T Choudhury and H Fenwick, 'The Impact of Counter-terrorism Measures on Muslim Communities' (2011) 25 *International Review of Law, Computers & Technology* 151–81; Sidhu (n 80).

[83] See ch 3, s II.B.iii.

[84] Universal Declaration of Human Rights (adopted 10 December 1948) UNGA Res 217 A(III) (UDHR) art 12; International Covenant on Civil and Political Rights (adopted 16 December 1966, entered into force 23 March 1976) 999 UNTS 171 (ICCPR) art 17.

[85] UDHR art 19; ICCPR art 19; Sidhu (n 80).

[86] Rome Statute art 7(1)(h).

jurisdiction of the Court.[87] Moreover, the Trial Chamber noted that 'connection' is meant in the sense of 'link to, or interrelated with', and that it is not necessary to demonstrate that the Article 7(1) acts connected to the persecution meet the contextual elements for crimes against humanity.[88] Therefore, in a scenario where the core conduct of persecution is intrusive digital surveillance, there would still need to be some link to another Article 7(1) crime, although as interpreted by the Trial Chamber, this connection can be broader than a specific direct nexus. This point is further clarified in the Office of the Prosecutor (OTP) Policy on Cyber-Enabled Crimes under the Rome Statute, which states (in relation to persecution) that '[c]onduct in cyberspace may be used to seriously deprive persons or groups of various fundamental rights' and as an example, that 'a particular ethnic or religious group may be subjected to a campaign of persecution, which may be facilitated or even partly constituted by the use of various intrusive surveillance techniques'.[89]

It was proposed during the 2024 negotiations for the Draft Articles on the Prevention and Punishment of Crimes Against Humanity (colloquially known as the 'Crimes Against Humanity Treaty') that the requirement of a connection to another crime be removed,[90] which if accepted, could be better suited to achieve accountability for persecution, including via the use of digital technologies for the reasons stated above. Negotiations for the Crimes Against Humanity Treaty are still ongoing, although at the time of writing, the connection requirement still appears in the Draft Articles (Article 2(1)(h)).[91]

Further, the nature of the harm of mass surveillance is that of an invasion of privacy, feelings of paranoia of being watched and a loss of dignity, all which can lead to chilling effects on freedom of expression, assembly, religion, and association. These harms have been considered prior to the development of modern technologies,[92] although as will be illustrated through a case study on Xinjiang, China in chapter seven,[93] the addition of digital technologies significantly exacer-

[87] *Prosecutor v Al Hassan* (Judgment) ICC-01/12-01/18, Trial Chamber X (26 June 2024) [1201]–[1211].

[88] ibid.

[89] Office of the Prosecutor, Policy on Cyber-Enabled Crimes Under the Rome Statute (December 2025) [77]–[78].

[90] Colombia and Portugal suggested a broader definition of persecution by aligning it with customary international law and other international instruments and jurisprudence. Australia stated that it was 'contemplating' addressing persecution as a 'standalone crime', and Brazil and Malta suggested that persecution be a 'standalone crime' and that the connection to another crime requirement should be deleted; UN Secretary General, 'Crimes against humanity' (1 January 2024) UN Doc A/78/717 [48]–[49]. Treaty negotiations are still ongoing at the time of writing; see also L Sadat, 'A Draft Treaty on Crimes Against Humanity Draws More Engagement from States' (Just Security, 22 May 2024) www.justsecurity.org/95850/crimes-against-humanity-draft-treaty-states-engagement/.

[91] International Law Commission, Draft Articles on Prevention and Punishment of Crimes Against Humanity (2019). See also Global Justice Center, 'Crimes Against Humanity Treaty Now', cahtreatynow.org.

[92] M Foucault, *Discipline and Punish: The Birth of the Prison* (Penguin Books, 1979); F Fanon, *Rencontre de la société et de la Psychiatrie: Notes de cours, Tunis 1959–60* (edited by Bensalem, Université d'Oran, 1984).

[93] See ch 7, s III of this book.

bates the harm. For instance, in his discussions of the panopticon, Foucault argued that the threat of surveillance is equally as traumatic as actually being watched – unsure of whether an authority would be watching, an individual would always try to conform to its perceived desires.[94] As noted by Fanon in relation to surveillance in the workplace, surveillance can be viewed as a form of 'control by quantification' that can result in embodied psychological effects like nervous tensions, insomnia, fatigue, or recurrent nightmares.[95] This is consistent with psychological studies that have found that surveillance increases feelings of anxiety and unease and general distress.[96] Taken together, these two points illustrate that surveillance can result in psychological harms (or as described by Richards, surveillance 'menaces intellectual privacy')[97] and lead to the suppression of certain behaviours to conform to what the authority deems acceptable.

The latter is commonly referred to as a 'chilling effect', meaning that surveillance 'can deter people from speaking or engaging in other legal, constitutionally protected, and even desirable activities'.[98] In addition to avoiding behaviours that may be undesirable to the authority, surveillance can also cause individuals to actively conform to the status quo (a 'conforming effect').[99] As explained by Kaminski and Witnov, these effects are particularly dangerous in the context of freedom of expression, as they are damaging to the development of diverse viewpoints and cultures and weaken minority influence.[100] As technology has developed, it has become easier for governments to monitor individuals on a large scale, both outside (ex. CCTV cameras) and inside (ex. tracking on personal devices) the home, which could amount to chilling and conforming effects on individual's cultural and religious practices. A key example is the current situation in Xinjiang, China, in which the Chinese government has imposed extreme digital surveillance measures upon the Uyghur Muslim population, arguably constituting an invasion of privacy that cannot be justified on the basis of legitimacy, necessity,

[94] Foucault (n 92); J Boyle, 'Foucault in Cyberspace: Surveillance, Sovereignty, and Hardwired Censors' (1997) 66 *University of Cincinnati Law Review* 177, 186.

[95] S Browne, *Dark Matters: On the Surveillance of Blackness* (Duke University Press, 2015) 5–6; Fanon (n 92).

[96] M Kaminski and S Witnov, 'The Conforming Effect: First Amendment Implications of Surveillance, Beyond Chilling Speech' (2014) 49 *University of Richmond Law Review* 465; GL White and PG Zimbardo, 'The Effects of Threat of Surveillance and Actual Surveillance on Expressed Opinions Toward Marijuana' (1980) *111 Journal of Social Psychology* 49, 59; JR Aiello, 'The Effects of Computer Monitoring, Standards, and Rewards on Work Performance, Job Satisfaction, and Stress' (1993) 23 *Journal of Applied Social Psychology* 499, 502–03; JR Aiello and KJ Kolb, 'Electronic Performance Monitoring and Social Context: Impact on Productivity and Stress' (1995) 80 *Journal of Applied Psychology* 339, 348; AM Watson et al, 'When Big Brother Is Watching: Goal Orientation Shapes Reactions to Electronic Monitoring During Online Training' (2013) 98 *Journal of Applied Psychology* 642, 643–44, 650; M Bhatia, 'Racial Surveillance and the Mental Health Impacts of Electronic Monitoring on Migrants' (2021) 62 *Race & Class* 18–36.

[97] NM Richards, 'The Dangers of Surveillance' (2013) 126 *Harvard Law Review* 1934, 1936.

[98] J Penney, 'Cybersecurity, Human Rights, and Empiricism: The Case of Digital Surveillance' in P Cornish (ed), *The Oxford Handbook of Cyber Security* (OUP, 2021) 411.

[99] Kaminski and Witnov (n 96).

[100] ibid.

and proportionality and which results in severe harm.[101] This example will be analysed in detail as a case study for how the digital harm may be encompassed by ICL frameworks in chapter seven.[102]

B. Online Hate Speech and Disinformation

Another example of a digital harm that has relevance for international crimes is the spread of hate speech and disinformation. Hate speech has no universal definition under international law, though it may generally be thought of as speech that targets a group or an individual based on inherent characteristics (such as race, religion, or gender) and that may threaten peace.[103] Disinformation refers to false information that is intentionally spread, as opposed to misinformation, which is false information spread unknowingly or by mistake.[104] Concerning ICL, disinformation has been linked to the commission of atrocity crimes at different stages of perpetration, including prompting such crimes, enabling their continuation as they occur, and concealing or denying them afterwards.[105] In the age of social media, hate speech and disinformation (which can include hateful false information or propaganda about a particular group) can be spread to a large audience with the click of a button. While these are two distinct concepts, hate speech and disinformation can overlap and may be used in tandem to target a particular individual or group. For instance, false information can constitute hateful speech that could be intended to sway others against (or even incite violence against) a group.

Online hate speech and disinformation could constitute the crimes of persecution and (incitement to) genocide.[106] First, in ICL jurisprudence, offline hate speech has been found to constitute an act of persecution.[107] This occurred at the International Criminal Tribunal for Rwanda (ICTR), in which the Trial Chambers for both the cases of *Ruggiu* and *Nahimana et al.* held that hate speech (regardless of whether it included calls for violence against the group) could constitute persecution.[108] In *Ruggiu*, the Trial Chamber noted that this was because the public

[101] Human Rights Watch, 'China's Algorithms of Repression: Reverse Engineering a Xinjiang Police Mass Surveillance App' (1 May 2019) www.hrw.org/report/2019/05/01/chinas-algorithms-repression /reverse-engineering-xinjiang-police-mass.

[102] See ch 7, s III of this book.

[103] United Nations, 'Strategy and Plan of Action on Hate Speech' (2019) www.un.org/en/genocide prevention/documents/advising-and-mobilizing/Action_plan_on_hate_speech_EN.pdf, 2.

[104] AM Guess and BA Lyons, 'Misinformation, Disinformation, and Online Propaganda' in N Persily and J Tucker (eds), *Social Media and Democracy: The State of the Field, Prospects for Reform* (CUP, 2020) 11.

[105] M Holvoet, 'International Criminal Liability for Spreading Disinformation in the Context of Mass Atrocity' (2022) 20 *Journal of International Criminal Justice* 223–50, 248.

[106] Rome Statute arts 7(1)(h) and 25(3)(e).

[107] R Kapoor and S Aravindakshan, 'Hate Speech as Persecution: Tackling the Gordian Knot'(EJIL: Talk!, 12 August 2020) www.ejiltalk.org/hate-speech-as-persecution-tackling-the-gordian-knot/.

[108] *Prosecutor v Ruggiu* (Judgment) ICTR-97-32-I, Trial Chamber I (1 June 2000) ('*Ruggiu* Trial Judgment') [22]; *Prosecutor v Nahimana, Barayagwiza and Ngeze* (Judgment) ICTR-99-52-T, Trial Chamber (3 December 2003) ('*Nahimana et al* Trial Judgment') [1073].

radio broadcasts were 'aimed at singling out and attacking' the groups 'on discriminatory grounds, by depriving them of the fundamental right to liberty and basic humanity enjoyed by members of wider society'.[109] Further, the Chamber found that '[t]he deprivation of [those] rights can be said to have as its aim the death and removal of those persons from the society in which they live alongside the perpetrators, or eventually even from humanity itself'.[110] In the case of *Nahimana et al.*, the Trial Chamber found that because the crime of persecution is defined in terms of impact as opposed to intent, '[i]t is not a provocation to cause harm' and is 'itself the harm'.[111] It is for this reason that, in the view of the Trial Chamber, 'there need not be a call to action in communications that constitute persecution'.[112] Yet, in the same case, the Appeals Chamber stated that hate speech in combination with calls for violence could constitute persecution, but was uncertain as to whether 'mere' hate speech without calls for violence could amount to persecution (and ultimately decided that it was not relevant to answer this question).[113]

On this note, an obstacle for prosecuting crimes before certain international criminal courts and tribunals (ICCTs) – most notably the ICC – is the gravity requirement, which refers to the focus on only the 'most serious crimes of concern to the international community', as provided in the Rome Statute.[114] There seems to be uncertainty amongst ICCTs as to whether hate speech that does not explicitly call for physical violence meets the gravity requirement for the crime against humanity of persecution.[115] For example, while the ICTR in the *Nahimana et al.* case ruled that hate speech can meet the threshold to constitute persecution,[116] the International Criminal Tribunal for the former Yugoslavia (ICTY) Trial Chamber in *Kordic and Čerkez* found that hate speech without any direct call for violence does not meet the gravity requirement to be considered a crime against humanity.[117] This uncertainty between ICL Chambers signals that in order for online hate speech to potentially constitute an act of persecution at a court such as the ICC, it may need to involve direct calls for violence.

Second, regarding incitement to genocide as its own offence under Article 25(3)(e) of the Rome Statute, this type of speech would need to be 'direct' and

[109] *Ruggiu* Trial Judgment (n 108) [22]. This case concerned charges of genocide and crimes against humanity against a journalist and broadcaster for the RTLM radio in Rwanda.

[110] ibid.

[111] *Nahimana et al* Trial Judgment (n 108) [1073]. This case concerned charges against three individuals in the media sector for their roles in the Rwandan genocide.

[112] ibid.

[113] *Prosecutor v Nahimana, Barayagwiza and Ngeze* (Judgment) ICTR-99-52-A, Appeals Chamber (28 November 2007) ('*Nahimana et al* Appeal Judgment') [987].

[114] Rome Statute, Preamble. For a comprehensive overview of the gravity requirement, see M deGuzman, 'Gravity and the Legitimacy of the International Criminal Court' (2008) 32 *Fordham International Law Journal* 1400–65.

[115] G S Gordon, 'Hate Speech and Persecution: A Contextual Approach' (2013) 46 *Vanderbilt Journal of Transnational Law* 303–73.

[116] *Nahimana et al* Trial Judgment (n 108); *Nahimana et al* Appeal Judgment (n 113).

[117] *Prosecutor v Kordic and Čerkez* (Judgment) IT-95-14/2-T, Trial Chamber (26 February 2001) ('Kordic and Čerkez Trial Judgment') [209].

'public' in its call for genocide against a protected group.[118] Under the Rome Statute, genocide is the only international crime in which incitement is expressly prohibited,[119] and it constitutes an inchoate offence, meaning the incitement is a crime regardless of whether a genocide subsequently occurs.[120] Historically, individuals have already been prosecuted whose hateful words directly incited acts of genocide to be committed against members of a targeted group. For example, at the Nuremburg Tribunal, Streicher and Fritzsche were tried, in part, for hate propaganda, as Streicher's genocidal rants were published in a weekly anti-Semitic newspaper. Fritzsche served as the head of the Radio Division of the Propaganda Ministry.[121] Additionally, at the ICTR, Akayesu was convicted of incitement to commit genocide for speeches urging a crowd to eliminate the Tutsis, and three men in the case of *Nahimana et al.* were prosecuted for similar hate speech made in newspapers and on the radio.[122]

A recent and ongoing example of the harm of online hate speech and disinformation is the suspected genocide in Myanmar against the Rohingya population. Social media websites, specifically Facebook (now under the parent company, Meta), have purportedly become tools used by the Myanmar military and its supporters to disseminate hateful and false messages about the Muslim Rohingya group.[123] For instance, Myanmar military personnel have allegedly posed as civilians on Facebook and posted various forms of hateful speech, such as that 'Islam is a global threat to Buddhism' or a false story about the rape of a Buddhist woman by a Muslim man.[124] As found by the Independent International Fact-Finding Mission on Myanmar, these posts are part of a systematic strategy used by the Myanmar military on Facebook to target the Rohingya population, allowing Facebook to serve as an 'echo chamber of virulent anti-Rohingya content' that 'pour[s] fuel on

[118] Rome Statute art 25(3)(e).

[119] C Stahn, *A Critical Introduction to International Criminal Law* (CUP, 2018) 47. As noted in the previous footnote, incitement is listed under Article 25 as a form of individual criminal responsibility rather than as an offence under Articles 6-8*bis*.

[120] WK Timmermann, 'Incitement in International Criminal Law' (2006) 88 *International Review of the Red Cross* 823.

[121] ibid 260–61; GS Gordon, 'The Propaganda Prosecutions at Nuremberg: The Origin of Atrocity Speech Law and the Touchstone for Normative Evolution' (2017) 39 *Loyola of Los Angeles International and Comparative Law Review* 209–45, 217.

[122] ibid 266.

[123] OHCHR, 'Report of the Independent International Fact-Finding Mission on Myanmar' (16 September 2019) UN Doc A/HRC/42/50; E Irving, '"The Role of Facebook is Significant": Facebook and the Fact Finding Mission on Myanmar' (Opinio Juris, 7 September 2018) opiniojuris.org/2018/09/07/the-role-of-social-media-is-significant-facebook-and-the-fact-finding-mission-on-myanmar/; P Mozur, 'A Genocide Incited on Facebook, With Posts from Myanmar's Military' (The New York Times, 15 October 2018) www.nytimes.com/2018/10/15/technology/myanmar-facebook-genocide.html. It is also worth noting that there is a growing body of literature focused on whether social media actors could be held responsible for the spread of hate speech under international law, see SR Singh, 'Move Fast and Break Societies: The Weaponisation of Social Media and Options for Accountability under International Criminal Law' (2019) 8(2) *Cambridge International Law Journal* 331–42; J Domino, 'Crime as Cognitive Constraint: Facebook's Role in Myanmar's Incitement Landscape and the Promise of International Tort Liability' (2020) 52 *Case Western Reserve Journal of International Law* 143–98.

[124] ibid.

the fire of long-standing discrimination and substantially increase[s] the risk of an outbreak of mass violence'.[125] The *New York Times* reported that as described by anonymous whistle-blowers, hundreds of military personnel created 'troll accounts' and fake news and celebrity pages on Facebook, then 'flooded them with incendiary comments and posts timed for peak viewership'.[126] This online hate speech has been argued to have incited murders, rapes, and 'the largest forced migration in human history',[127] all of which have contributed to the alleged genocide in Myanmar (which is currently under investigation by the ICC). This practice of spreading hate speech has even been confirmed by Facebook's parent company, Meta, whose Head of Security Policy stated that they had found 'clear and deliberate attempts to covertly spread propaganda that were directly linked to the Myanmar military'.[128]

What sets the harm of online hate speech and disinformation apart from offline speech of a similar nature is its ability to spread to much wider audiences in a very short timeframe. For example, while shouting something hateful about a minority group in a public town square might be heard by those in the immediate vicinity, posting the same comment on a website can allow for anyone around the world to see it and potentially act upon that message. In the context of the Rohingya situation, Facebook is many times equated with the internet itself, with an estimated 20 million users in Myanmar as of 2018 that is 'growing exponentially'.[129] As reported by Amnesty International following interviews conducted in Myanmar, it is also apparent that the rapid transformation of the country's telecommunications landscape and the rise of Facebook meant that digital media literacy is still fairly low, and the combination of Facebook being an American platform 'populated by trusted friends and family' and also used by the government for official announcements contributes to users' perceptions of the social media website as a reliable source of information.[130] Amnesty International further observed that Facebook 'was used not only as a means of communicating with friends, but for many people in Myanmar, it became their primary news source, business directory, online marketplace, and go-to search engine'.[131] Therefore, when anti-Rohingya groups and the government itself allegedly used Facebook to spread hateful messages and incite violence, they were able to influence an extremely wide audience in a short span of time, which would not have been possible without the online element.

In this sense, a comparison can be drawn with the Rwandan genocide, in which the hate speech spread on the Hutu radio stations about the Tutsi population were used to incite Hutu to 'hate and kill the Tutsi'.[132] In the case of *Nahimana*

[125] ibid; Amnesty International, 'The Social Atrocity: Meta and the Right to Remedy for the Rohingya' (September 2022) www.amnesty.org/en/documents/ASA16/5933/2022/en/, 6.
[126] Mozur (n 123).
[127] ibid.
[128] ibid.
[129] Amnesty International (n 123) 17.
[130] ibid.
[131] ibid; OHCHR (n 123) [1345].
[132] A Hefti and L Ausserladscheider Jonas, 'From Hate Speech to Incitement to Genocide: The Role of the Media in the Rwandan Genocide' (2020) 38 *Boston University International Law Journal* 15.

et al. at the ICTR, two defendants were found guilty of incitement to genocide for broadcasting hateful speech on their radio station, *Radio Télévision Libre des Mille Collines* (RTLM), and the third for speech published in a newspaper.[133] The two defendants charged in relation to the radio station RTLM, which was very popular in Rwanda at the time,[134] were found to have perpetuated ethnic stereotyping against the Tutsis through their broadcasts and deliberately called for violence against the group.[135] Just as hate speech and other propaganda spread through the radio could be classified as incitement to genocide in Rwanda, it is possible and even probable that the same type of speech directed against a group (such as the Rohingya) on social media could also meet this threshold. Online hate speech can be especially severe given that the internet can reach a much wider audience in quicker and more extended amounts of time (as posts remain visible on the internet after being uploaded, unlike speech given on live radio broadcasts).

Though there has not yet been an international criminal trial in which *online* hate speech or disinformation has been considered, it is coming. In its request for authorisation of an investigation into the situation of Bangladesh and Myanmar in 2019, the ICC OTP referred to numerous instances of hate speech attacking the Rohingya and other Muslims posted to Facebook.[136] The case is still currently in the investigation phase, though it is foreseeable that should warrants of arrest be issued and a trial occur, that the ICC will consider the harms of online hate speech in the context of the alleged genocide depending on which crimes the Prosecutor decides to focus on. However, a key challenge which would likely emerge should hate speech and disinformation on social media websites be a main element of the OTP's case, would be the acquisition of evidence. As has already been an issue at proceedings for the same situation at the International Court of Justice (ICJ) (*The Gambia v Myanmar*), Meta will likely refuse to disclose information to an international court without a legal obligation to do so, as shown by its limited cooperation to provide evidence that led The Gambia to bring a case in relation to the handover of information against it in a United States domestic court.[137] Thus, should cases considering online hate speech or disinformation be heard at the ICC, which cannot compel a company to cooperate with it, there could be barriers to accessing the original posts containing the speech. In these instances, the ICC would need to take other measures, such as asking a State Party to request the content from social

[133] *Nahimana et al* Trial Judgment (n 108). The third defendant, Barayagwiza, was the government minister who provided the political framework for the killings.

[134] ibid [342].

[135] ibid [371].

[136] *Situation in the People's Republic of Bangladesh/Republic of the Union of Myanmar* (Request for authorisation of an investigation pursuant to article 15) ICC-01/19 (4 July 2019) [59]–[60].

[137] P Pillai, 'The Republic of The Gambia v Facebook, Inc: Domestic Proceedings, International Implications' (Opinio Juris, 8 August 2020) opiniojuris.org/2020/08/08/the-republic-of-the-gambia-v-facebook-inc-domestic-proceedings-international-implications/; A Koenig, 'Q&A on Court Ordering Facebook to Disclose Content on Myanmar Genocide' (Just Security, 24 September 2021) www.justsecurity.org/78358/qa-on-court-ordering-facebook-to-disclose-content-on-myanmar-genocide/.

media companies. Cooperation between the ICC and States and private corporations will be considered further in chapter six, section IV.[138]

Additionally, another challenge which could emerge should online hate speech and disinformation become a crime under ICL is that of jurisdiction. In some cases with very specific contexts, such as government officials in Myanmar posting hateful speech on Facebook, it may be fairly straightforward to determine whether a court such as the ICC has jurisdiction, as some of the alleged crimes took place in Bangladesh (a State Party to the ICC), and the government officials posting are in the area and involved with the conflict. However, in other cases where online hate speech is perpetrated from multiple States (some of which might not even be known, as users can be anonymous and hide their locations), it would be difficult to determine a jurisdictional or legal basis for prosecution.[139] Jurisdictional issues associated with prosecuting individuals for content that is posted online will be considered in detail in chapter six, section II.B.[140]

C. Sharing Footage of Crimes Online

In recent years, non-State armed groups have included an online element while committing acts of torture and murder on their victims, either by posting footage of physical torture and killings online to further humiliate the victims and their families, or by forcing individuals (including children) to watch execution videos.[141] This example encompasses three different scenarios, all inflicting different harms.

First, the element of recording and/or sharing a video of someone being tortured causes an additional amount of humiliation and degradation to the 'direct' victim. This harm was alluded to by the OTP in the case of *Al Hassan* at the ICC, which stated that the public nature of executions by the non-State armed terrorist group Ansar Dine, with whom the accused was affiliated, who also posted videos of executions on social media, was particularly humiliating for the victims.[142] The OTP also submitted that the videos posted to YouTube by Ansar Dine depicted the victims 'bent over in pain' and with 'private parts exposed for all to see', which contributed to 'a sense of public humiliation'.[143] A similar issue was also held by the Pre-Trial Chamber in the case of *Al Werfalli*, where execution videos were posted

[138] See ch 6, s IV of this book.

[139] For a relevant discussion of jurisdictional challenges faced when prosecuting transnational cyber offences, see A Perloff-Giles, 'Transnational Cyber Offenses: Overcoming Jurisdictional Challenges' (2018) 43 *Yale Journal of International Law* 191.

[140] See ch 6, s II.B of this book.

[141] See, eg Report of the Independent International Commission of Inquiry on the Syrian Arab Republic (5 February 2015) which details multiple incidents of this nature committed by ISIS in Syria.

[142] *Prosecutor v Al Hassan* (Requête urgente du Bureau du Procureur) ICC-01/12-01/18, La Chambre Préliminaire (20 mars 2018) [136]. This case concerned charges of crimes against humanity and war crimes against the *de facto* chief of the Islamic police in Mali.

[143] ibid [304].

on social media.[144] The Pre-Trial Chamber stated in its two arrest warrants that 'the posting on social media of the videos depicting executions' and 'the manner in which the crime was committed and publicized was cruel, dehumanizing, and degrading'. However, the Court never addressed this issue, as the case did not move forward past the arrest warrant stage due to Al Werfalli's death.

The posting of videos of torture and executions online further degrades victims before a large audience, and can extend their suffering, as once something is shared online, it can be extremely difficult to remove it completely and stop its circulation[145] – an act which is usually a singular instance fixed in time is changed to one that is continuous and constantly available to taunt victims and their communities. As Irving and I have argued, in the Chamber's gravity assessment in *Al Hassan*, more focus should have been placed on the additional harm suffered by victims by having their suffering posted to public online platforms, which 'extended the audience of this suffering far beyond the group of onlookers on the street that day' and likely heightened their sense of humiliation and degradation immensely.[146] This is because the posting of videos of executions to social media by Ansar Dine itself demonstrated a desire to further degrade victims before a widespread audience, which the authors argue should have been considered by the Pre-Trial Chamber as aggravating the offence.[147] This analysis is also consistent with the ICTY Trial Chamber's findings in *Kvočka et al.* – that '[t]he presence of onlookers, particularly family members, also inflicts severe mental harm amounting to torture'.[148]

The harms experienced by victims when footage of crimes is shared online are seemingly similar in their nature of severe humiliation and degradation to the harms encompassed by torture, other inhumane acts, and the war crimes of inhuman treatment, wilfully causing great suffering, and outrages upon personal dignity, which were discussed previously.[149] This is because all of these crimes have addressed harms in which either a victim suffers severe mental harm and a loss of dignity from the presence of onlookers, or witnesses to a violent act suffer mental distress. In relation to war crimes, though these crimes have not been prosecuted yet at ICCTs tribunals for online acts, domestic criminal courts have prosecuted them primarily in relation to open-source photos and videos. For instance, in The Netherlands, a man was convicted for degrading treatment and an assault on

[144] *Prosecutor v Al Werfalli* (Warrant of Arrest) ICC-01/11-01/17, PTC I (15 August 2017) [29]; *Prosecutor v Al Werfalli* (Second Warrant of Arrest) ICC-01/11-01/17, PTC I (4 July 2018) [31]. This case concerned charges of war crimes against a major in the Al-Saiqa Brigade in Libya.

[145] S Zarmsky and E Irving, 'Digital Evidence in the Al Hassan Warrant' in K McLoughlin, R Grey, L Chappell, and S Varrall (eds), *Feminist judgments: Reimagining the International Criminal Court* (CUP, 2025) 470–78.

[146] ibid.

[147] ibid.

[148] *Prosecutor v Kvočka et al* (Judgment) IT-98-30/1-T, Trial Chamber (2 November 2001) ('*Kvočka et al* Trial Judgment') [149]. However, the Trial Chamber did not provide further reasoning as to why it came to this finding.

[149] See ch 3 of this book.

personal dignity for posting a photo of himself with a crucified individual in Syria to Facebook.[150] In this case, the Hague Court of Appeal found:

> By posing next to the deceased person and having a photo taken, the suspect has contributed to further deepening the humiliation and/or dishonor of the deceased. The suspect has expressed that the body of the deceased should be seen as a trophy and that he is superior to the deceased. This humiliating and/or degrading behaviour is of such gravity that it is simply seen as an assault on the personal dignity of the deceased person. By subsequently posting the photo on his Facebook account, the suspect ensured that a large number of people were given the opportunity to take note of the photo.[151]

In this ruling, the Hague Court of Appeal considered what the ICC Pre-Trial Chamber arguably overlooked in *Al Werfalli* and *Al Hassan* – that the posting of footage of victims in such a violent and vulnerable state onto social media was not just evidence of other crimes, but an act worthy of being a crime itself. In doing so, the Hague Court of Appeal was able to deliver more tailored justice to the victim and his family through acknowledging the additional harm the defendant knowingly inflicted when choosing to share the image.

Another man in The Netherlands was convicted of the same crimes for posting a video of himself kicking and spitting on bodies of the dead in Syria to YouTube.[152] The Hague District Court found in this case that uploading the video to YouTube 'continu[ed] the humiliation and dishonor by allowing a large audience to learn about it'.[153] In this case, the Hague Court referenced the *Kunarac* case at the ICTY, which defined an assault on personal dignity as when 'the accused intentionally committed or participated in an act or omission which would be generally considered to cause serious humiliation, degradation or otherwise be a serious attack on human dignity' – a definition that was, in the Court's view, met by posting a video desecrating dead bodies to YouTube.[154] Additionally, the Hague District Court recalled Article 13 of Geneva Convention III concerning the human treatment of prisoners, which states that prisoners (presumably alive or dead) must be protected 'against insults and public curiosity'.[155] The Court noted the 2020 International Committee of the Red Cross (ICRC) Commentary on Article 13, which states:

> In modern conflicts, the prohibition also covers, subject to the considerations discussed below, the disclosure of photographic and video images, recordings of interrogations or private conversations or personal correspondence or any other private data, irrespective

[150] ECLI:NL:GHDHA:2021:103.
[151] ibid, translated from Dutch.
[152] ECLI:NL:RBDHA:2021:3998.
[153] ibid, translated from Dutch.
[154] ibid; *Prosecutor v Kunarac et al* (Judgment) IT-96-23-7 & IT-96-23/1-T, Trial Chamber (22 February 2001) ('*Kunarac et al* Trial Judgment') [514].
[155] ibid; Convention (III) relative to the Treatment of Prisoners of War, Geneva, 12 August 1949, art 13.

> of which public communication channel is used, including the internet. Although this is seemingly different from being marched through a hostile crowd, such disclosure could still be humiliating and jeopardize the safety of the prisoners' families and of the prisoners themselves once they are released.[156]

The Hague District Court applied the reasoning described in the ICRC Commentary to demonstrate that the acts which violate the prohibition of curiosity, first written in 1949, have changed to encompass modern technological advancements. It is thus possible that in a similar vein, the acts which violate other international prohibitions and constitute crimes may evolve to accommodate other digital harms.

However, the charge of outrages upon personal dignity in this case was overturned by the Court of Appeal.[157] The Court of Appeal stated that this was because although the 'acts by the fighters [were] extremely distasteful and demonstrate a disrespectful attitude towards the deceased soldiers', '[t]his does not necessarily mean that there has been an "outrage upon personal dignity, in particular humiliating and degrading treatment"'.[158] The Court then stated that '[t]he bar for that is higher'. To explain this finding, the Court recalled that 'despite the deceased enjoying protection' under Common Article 3 of the Geneva Conventions, 'they cannot be said to be suffering severely physically or mentally' as a result of the accused's actions (namely, desecrating the corpses and posting the footage on social media).[159] The Court further noted that the actions of the accused lasted 'only a few minutes' which 'detracts to some extent from the gravity' of the behaviour, and that it could not consider the interests of surviving relatives in this case because it did not have enough information about them from the case file.[160] In this case, the Court was concerned with the Dutch International Crimes Act Section 6(1)(c), which criminalises outrages upon personal dignity in the Dutch penal code.[161] This is notably distinct from the crime as defined in the Rome Statute because it does not include the provision that outrages upon personal dignity shall also apply to deceased persons.[162] It is therefore possible that should the same case have been tried before the ICC, the conviction would not have been overturned as the Court of Appeal seemed to have the largest issue with the fact that the victims were already deceased, and thus in its view, 'not suffering'.[163]

[156] 'Convention (III) relative to the Treatment of Prisoners of War, Geneva, 12 August 1949, Commentary of 2020: Article 130 (Grave Breaches)' (ICRC IHL Treaties Database) ('ICRC 2020 Commentary')ihl-databases.icrc.org/en/ihl-treaties/gciii-1949/article-130/commentary/2020?activeTab=#_Toc42767226 [1624].

[157] ECLI:NL:GHDHA:2022:2858.

[158] ibid; translated from Dutch.

[159] ibid.

[160] ibid.

[161] ibid; International Crimes Act (2003) section 6(1)(c).

[162] ibid; Elements of Crimes art 8(2)(c)(ii), fn 57.

[163] ibid.

Similar cases in which individuals were prosecuted for assaults on personal dignity for filming and posting footage of crimes to social media have also occurred in Finland, Germany, and Sweden.[164] For example, in Finland, two men were convicted for posting images of themselves holding decapitated heads on Facebook – one was convicted for desecrating the corpse of the dead fighter, and the other was convicted for an outrage upon the personal dignity of the deceased for circulating degrading footage of the victim online.[165] In Germany, one man was prosecuted for posing with severed heads of enemy combatants impaled on metal rods and uploading the photos to Facebook 'with limited privacy settings', and another was convicted on similar grounds for recording himself mutilating the bodies of dead soldiers.[166] In Sweden, a man was convicted for posing next to multiple severed heads and posting the photos on Facebook.[167] Given the fact that the digital harms which come from posting videos of crimes to social media have been successfully prosecuted as international crimes at the domestic level, it is plausible that this type of harm could be prosecuted at an international court like the ICC. Indeed, the OTP Policy on Cyber-Enabled Crimes under the Rome Statute expressly states that outrages upon personal dignity may be committed through 'the production and publication of humiliating images of persons in captivity, or deceased persons, which can be carried out online and exploit existing platforms and channels such as popular social media'.[168] Further, while it could be raised that the criminal frameworks governing international crimes in such domestic jurisdictions may not explicitly contain a gravity requirement as is provided by Article 17 of the Rome Statute, as will be explained further in chapter six, section II.A,[169] international crimes are grave in their nature and as such, the domestic analysis often includes a gravity consideration.[170] It is therefore not unreasonable to infer that those successfully prosecuted by domestic courts are similar in gravity to those which would be at international courts.

In addition to the harm experienced by the immediate victims, once footage of torture is recorded and shared, those close to them and other internet users who stumble across the content can experience serious mental harm. As discussed in chapter three, section II,[171] ICL jurisprudence has recognised the 'serious mental harm' that can come to third parties, particularly family or friends of the victim,

[164] Eurojust, 'Prosecuting war crimes of outrage upon personal dignity based on evidence from open sources - Legal framework and recent developments in the Member States of the European Union' (2018) www.eurojust.europa.eu/sites/default/files/Partners/Genocide/2018-02_Prosecuting-war-crimes-based-on-evidence-from-open-sources_EN.pdf, 7-10.

[165] ibid.

[166] ibid.

[167] ibid.

[168] Office of the Prosecutor (n 89) [95].

[169] See ch 6, s II.A of this book.

[170] For example, in the Dutch case mentioned above that was reversed on appeal, the Hague Court of Appeal expressly mentioned that the fact that the videos were brief, in combination with other factors, detracted from the 'gravity' of the acts, indicating the Court's consideration of gravity in the decision; (n 157).

[171] See ch 3, s II of this book.

when witnessing violent acts committed against others.[172] On this note, international criminal jurisprudence has demonstrated that viewing torture of another person can be enough to constitute torture itself. For example, as was discussed previously in relation to the *Furundžija* case, the ICTY Trial Chamber found that being forced to watch sexual attacks on a female acquaintance constituted the severe mental suffering threshold needed to be considered an act of torture.[173] Though this offence occurred in person and not through a computer screen, the harms can still be connected between the offline and online situations because viewing extremely violent content has been shown to cause the same types of effects as when individuals witness real-life violence, such as anxiety, depression, PTSD, or alcohol consumption.[174] For example, a study of journalists frequently exposed to violent images found that the frequency of exposure to violent content consistently predicted incidents of psychopathology, including those related to anxiety, depression, PTSD, and alcohol abuse.[175] These harms are very similar to the kinds of psychological issues faced by victims of in-person torture, which are known to also include frequent instances of depression and PTSD.[176]

While there is arguably a distinction between being forced to watch an act of torture and choosing to watch the act (ie as part of one's job or out of curiosity online), it should not be assumed that the means of viewing the torture, whether it be in real life or through a screen, lessens the harm caused. Over four clinical psychological studies, Ramsden found that participants were significantly affected by events they witnessed only through social media (and never in real life).[177] In one of the studies, 22 per cent of participants 'scored highly on clinical assessments of PTSD, despite only being exposed to videos and images of the traumatic events, not the events themselves'.[178] In addition, the more often the participants viewed the imagery, the more affected they were.[179] Further, as observed by Koenig and Lampros, imagery can be even more harmful if they have a personal connection to what is depicted. The authors state that '[s]ometimes, it's less about the graphic nature of imagery than the history a moment carries with it that gets to us – and people's relationship to that history, and thus their identities, that determines their

[172] *Prosecutor v Fofana and Kondewa* (Judgment) SCSL-04-14-T, Trial Chamber I (2 August 2007) ('*Fofana and Kondewa* Trial Judgment') [153].

[173] *Prosecutor v Furundžija* (Judgment) IT-95-17/1-T, Trial Chamber (10 December 1998) ('*Furundžija* Trial Judgment') [267(ii)].

[174] A Feinstein, B Audet, and E Waknine, 'Witnessing Images of Extreme Violence: A Psychological Study of Journalists in the Newsroom' (2014) 5 *JRSM Open* 1–7.

[175] ibid.

[176] M Basoglu et al, 'Psychological Effects of Torture: A Comparison of Tortured with Nontortured Political Activists in Turkey' (1994) 152 *American Journal of Psychiatry* 76–81.

[177] P Ramsden, 'Vicarious Trauma, PTSD and Social Media: Does Watching Graphic Videos Cause Trauma?' (2017) Journal of Depression and Anxiety 3rd International Conference on Depression, Anxiety and Stress Management; see also A Koenig and A Lampros, *Graphic: Trauma and Meaning in Our Online Lives* (CUP, 2023) 44.

[178] ibid.

[179] ibid; ''Trigger Warning': Violence on Social Media Can Cause PTSD-Like Symptoms' (Medaxs, 26 May 2015) medaxs.com.au/2015/05/26/trigger-warning-violence-on-social-media-can-cause-ptsd-like-symptoms/.

differing reactions'.[180] Overall, these findings demonstrate that viewing graphic content, even through a screen, can manifest in serious psychiatric ailments, and that these effects can be worsened by factors such as the number of times the individual views the content or their relationship to it.

However, even if the harms between viewing violent acts against someone (and particularly a family member) in person versus online may be comparable, a major obstacle in considering this 'digital harm' as torture as a crime against humanity is the requirement under Article 7(2)(e) of the Rome Statute that the victim be in the custody or under the control of the perpetrator.[181] This requirement was added in order to establish an imbalance of power between the perpetrator and the victim, as the requirement that the perpetrator be a public official that exists in the Torture Convention was removed in the Rome Statute.[182] In this case, a victim's family member simply viewing the footage from a remote location voluntarily (or even stumbling across it) without being under the immediate control of the perpetrator may not amount to torture, regardless of the level of harm caused. Thus, torture may not be the most appropriate offence to consider, and further, may not be well equipped to encompass potential new modes of perpetrating the crime in a digital age where physical custody or control over the victim is not possible but the harm remains severe.

In these instances, it would be easier to envision such digital harms as falling under other inhumane acts, wilfully causing great suffering, cruel or inhuman treatment, or outrages upon personal dignity, which do not possess custody requirements, unless the family members were physically forced to watch the footage on a screen. However, torture as a war crime under Article 8(2)(a)(ii) does not contain a custody criterion, only that the offence take place in the context and be associated with an international armed conflict.[183] This is because, as implied in the Elements of Crimes, the power imbalance between the perpetrator and victim is already established because Element 3 of Article 8(2)(a)(ii) requires that the victim be a protected person under the Geneva Conventions.[184] It is thus possible that should the act take place in the context of a conflict (such as in a situation where a party to a conflict films footage of crimes and shares it), sharing this footage with the victim's family members who are protected persons could potentially constitute a form of torture even if they were not in the custody of the perpetrator.

A third potential effect of footage of torture and killings being recorded and shared relates to those who are targeted as recruits by terrorist organisations, particularly children. Generally, viewing violent and graphic content is known to cause emotional distress, which can result in vicarious psychological trauma to

[180] Koenig and Lampros (n 177) 48.
[181] Rome Statute art 7(2)(e).
[182] RS Lee (ed), *The International Criminal Court: Elements of Crimes and Rules of Procedure and Evidence* (Ardsley, 2001) 90.
[183] Rome Statute Elements of Crimes art 8(2)(a)(ii-1).
[184] ibid fn 35.

the viewer.[185] More specifically, when that violent content is tailored to and strategically distributed to a vulnerable population, such as children, who may not be as resilient as adults,[186] the effects can be harmful. Further, terrorist groups have increasingly used social media platforms to target young audiences, using techniques such as 'targeted advertising' to those most vulnerable to propaganda and 'grooming', when the perpetrator learns about the child's interests in order to tailor the approach and build a trusting relationship.[187] Thus, the harm of posting footage of a crime online has the potential to set off a cascade of more harm, as it could potentially be framed in a certain way or shared intentionally with a vulnerable audience in order to recruit more individuals and perpetuate more crimes (such as the recruitment of children to engage them in hostilities).

D. Online Sexual Violence

'Sexual violence' is an umbrella term which encompasses any unwanted sexual act or activity, from verbal harassment, to sexual abuse, to forced marriage or forced pregnancy.[188] In the context of digital harms, online sexual violence is closely linked to personal dignity, as the physical harms that can result from the sexual violence are not typically present given the nature of the digital space. Parallels can be drawn between online sexual violence and ICL cases dealing with public rapes and sexual assaults. For example, in *Furundžija*, the ICTY Trial Chamber found that the fact that victims were raped and sexually assaulted in front of soldiers who were watching and laughing caused 'severe physical and mental pain, along with public humiliation' and thus amounted to outrages upon personal dignity and sexual integrity.[189] Additionally, in the *Akayesu* case, the ICTR Trial Chamber found that forcing a female student to undress and do gymnastics naked in a public courtyard in front of a crowd also constituted the amount of seriousness to be considered sexual violence.[190] The idea of being naked or sexualised in front of a wider audience therefore seems to increase the severity of the act in the eyes of ICCTs due to the additional harm it causes in terms of humiliation to the victim.

[185] See C Newton, 'The Trauma Floor: The Secret Lives of Facebook Moderators in America' (The Verge, 25 February 2019) www.theverge.com/2019/2/25/18229714/cognizant-facebook-content-moderator-interviews-trauma-working-conditions-arizona.

[186] M Stoilova, S Livingstone, and R Khazbak, 'Investigating Risks and Opportunities for Children in a Digital World: A Rapid Review of the Evidence on Children's Internet Use and Outcomes' (UNICEF Innocenti Discussion Paper 2020-03, February 2021).

[187] UNODC, 'Handbook on Children Recruited and Exploited by Terrorist and Violent Extremist Groups: The Role of the Justice System' (2017) 13–14.

[188] OHCHR, 'Sexual and gender-based violence in the context of transitional justice' (October 2014) www.ohchr.org/sites/default/files/Documents/Issues/Women/WRGS/OnePagers/Sexual_and_gender-based_violence.pdf.

[189] Eurojust (n 164); *Furundžija* Trial Judgment (n 173) [272].

[190] *Prosecutor v Akayesu* (Judgment) ICTR-96-4-T, Trial Chamber I (2 September 1998) ('*Akayesu* Trial Judgment') [688].

This same harm is present in many cases of sexual violence perpetrated through online environments, for instance in relation to image-based sexual abuse, or 'revenge porn'.[191] In some cases, intimate images or live-streams of individuals are posted online without permission from the person depicted, and are extremely difficult to remove from the internet once they have been uploaded, resulting in 'immeasurable harm' to victims.[192] It is also possible that sexual imagery of a person is created without consent using AI technology (or 'deepfakes').[193] Both of these acts can also be perpetrated towards children, which can cause an irreparable amount of psychological trauma.[194] In addition, image-based sexual abuse subjects victims to the possibility of other types of harm, such as cyberbullying from other users who see the photos.[195] It is for these reasons that scholars have argued for the general or domestic criminalisation of image-based sexual abuse,[196] and new domestic criminal laws have been enacted by multiple States to accommodate this harm.[197]

Aside from the harm to direct victims of sexual violence, importantly, ICL has also recognised the harm to those who are forced to watch sexual violence as also being sexual in nature. For example, at the Special Court for Sierra Leone (SCSL), the Trial Chamber recognised the harm caused to a man being forced to watch the rape and death of his wife as 'fomenting terror by sexual means'.[198] This is also a relevant consideration for accommodating online sexual violence under ICL, since family members or friends of victims could also experience a form of sexual

[191] C Rigotti and C McGlynn, 'Towards an EU Criminal Law on Violence Against Women: The Ambitions and Limitations of the Commission's Proposal to Criminalise Image-Based Sexual Abuse' (2022) 13 *New Journal of European Criminal Law* 452–77.

[192] A Dodge, 'Nudes are Forever: Judicial Interpretations of Digital Technology's Impact on "Revenge Porn"' (2019) 34 *Canadian Journal of Law and Society* 121–43.

[193] Rigotti and McGlynn (n 191) 455.

[194] See for instance M Joleby, S Landström, C Lunde, and LS Jonsson, 'Experiences and Psychological Health Among Children Exposed to Online Sexual Abuse – A Mixed Methods Study of Court Verdicts' (2021) 27 *Psychology, Crime & Law* 159–81. Online child sexual abuse (or 'child pornography') has been widely discussed in literature and well-developed in domestic law, and thus falls outside the scope of this book. However, for a comprehensive overview of transnational and international responses to online child sexual abuse, see SK Witting, 'Transnational by Default: Online Child Sexual Abuse Respects No Borders' (2021) 29 *International Journal of Children's Rights* 731–64.

[195] A Dodge, 'Digitizing Rape Culture: Online Sexual Violence and the Power of the Digital Photograph' (2016) 12 *Crime, Media, Culture* 65–82.

[196] M Goudsmit Samaritter, 'What Makes a Sex Crime? A Fair Label for Image-based Sexual Abuse' (2021) 2 *BJU Strafblad* 67; RT Toparlak, 'Criminalising Deep Fake Pornography: A Gender-Specific Analysis of Image-Based Sexual Abuse' (2023) 1 *cognitio – studentisches Forum für Recht und Gesellschaft* 1–16; S Bloom, 'No Vengeance for "Revenge Porn" Victims: Unraveling Why This Latest Female-Centric, Intimate-Partner Offense Is Still Legal, and Why We Should Criminalize It' (2015) 42 *Fordham Urban Law Journal* 233–90.

[197] For example, as of 2017, laws had been enacted in England and Wales, Scotland, Israel, Japan, Canada, Australia, New Zealand, and the United States; C McGlynn and E Rackley, 'Image-Based Sexual Abuse' (2017) 37 *Oxford Journal of Legal Studies* 534–61, 554, fn 100.

[198] V Oosterveld, 'Sexual Violence Directed against Men and Boys in Armed Conflict or Mass Atrocity: Addressing a Gendered Harm in International Criminal Tribunals' (2014) 10 *Journal of International Law and International Relations* 110, 114.

violence should they be forced to watch a video of a sexual assault or come across one online.

Overall, distributing footage of sexual assaults or sharing nude images without consent online or being made to watch such footage is an example of a digital harm that existing ICL frameworks on sexual violence should be able to address. This is because even though they differ from 'traditional' offences where international courts have recognised being sexually assaulted or nude in public or physically witnessing a sexual offence as a crime, the fact that the harm occurs through a screen does not detract from its severity. Moreover, as was argued in relation to sharing footage of crimes,[199] the wide reach and instantaneousness of the online environment can exacerbate the sense of humiliation experienced by victims. As exemplified by the Rome Statute, provisions criminalising forms of sexual violence are often vague – the lists of acts included under Articles 7(g) (crimes against humanity) and 8(2)(b)(xxii) and 8(2)(e)(vi) (war crimes) are, indeed, non-exhaustive and allow for room for interpretation.[200] It is thus plausible, given the similar nature of the harms previously recognised as grave enough to constitute sexual violence at ICCTs and the sharing of footage of sexual crimes or other nude imagery, that online sexual violence could also be considered a crime under ICL.

A final category of online sexual violence consists of when traditional international crimes, such as sexual slavery, are perpetrated directly through the online space. For example, in the context of the genocide against the Yazidi population in northern Iraq, ISIS used the internet to auction women and children, using posts with their registration information, photos, and minimum purchase prices.[201] The crime of sexual slavery already exists under the Rome Statute,[202] and in this instance, using the internet as a forum to purchase or sell persons could constitute the offence as a crime against humanity or a war crime should the other elements of the crimes be met.[203] However, as noted by Koenig and Egan, using such online auctions also implied the sharing of a wealth of data about the victims to a global internet audience.[204] In this situation, in addition to the crime of sexual slavery being committed, victims are further humiliated through their images and data being circulated online and their right to privacy is infringed upon when their personal information is shared. For this example of a digital harm, though an offence is already available under ICL, the online component that exacerbates the

[199] See ss III.C and IV.C of this chapter.

[200] For instance, Art 7(g) (crimes against humanity) includes 'any other form of sexual violence of comparable gravity' to the listed acts, and both provisions under Art. 8(2) (war crimes) include 'any other form of sexual violence also constituting a grave breach of the Geneva Conventions'. Rome Statute arts 7(g), 8(2)(b)(xxii), and 8(2)(e)(vi).

[201] A Koenig and U Egan, 'Power and Privilege: Investigating Sexual Violence with Digital Open Source Information' (2021) 19 *Journal of International Criminal Justice* 55–84, 66; P Sellers and J Kestenbaum, 'Missing in Action: The International Crime of the Slave Trade' (2020) 18 *Journal of International Criminal Justice* 517–542, 524–25.

[202] Rome Statute arts 7(1)(g), 8(2)(b)(xii), and 8(2)(e)(vi).

[203] Rome Statute Elements of Crimes art 7(1)(g)-2, 8(2)(b)(xii)-2, and 8(2)(e)(vi)-2.

[204] ibid.

harm can and should be considered as either aggravating the offence, such as in the gravity assessment or at sentencing, or as its own additional crime, such as the crime against humanity of other inhumane acts or the war crimes of inhuman or cruel treatment or outrages upon personal dignity (if the link to an armed conflict is established).

V. Conclusion

This chapter demonstrated that there are critical differences between harm in general and digital harm. In summary, digital harms can consist both of new ways of perpetrating 'traditional' harms, and of novel forms of harm that could not come to fruition without the development of digital technologies. Digital harms on an individual level tend to be more easily and quickly inflicted than their non-digital counterparts, and can reach more victims regardless of physical distance from the perpetrator. At the level of hate speech directed towards groups, racist, misogynistic, homophobic, and other problematic attitudes can be easily spread and amplified through 'online echo chambers' and can many times act as precursors to violence against members of those groups. Finally, at the societal level, online terrorist or violent content can quickly and easily instil fear in a population, and mis/disinformation and cyber-meddling can pose harms to democracy and self-determination in an efficient manner.

Some examples of digital harm discussed may fit already under the definitions of existing international crimes. For example, in the case of the spread of hate speech, the digital harm could likely fall under existing definitions of incitement to genocide, or when footage of crimes is shared online, it could likely amount to an outrage upon personal dignity. On the other hand, some examples of digital harm may not be encompassed as easily within existing crimes, such as the use of digital mass surveillance to infringe upon the rights of a group, which at present could not be prosecuted as persecution on its own under the Rome Statute due to the need for a connecting crime. In this case, I argue that the definition of persecution within the Rome Statute would be better suited for a digital age if this connection requirement were removed.

It is important to note that this chapter does not go so far as to make a case for criminalising certain digital harms under specific provisions of ICL. The process of either incorporating digital harms into existing ICL frameworks or amending a crime will require a more specified and complex analysis and would need to take various challenges into account that will be analysed in chapter six,[205] such as the acquisition and use of digital evidence or potential issues with jurisdiction for crimes committed in 'cyberspace'. Instead, this chapter provided a survey of digital harms that could imaginably be connected to the perpetration of international crimes and proposed some ideas for where those harms might fit best given the

[205] See ch 6 of this book.

nature of already-recognised harms. The aim of this chapter was to outline how digital harms may foreseeably be included in future ICL cases in order to ensure greater accountability for digital acts and justice for victims, which will likely be more or less difficult depending on the digital act.

Ultimately, an element present amongst the digital harms discussed is the ability of the perpetrator, using technology, to amplify and extend the suffering of victims. This occurs in the case of mass surveillance, where digital tools have made it possible for a targeted group to be watched almost any time and anywhere, and in the case of hate speech and disinformation, where the spread of hateful or false language can reach a much wider audience. It is also especially the case for when footage of crimes or sexual images are shared online, as those depicted are continuously subject to humiliation and ridicule even after the initial events occur. Therefore, in the interests of bringing more justice to victims, digital harms are not insignificant and should be an issue at the forefront of ICL, as technology will only continue to evolve and inevitably enable more forms of harm. The reasons why criminalisation under ICL is the answer to accounting for harms in a digital age will be considered in the next chapter.

5

Criminalising Digital Harm

I. Introduction

The purpose of this chapter is to answer the questions of why and how digital harm should be criminalised under international criminal law (ICL). However, it is first necessary to address why ICL is a valuable and necessary tool for pursuing justice for victims of digital harm, as opposed to other accountability avenues such as domestic law.

ICL concerns itself with acts 'of concern to the international community as a whole' or 'which violate a fundamental interest protected by international law'.[1] ICL formally originated in the aftermath of the Second World War, in which the crimes committed by the Nazis (ie genocide, crimes against humanity, and war crimes) were so horrific that the allied powers established an international military tribunal (IMT) to hold them to account and condemn this level of atrocity, followed by the creation of a similar tribunal for the crimes committed by the Japanese one year later.[2] As defined in the *Hostage* case at the IMT, an 'international crime' is 'an act universally recognized as criminal, which is considered a grave matter of international concern and for some valid reason cannot be left within the exclusive jurisdiction of the State that would have control over it under ordinary circumstances'.[3] Thus, a key part of international criminalisation is the consensus within the international community that an act is so heinous that it should be universally prohibited. As argued by Randhawa, this entails a two-stage process that requires (1) the emergence of an international criminal norm, and (2) the translation of that norm into an international legal proscription (a formal

[1] R Cryer, H Friman, D Robinson, and E Wilmshurst (eds), *An Introduction to International Criminal Law and Procedure* (3rd edn, CUP, 2014) 6.

[2] 'The Nuremberg Trial and the Tokyo War Crimes Trials (1945–1948)' (US Department of State Office of the Historian) history.state.gov/milestones/1945-1952/nuremberg. Notably, international crimes existed before the Nuremberg and Tokyo trials, such as prohibitions against piracy or regulations of the slave trade. However, the IMT and IMTFE launched the modern regime of ICL by formally codifying core international crimes and establishing international criminal tribunals. See B Van Schaack and R Slye, 'A Concise History of International Criminal Law' (2007) *Santa Clara Law Digital Commons* 7–47.

[3] *Hostage Case* (Judgment) US Military Tribunal, Nuremberg (19 February 1948) [1241].

law).[4] International legal proscriptions can be generated through a variety of sources, including (but not limited to) treaties and statutes, customary international law, and ICL case law. This book focuses mostly on the ICC, and therefore this chapter will mainly explore the potential international criminalisation of digital harms through linkages to existing crimes within the Rome Statute or the addition of new crimes.

This chapter will first consider reasons for international criminalisation that can be applied to digital harm, including harm prevention, punishment theories, and expressivism. The chapter concludes with an analysis of how digital harm can be criminalised under international law in practice.

II. Why International Criminal Law?

In the context of digital harms, the reasons for criminalisation are not necessarily new, as many of the theories applicable to 'traditional' crimes still apply. This chapter aims to demonstrate that novel harms or the perpetration of existing crimes via new technologies can and should be encompassed within existing criminalisation theories. This section is broken up into subsections, each of which adapts some of the most relevant ICL theories to digital harm: preventing harm (the harm principle), punishment, and sending a message (expressivism).

Though other theories of international criminalisation exist, this chapter only considers those that, in my view, would suit the purpose of criminalising of digital harm. For instance, victim-centred justice theories such as restorative and reparative justice are discussed in the literature, but have been heavily criticised for their inability to work properly in the current ICC system.[5] At present, the victim-centred justice mechanisms that ICC currently provides would likely not be adequate to address digital harms – for example, it seems unlikely that the Court, given previous decisions, would order reparations such as compensation to be specifically used for psychological treatment, which would be helpful for victims of digital harm. Restorative and reparative justice aims would likely therefore be better achieved at the domestic level, or through regulatory approaches by technology companies, which are outside the scope of this book.[6]

[4] SH Randhawa, 'International Criminalization and the Historical Emergence of International Crimes' (2022) 14 *International Theory* 460–502, 460.

[5] E van Sliedregt, 'Punishment and the Domestic Analogy: Why it Can and Cannot Work' in F Jeßberger and J Geneuss (eds), *Why Punish Perpetrators of Mass Atrocities?: Purposes of Punishment in International Criminal Law* (CUP, 2020) 83.

[6] See also NT Navarro, 'Collective Reparations and the Limitations of International Criminal Justice to Respond to Mass Atrocity' (2018) 18(1) *International Criminal Law Review* 67–96; AA Hasinoff, AD Gibson, and N Salehi, 'The promise of restorative justice in addressing online harm' (Tech Stream, 27 July 2020) www.brookings.edu/techstream/the-promise-of-restorative-justice-in-addressing-online-harm/.

A. The Harm Principle and Preventing Harm

One reason for criminalising conduct under ICL is to prevent harm, which is derived from what is generally known as the 'harm principle'. As considered in chapter four,[7] digital harms may be different from harms traditionally encompassed by the law through the way they are perpetrated but have many similarities regarding their seriousness and the ways they manifest. It is therefore possible that digital harms could also be criminalised, at least in part, to prevent them from happening.

The harm principle is a key theory of criminalisation for both domestic and international law. It was first coined by Mill in his essay *On Liberty*, in which he explained that 'the only purpose for which power can be rightfully exercised over any member of a civilised community against his will is to prevent harm to others'.[8] Regarding criminal law, this principle provides a basis for criminalising conduct that can cause harm to others. In other words, the harm principle serves as a control for lawmakers as to when activity can be limited – it allows only for harmful acts to be criminalised and gives authorities the power to intervene with criminal sanctions to stop such acts from taking place, resulting in harm prevention.

Mill's position was reinforced and expanded upon by Feinberg in the *Moral Limits of the Criminal Law*, in which Feinberg stated that 'it is always a good reason in support of penal legislation that it would be effective in preventing (eliminating, reducing) harm to persons other than the actor', and further that 'it is always a good reason in support of a proposed criminal prohibition that it is probably necessary to prevent serious offense to the persons other than the actor'.[9] A key difference in Feinberg's approach in comparison with Mill's is that whereas Mill seems to present the harm principle as a 'negative constraint' where the State is not entitled to intervene in the absence of a risk of harm, Feinberg places emphasis on the State's moral positive obligation to prohibit harm and act before there is even a tangible risk.[10] This approach therefore seems to allow for greater restrictions of individuals' freedom to act in favour of preventing harm than Mill's approach. Feinberg's approach demonstrates an evolution of the harm theory in the sense that it does not just serve as a justification for criminalising acts that can cause harm but is more of a requirement for governing bodies to act to prevent harm, which is positive because it focuses on further minimising harm to victims.

Additionally, a core part of the harm principle is the distinction between harmful and wrongful conduct, which are not the same (though they may overlap) – for example, it could be argued that amputating a limb that would otherwise infect the rest of the body causes physical harm to a person, but doing so would not necessarily be wrongful if it is a means to a positive result and helps to prevent

[7] See ch 4 of this book.

[8] JS Mill, *On Liberty* (1859).

[9] J Feinberg, *Harmless Wrongdoing – The Moral Limits of the Criminal Law* (OUP, 1990) 26.

[10] AP Simester and A von Hirsch, *Crimes, Harms, and Wrongs: On the Principles of Criminalisation* (Bloomsbury, 2011) 35.

further harm (ie not dying from infection) that the individual validly consented to. As identified by Feinberg, a harm can be a wrong to another person,[11] but harm is not always wrongful. For example, harm could be caused to a person by way of a volcano erupting, in which no wrongdoing occurred. It is therefore not merely harm that is criminalised, but harm that results from wrongful conduct that entails a fault or malicious intent.

Feinberg argues that the type of harm to be employed with the harm principle (or considered for criminalisation, in this context) needs to also be wrongful.[12] This is an important distinction to consider for criminalising digital harm, especially the sharing of graphic footage of international crimes, and ties in with the issue of intent. As considered in chapter four, individuals may share photos or videos of atrocity crimes to social media maliciously, especially in the context of terrorism, to further degrade the victims depicted or spread fear.[13] However, it has become increasingly common for individuals to share content with a genuine aim to raise awareness about a conflict or try to attract the attention from authorities. For example, the current conflict in Ukraine has led to a large influx of photos and videos being shared by civilians on a daily basis to call attention to war crimes committed by Russian soldiers.[14] In April 2023, a gruesome video alleged to show the beheading of a live Ukrainian soldier by Russian soldiers circulated on social media.[15] The video was allegedly captured by one of the Russian soldiers, but was shared and reshared by many accounts with the intention of condemning the incident.[16] This phenomenon also occurred prior to the Russian invasion of Ukraine and in other parts of the world, such as in the context of the conflicts in Syria and Cameroon.[17] In the Syrian context, photos and videos have been shared about the conflict on platforms such as YouTube since the early 2010s,[18] and in Cameroon, it

[11] Feinberg (n 9); RA Duff, 'Harms and Wrongs' (2001) *Buffalo Criminal Law Review* 13–45, 17.

[12] Feinberg defines harm in relation to the harm principle as a '*wrongful* setback of interests' (emphasis added). Feinberg (n 9); see also MD Bayles, 'Book Review: Offense to Others: The Moral Limits of the Criminal Law, Vol. 2 by Joel Feinberg' (1986) 5 *Law and Philosophy* 113–20, 114.

[13] See ch 4, ss III and IV of this book.

[14] 'Video appears to show Russians beheading Ukrainian soldier - as "appalled" UN says incident not isolated' (Sky News, 12 April 2023) news.sky.com/story/volodymyr-zelenskyy-condemns-video-appearing-to-show-russian-beasts-beheading-a-ukrainian-captive-12855811. See also S Zarmsky, 'ICL's Potential to Address Online Harms in Ukraine, Palestine, and Beyond' (Opinio Juris, 10 September 2024) opiniojuris.org/2024/09/10/contemporary-international-criminal-law-after-critique-symposium-icls-potential-to-address-online-harms-in-ukraine-palestine-and-beyond/; A Koenig, 'From 'Capture to Courtroom': Collaboration and the Digital Documentation of International Crimes in Ukraine' (2022) 20 *Journal of International Criminal Justice* 829–42.

[15] Sky News (n 14) and Zarmsky (n 14).

[16] ibid.

[17] See, eg A Katz, 'Dramatic Footage Shows Syrian Girl's Rescue from Rubble' (Time Magazine, 23 September 2016) time.com/4505749/syria-aleppo-girl-rescue/ (this piece reports on a video that went viral on YouTube of a child being pulled from the rubble after an airstrike); Cameroon Database of Atrocities, 'Verified Incident: Shooting of Five Civilians in Mile 90, Nsongwa' (April 2021) borealisdata.ca/file.xhtml?fileId=411399&version=1.0.

[18] ibid

is common for civilians to post imagery to Facebook and X about the Anglophone Crisis.[19]

The issue that arises here is that though sharing footage with the purpose of trying to help the situation might not be morally wrongful due to good intentions behind the act (even though it might be potentially inconsiderate),[20] it can still be equally harmful to victims and their families if the necessary precautions are not taken (such as blurring faces and removing metadata to protect privacy).[21] In addition, some images may be so harmful that no matter what the justification for doing so, sharing them will always be wrongful. This would be the case for particularly sensitive images, such as images of sexual abuse or those of unclothed individuals taken without their consent, which is already a crime in many domestic jurisdictions, including multiple countries in Europe, the United States, Canada, and Australia.[22] Therefore, whether there is a good intention behind sharing such images or an absence of malicious intent, while this could be a valuable consideration for whether a harm is wrongful, it does not automatically exclude the harm from being wrongful.

Nevertheless, regardless of whether the harm is considered wrongful, considering what makes an 'international crime' as explained previously in this chapter, sharing footage of crimes for the purposes of raising awareness or calling for help may still not be suitable for criminalisation at the international level due to a lack heinousness and intent to degrade victims, and thus may be better addressed by content moderation policies of social media platforms (as all major social media platforms at the time of writing, such as Facebook, Instagram, X, and TikTok have policies in place to remove graphic content). This is because should sharing footage of crimes online be prosecuted at the ICC, the accused would need to have the intent 'to cause that consequence' or must be 'aware that it will occur in the ordinary course of events',[23] and it could be argued that someone sharing a video as a way of calling for help or condemning the crime would not have meant for additional harm to be caused to the victim. In this situation, criminalisation and prosecution would also likely infringe too far upon the individual's freedom of speech if there was zero intent to cause harm or awareness that harm could be caused.[24]

[19] ibid.

[20] See M Bair, 'Navigating the Ethics of Citizen Video: The Case of a Sexual Assault in Egypt' (2014) 19 *Arab Media & Society* 1–7; A Conti, 'The Ethics of Watching and Sharing Violent Viral Videos' (Vice News, 27 August 2015) www.vice.com/en/article/jmajx7/is-it-ethical-to-watch-or-share-violent-videos-like-the-virginia-news-crew-shooting-816.

[21] WITNESS, 'Ethical Guidelines: Using Eyewitness Videos in Human Rights Reporting & Advocacy' (October 2015) library.witness.org/product/video-as-evidence-ethical-guidelines/.

[22] Revenge porn laws across the world' (The Centre for Internet and Society, 25 April 2018) cis-india.org/internet-governance/blog/revenge-porn-laws-across-the-world.

[23] Rome Statute art 30(2)(b).

[24] This is also in accordance with 'harm' as defined through excessive restrictions on personal liberties and autonomy, which was described in reference to Mill and Raz in ch 2, s II.A of this book.

However, a lack of intent to cause harm to the victim does not necessarily mean that there is a lack of wrongfulness – while someone may share a video for a non-malicious reason, it still may not be the right thing to do. In line with Feinberg's view that criminalisable harms must be wrongful, it could therefore still be possible for digital harms to constitute crimes even if the perpetrator did not intend to cause serious harm or had 'good' intentions. In terms of legal framing, a lack of intent could still constitute a crime through the common law concept of recklessness,[25] which could be argued, in line with the International Committee of the Red Cross (ICRC)'s Customary International Law Rule 156 and jurisprudence from the International Criminal Tribunal for the former Yugoslavia (ICTY), is a sufficient mens rea for war crimes prosecutions as a matter of customary international law.[26] In this instance, if an individual shares disinformation that leads to violence or an image that further degrades a victim and their family, even if they did not mean to cause harm, it could be argued that they should have been aware of the possibility of that consequence and therefore acted in a reckless manner. Yet, it has been debated whether recklessness would be a sufficient basis to prosecute crimes at the ICC, given that it was not included in the Rome Statute.[27] Even so, if recklessness can constitute the mens rea for a crime under the Rome Statute, a foreseeable challenge would be meeting the gravity threshold for case selection and prosecution at the ICC, which will be considered in the next chapter.

[25] 'Recklessness' in common law systems refers to when an individual is aware of the risk of a particular consequence arising from their actions but decides to continue with their actions and take the risk where it is unreasonable to do so. *R v G* [2004] 1 AC 1034 (HL); see also 'Recklessness' in *Oxford Dictionary of Law* (10th edn, OUP, 2022).

[26] The ICRC's position as to the state of Customary International Law, Rule 156 states that 'international case law has indicated that war crimes are violations that are committed wilfully, ie, either intentionally (*dolus directus*) or recklessly (*dolus eventualis*)', and cites to the *Delalić* Trial Judgment in which the ICTY Trial Chamber found that recklessness is recognised by the Geneva Conventions and can constitute the mens rea for war crimes; 'Rule 156. Definition of War Crimes' (ICRC Customary IHL Database) ihl-databases.icrc.org/en/customary-ihl/v1/rule156#Fn_41B4CBC3_00032; *Prosecutor v Delalić et al.* (Judgment) IT-96-21-T, Trial Chamber (16 November 1998) ('*Delalić et al* Trial Judgment') [437]–[439]. However, this interpretation remains controversial, see B L Cox, 'Recklessness, Intent, and War Crimes: Refining the Legal Standard and Clarifying the Role of International Criminal Tribunals as a Source of Customary International Law' (2020) 52 *Georgetown Journal of International Law* 1.

[27] For instance, Cassese notes that it was 'questionable' that recklessness was excluded as a culpable mens rea under Article 30 of the Rome Statute, and Werle and Jeßberger argue that it follows 'from the wording of Article 30(2)(b) that recklessness and *dolus eventualis* do not meet the requirement'; A Cassese, 'The Statute of the International Criminal Court: Some Preliminary Reflections' (1999) 10 *European Journal of International Law* 158, 153; G Werle and F Jeßberger, '"Unless Otherwise Provided": Article 30 of the ICC Statute and the Mental Elements of Crimes under International Criminal Law' (2005) 3 *Journal of International Criminal Justice* 35–55, 53. Conversely, Piragoff and Robinson argue that even though recklessness is not included under Article 30, that the Court can still interpret the provision to allow for it, and Jescheck argues that the definition of 'knowledge' under Article 30 includes the concept of *dolus eventualis*; DK Piragoff and D Robinson, 'Article 30: Mental Element' in O Triffterer and K Ambos (eds), *The Rome Statute of the International Criminal Court: A Commentary* (3rd edn, Bloomsbury, 2016) 1122; H Jescheck, 'The General Principles of International Criminal Law Set Out in Nuremberg, as Mirrored in the ICC Statute' (2004) 2 *Journal of International Criminal Justice* 38–55, 45.

Building upon the discussion of harms needing to also be wrongful, Duff insists that criminalisable harms must further be *public* wrongs (or wrongful to the public in some way, such as a robbery that could make the public environment less safe and impact security) that therefore require collective responses, such as the enactment of a law.[28] On the surface, one may then assume that harms that occur in private, such as inside the home or on a closed online messaging platform, would not be criminalisable. However, it can be argued that Duff's requirement of being a 'public wrong' does not necessarily mean a harm has to occur in a public forum, as harms that occur in a private space can still have significant effects on the community of the victim.[29] For instance, as noted by Hudson, '[a] crime is different from a tort in that it is an offence against public behavioural norms as well as something that is harmful to an individual victim'.[30] In addition, taking into account May's and Cain and Howe's arguments about group harm as considered in chapter two,[31] instances of domestic violence in private against a woman by her husband can also form part of the endemic violence against women that perpetuates negative stereotypes and results in harm to all women. In line with this view, it has since been recognised that harms occurring in domains traditionally understood as 'private', such as in the home,[32] or perhaps in certain closed online spaces such as direct messages, should also be considered for criminalisation in the appropriate circumstances.[33]

However, criminal lawmakers have historically been reluctant to accommodate such harms (that frequently occur against women or minority groups) to the same level as harms that take place in public spaces.[34] This could mean that some digital harms, that can be perceived as private in nature if they are through a closed forum for example, could be similarly overlooked. On a more abstract level, the appropriate response to overcome this would be for ICL prosecutors or judges to be more inclusive and recognise harms occurring both behind and in front of

[28] RA Duff, 'Towards a Modest Legal Moralism' (2012) 8 *Criminal Law and Philosophy* 217, 230.

[29] See also B Stellings, 'Public Harm of Private Violence: Rape, Sex Discrimination and Citizenship' (1993) 28 *Harvard Civil Rights-Civil Liberties Law Review* 185.

[30] B Hudson, 'Restorative Justice and Gendered Violence: Diversion or Effective Justice?' (2002) 42 *British Journal of Criminology* 616–34, 628.

[31] See ch 2, s II.D of this book; L May, *The Morality of Groups: Collective Responsibility, Group-Based Harm, and Corporate Rights* (University of Notre Dame Press, 1987) 135; M Cain and A Howe, 'Introduction' in Maureen Cain and Adrian Howe (eds), *Women, Crime and Social Harm: Towards a Criminology for the Global Era* (Hart Publishing, 2008) 3.

[32] See, eg H Charlesworth, C Chinkin and S Wright, 'Feminist Approaches to International Law' (1991) 85 *American Journal of International Law* 613–45.

[33] A key example of this is image-based sexual abuse, where nude images originally intended for private use between individuals are shared (either publicly, such as a post on social media, or privately, such as sending to other individuals in a closed forum) without the consent of the person depicted. Depending on the nature of the distribution, this might not be an overtly public wrong, but is still potentially equally as harmful and is therefore argued by scholars to be deserving of explicit criminalisation. See DK Citron and M Franks, 'Criminalizing Revenge Porn' (2014) 49 *Wake Forest Law Review* 345–91; M Goudsmit Samaritter 'What Makes a Sex Crime? A Fair Label for Image-based Sexual Abuse' (2021) 2 *BJU Strafblad* 67.

[34] ibid; see also B Hudson, 'Beyond White Man's Justice: Race, Gender and Justice in Late Modernity' (2006) 10 *Theoretical Criminology* 29–47.

closed doors – this has already begun to take place over time, such as rape, forced marriage, and forced pregnancy, which are often instances of violence in private, have begun to be considered by prosecutors,[35] and are increasingly being prosecuted before international criminal courts and tribunals (ICCTs).[36] It is therefore plausible that given this trend that ICL actors would be able to extend this focus to also include acts within the digital space. On a more specific level, it could be argued that a reason harms occurring in private (which are many times gender-based crimes) are prosecuted less is because of failures of investigations to tailor themselves in a way to obtain evidence, and also because of potential tendencies of judges to require higher evidentiary standards for the prosecution than in other cases.[37] In a similar way to harms that may occur in private spaces, such as sexual violence, international criminal investigators will not simply happen upon the evidence of digital harms during field visits, and will instead need to have the expertise to find this information. To avoid under recognition of digital harms, it would be imperative for international prosecutors to develop a strategy of how to best collect and preserve the kind of evidence that is needed to secure prosecutions, including how to protect it from possible deletion by individual users or social media companies.[38]

In chapter three, the harms that ICL has previously sought to prevent were identified and later compared with 'newer' digital harms in chapter four.[39] A key conclusion was that ICL encompasses both physical and psychological harms in many of its existing core crimes, and that digital harms can be very similar in nature to those psychological harms. For instance, violations of human dignity are serious forms of harm that are clearly emphasised in crimes against humanity and war crimes, especially for crimes such as torture, inhuman treatment, sexual violence, outrages upon personal dignity and desecration of corpses. The similarity between the humiliation and degradation that comes from these existing crimes and that which comes from serious digital harms, as established in chapter four through reference to jurisprudence, is clear – for example, the horrific loss of dignity experienced by victims who are executed in a public square, or who are

[35] Office of the Prosecutor, Policy Paper on Sexual and Gender Based Crimes (June 2014).

[36] K Grewal, 'International Criminal Law as a Site for Enhancing Women's Rights? Challenges, Possibilities, Strategies' (2015) 23 *Feminist Legal Studies* 149–65; M D'Aoust, 'Sexual and Gender-based Violence in International Criminal Law: A Feminist Assessment of the *Bemba* Case' (2017) 17 *International Criminal Law Review* 208–21.

[37] S Sacouto and K Cleary, 'The Importance of Effective Investigation of Sexual Violence and Gender-Based Crimes at the International Criminal Court' (2009) 17 *American University Journal of Gender, Social Policy & the Law* 337, 348.

[38] Guidelines for how to best collect and archive content for international prosecutions can be found in OHCHR and Human Rights Center at the University of California, Berkeley, School of Law, 'Berkeley Protocol on Digital Open Source Investigations: A Practical Guide on the Effective Use of Digital Open Source Information in Investigating Violations of International Criminal, Human Rights and Humanitarian Law' (3 January 2022) ('The Berkeley Protocol') www.ohchr.org/en/publications/policy-and-methodological-publications/berkeley-protocol-digital-open-source, and in Human Rights Center, UC Berkeley School of Law, 'Digital Lockers: Archiving Social Media Evidence of Atrocity Crimes' (2021) humanrights.berkeley.edu/sites/default/files/digital_lockers_report5.pdf.

[39] See chs 3 and 4 of this book.

sexually assaulted in front of other soldiers, is no less severe when their suffering is displayed through an online space, and is arguably exacerbated further due to the internet's ability to reach a much wider audience in a quicker timeframe.

This is relevant to criminalisation through the harm principle because, as observed by multiple scholars,[40] and as demonstrated through ICL jurisprudence,[41] one of the aims of international (and domestic) criminalisation is to prevent serious harm to dignity. Dignity can generally be thought of as the basic worth that belongs to all by virtue of being human,[42] and therefore violations of dignity can lead to someone feeling or being treated as 'inhuman'. This exact wording is reflected in international crimes, for instance 'cruel and inhuman treatment', 'other inhumane acts', and 'outrages upon personal dignity',[43] demonstrating a clear emphasis on preventing harms to dignity. Further, ICL Chambers have described how central protecting dignity is to the international criminal, international humanitarian and human rights regimes. For instance, in *Furundžija*, the ICTY Trial Chamber stated:

> The general principle of respect for human dignity is the basic underpinning and indeed the very raison d'être of international humanitarian law and human rights law; indeed in modern times it has become of such paramount importance as to permeate the whole body of international law. This principle is intended to shield human beings from outrages upon their personal dignity, whether such outrages are carried out by unlawfully attacking the body or by humiliating and debasing the honour, the self-respect or the mental well being of a person.[44]

In this case, the Trial Chamber used the concept of human dignity to expand the definition of rape, arguing that forced oral penetration constituted an egregious assault on dignity equally severe as vaginal or anal penetration and therefore should be treated as the crime of rape.[45] The practice of using human dignity to help to progress the law has also been seen in other cases at the ICTY, such as *Vasiljević* in

[40] See T Hörnle, 'Criminalizing Behaviour to Protect Human Dignity' (2012) 6 *Criminal Law and Philosophy* 307–25; G Le Moli, 'Human Dignity in International Criminal Law' in G Le Moli, *Human Dignity in International Law* (CUP, 2021); JB Heath, 'Human Dignity at Trial: Hard Cases and Broad Concepts in International Criminal Law' (2012) 44 *George Washington International Law Review* 317; MM deGuzman, *Shocking the Conscience of Humanity: Gravity and the Legitimacy of International Criminal Law* (OUP, 2020).

[41] See, eg *Prosecutor v Furundžija* (Judgment) IT-95-17/1-T, Trial Chamber (10 December 1998) ('*Furundžija* Trial Judgment'); *Prosecutor v Vasiljević* (Judgment) IT-98-32, Trial Chamber II (29 November 2002) ('*Vasiljević* Trial Judgment'); *Prosecutor v Akayesu* (Judgment) ICTR-96-4-T, Trial Chamber I (2 September 1998) ('*Akayesu* Trial Judgment'); *Prosecutor v Niyitegeka* (Judgment) ICTR-96-14-T, Trial Chamber I (16 May 2003) ('*Niyitegeka* Trial Judgment'); and *Prosecutor v Nahimana, Barayagwiza and Ngeze* (Judgment) ICTR-99-52-T, Trial Chamber (3 December 2003) ('*Nahimana et al* Trial Judgment').

[42] The definition of dignity is complex and debated by philosophers, but this discussion falls outside the scope of this book. 'Dignity' (Stanford Encyclopedia of Philosophy, 18 February 2023) plato.stanford.edu/entries/dignity/#FourOrigStor.

[43] Rome Statute arts 7 and 8.

[44] *Furundžija* Trial Judgment (n 41) [183].

[45] ibid.

which the Trial Chamber employed dignity as a key element of other inhumane acts,[46] and also at the International Criminal Tribunal for Rwanda (ICTR), where in *Akayesu* the Trial Chamber used dignity to equate rape to torture,[47] and in *Niyitegeka* the Trial Chamber found that defilement of corpses was an attack on dignity.[48] In addition, outside the context of torture and inhuman treatment, in *Nahimana et al.*, the Trial Chamber used dignity to find that hate speech could amount to persecution and that radio broadcasts and newspapers themselves (not just the violence they allegedly incited with the speech) could constitute acts of genocide.[49] The Trial Chamber noted that hate speech was a 'discriminatory form of aggression that destroys the dignity of those in the group under attack' and that '[i]t creates a lesser status not only in the eyes of the group members themselves but also in the eyes of others who perceive and treat them as less than human'.[50] From these cases, it is evident that preventing harm to dignity has been a critical consideration by ICCTs when interpreting the elements of crimes and expanding the law to encompass a broader array of acts and omissions. The same logic could be applied to account for digital harms.

For instance, in the case of online hate speech, the harmful effects on dignity would be, at the very least, the same regardless of the type of forum used to spread the speech. It can be argued that online hate speech is even more severe and therefore would have greater effects on dignity because of its potential to reach a much wider audience, and the fact that anonymity can lead to even more egregious hate speech when there is little fear of accountability and a perceived sense of power imbalance between the victim and perpetrator because the perpetrator knows the identity of the victim but the victim does not know who the perpetrator is.[51] Further, these equally severe harms to dignity can occur through hateful or sexual content generated by AI, including 'deepfakes', which have already been reported by the United Nations as being used for malicious purposes including to spread disinformation and to incite hatred.[52] For example, voice-cloning technology has

[46] In this case, the Trial Chamber found that other inhumane acts were committed against two survivors of a shooting because 'the attempted murder of [the victims] constitutes a serious attack on their human dignity'. The case concerned charges of war crimes and crimes against humanity against a member of a Bosnian Serb paramilitary unit; see *Vasiljević* Trial Judgment (n 41) [239]; Heath (n 40) 321.

[47] *Akayesu* Trial Judgment (n 41) [597].

[48] *Niyitegeka* Trial Judgment (n 41) [465]. This case concerned charges of genocide and crimes against humanity against a journalist and news presenter at Radio Rwanda.

[49] *Nahimana et al* Trial Judgment (n 41); Heath (n 40) 319.

[50] *Nahimana et al* Trial Judgment (n 41) [1072]; CA MacKinnon, 'Prosecutor v. Nahimana, Barayagwiza, & Ngeze. Case No. ICTR 99-52-T' (2004) 98 *American Journal of International Law* 325–30.

[51] A Brown, 'What Is So Special About Online (as Compared to Offline) Hate Speech?' (2017) 18 *Ethnicities* 297–326; PK Smith, 'The Nature of Cyberbullying and What We Can Do About It' (2015) 15 *Journal of Research in Special Educational Needs* 176–84.

[52] United Nations, 'Information and Integrity on Digital Platforms' (Common Agenda Policy Brief 8, June 2023); See also M Pawalec, 'Deepfakes and Democracy (Theory): How Synthetic Audio-Visual Media for Disinformation and Hate Speech Threaten Core Democratic Functions' (2022) 1 *Digital Society* 19; N Brown, 'Deepfakes and the Weaponization of Disinformation' (2020) 23 Virginia Journal of Law and Technology 1.

been used to create convincing audio clips of politicians and celebrities reciting extremely harmful rhetoric, such as the actress Emma Watson reading Hitler's *Mein Kampf*, an individual saying 'trans rights are human rights' then being strangled, and the character Rick from the series *Rick & Morty* encouraging violence against women.[53] In addition, deepfake technology is becoming increasingly used to generate pornographic content, where real individuals' faces are imposed onto nude imagery without their consent and circulated throughout the porn industry, constituting a form of sexual abuse.[54]

In the case of sharing footage of crimes, as discussed in chapter four, humiliation and degradation are central to the harm of posting images of victims in their most vulnerable state to social media.[55] As also outlined in chapter four, this has already been recognised by a number of domestic courts who have convicted individuals for the war crime of outrages upon personal dignity for sharing images of executions and defilement of corpses to social media platforms.[56] In terms of preventing harms to dignity, it is foreseeable that an international court such as the ICC could prosecute individuals under the war crime of outrages upon personal dignity as well. This was explicitly mentioned in the Office of the Prosecutors (OTP) Policy on Cyber-Enabled Crimes Under the Rome Statute.[57] In reference to acts that could constitute outrages upon personal dignity, the Policy states:

> Typical examples may include graphic depictions of criminal conduct especially violence to the person, including gender based crimes. The production and publication of such images not only reflects a further dimension of the victimisation of the person depicted, but also frequently serves or is intended to serve the interests of the perpetrator, including potentially calling for or encouraging the commission of further crimes and thereby endangering others.[58]

Further, the idea of paying specific attention to these harms has already been apparent in the minds of ICC judges, as in the first arrest warrant in the *Al Werfalli* case, the Pre Trial Chamber explicitly noted 'the staging of these executions in front of the camera and the posting of the videos to social media'.[59]

[53] J Cox, 'AI-Generated Voice Firm Clamps Down After 4chan Makes Celebrity Voices for Abuse' (Vice News, 30 January 2023) www.vice.com/en/article/dy7mww/ai-voice-firm-4chan-celebrity-voices-emma-watson-joe-rogan-elevenlabs.

[54] K Tenbarge, 'Found through Google, bought with Visa and Mastercard: Inside the deepfake porn economy' (NBC News, 27 March 2023) www.nbcnews.com/tech/internet/deepfake-porn-ai-mr-deep-fake-economy-google-visa-mastercard-download-rcna75071.

[55] See ch 4, s III.C of this book.

[56] ibid.

[57] Office of the Prosecutor, 'Policy on Cyber-Enabled Crimes under the Rome Statute' (December 2025) [76] and [95].

[58] ibid [95], footnotes omitted.

[59] However, as noted in the previous chapter, this case did not proceed beyond the Arrest Warrant stage due to the death of the accused. *Prosecutor v Al Werfalli* (Warrant of Arrest) ICC-01/11-01/17-2, PTC I (15 August 2017) [27] fn 70.

Overall, preventing harm, and especially harm to dignity, is a compelling reason to criminalise digital harm under ICL because it can allow for the interpretation of what constitutes existing ICL crimes to be expanded. Keenan has argued that ICL Chambers rely on a harms-based approach to define new crimes that can help to prevent novel forms of harm.[60] He argues that this occurs mainly in a ground-up manner, meaning that prosecutors listen to victims to understand the true harms caused by perpetrators and then 'craft charges' to fit these harms.[61] Though this differs from the traditional harm principle, Keenan's discussion of the 'harms-based approach' to defining new areas of ICL reinforces the same overall principle that crimes are based on harms, because it is the nature of the harm that he argues ICL should consider to then determine whether a new crime is necessary to prevent future harm. Keenan substantiates his argument with examples in which ICL Chambers relied on an analysis of 'the type and magnitude of harm caused by the underlying conduct to determine whether novel conduct may be subject to prosecution', including the addition of forced marriage as a crime against humanity at the Special Court for Sierra Leone (SCSL).[62] In the *Brima* case, prosecutors charged defendants with the new crime against humanity of forced marriage despite having evidence of existing crimes such as rape, kidnapping, and forced labour.[63] In Keenan's view, this decision was taken deliberately because the prosecution was convinced by victims that the harms associated with forced marriage were different from the harms associated with the other existing crimes.[64] The Appeals Chamber agreed, finding that while forced marriage was similar to crimes such as sexual slavery in several ways, it also had distinct harms, including a 'forced conjugal association' that 'implies a relationship of exclusivity' between the perpetrator and his purported wife, with the wife risking disciplinary action for a breach of this arrangement.[65]

Keenan uses examples such as the *Brima* case to develop a theory about how ICL prosecutors approach novel conduct.[66] First, the prosecutors identify the harms associated with the conduct. Second, they demonstrate that those harms are 'similar in type and magnitude to harm associated with established crimes', and third, they 'show that the new crime is different enough from the established crime to justify using the novel crime'.[67] This theory could be useful in criminalising digital harm due to its similarities to the harm of established crimes, especially

[60] P Keenan, 'Doctrinal Innovation in International Criminal Law: Harms, Victims, and the Evolution of the Law' (2020) 42 *University of Pennsylvania Journal of International Law* 407.

[61] ibid.

[62] ibid 415.

[63] ibid 420. The *Brima* case concerned charges of war crimes and crimes against humanity against high-ranking military officials in the Armed Forces Revolutionary Council in Sierra Leone.

[64] ibid.

[65] ibid 422; *Prosecutor v Brima* (Judgment) SCSL-2004-16-A, Appeals Chamber (22 February 2008) ('*Brima* Appeal Judgment') [187]–[196].

[66] ibid 407.

[67] ibid 407–08.

concerning online speech harms as described in chapter four,[68] but could also be limiting in the sense that it would only allow for new harms to be criminalised that are similar enough to existing crimes. Thus, while this might be beneficial for digital harms such as online hate speech or sharing footage of crimes, that can be likened to existing crimes encompassing hate speech or outrages upon personal dignity, digital harms that are more 'novel' might be too far removed to accommodate.

In addition, a counterargument to Keenan's approach is that ICL Chambers need to exercise caution about how they interpret the law to avoid venturing too much into the realm of 'judicial activism'.[69] As observed by Schabas, the judges of ad hoc tribunals, particularly the ICTY, sometimes offered 'radical interpretations' of their Statutes and the definitions of crimes.[70] For example, Schabas notes that when the ICTY Statute was adopted, the concept of war crimes did not apply to non-international armed conflicts (NIACs), but the Chamber's 'creative interpretation' of Article 3 of the ICTY Statute in Tadic 'changed that situation forever'.[71] This could also be argued in relation to the *Brima* case discussed above, where forced marriage was not a part of the Statute for the SCSL, but the Appeals Chamber found the accused to be guilty of the 'new' crime against humanity.[72]

However, Schabas argues that Article 22(b) of the Rome Statute, which states that 'the definition of a crime shall be strictly construed and shall not be extended by analogy', 'clearly' demonstrates that the drafters 'contemplated a more conservative institution' at the ICC.[73] While this provision indeed limits the ability of ICC Chambers to broadly extend definitions of crimes to encompass any related harm, it arguably does not prohibit new interpretations to be made if the harm can match the elements of the offence (as has been demonstrated in relation to digital harms such as online hate speech, sharing footage of crimes online, and online sexual violence in chapter four).[74] Further, as provided in Article 21(3) of the Rome Statute, provisions of the Statute (including offences) must be interpreted in accordance with internationally recognised human rights protections,[75] such as fair trial rights and freedom of expression. Therefore, while digital harms cannot be encompassed by ICL through mere analogy, and Rome Statute crimes cannot be interpreted in a way that would unduly undermine human rights protections, this should not be an issue where the elements of crimes are directly fulfilled by digital harm and other admissibility criteria (i.e. gravity) are met. This is indeed

[68] See ch 4, s II of this book.
[69] W Schabas, 'Prosecutorial Discretion v. Judicial Activism at the International Criminal Court' (2008) 6 *Journal of International Criminal Justice* 731–61.
[70] ibid 755.
[71] ibid.
[72] *Prosecutor v Brima* (Judgment) SCSL-2004-16-A, Appeals Chamber (22 February 2008) ('*Brima* Appeal Judgment').
[73] Rome Statute art 22(b); Schabas (n 69) 760.
[74] See ch 4, s III of this book.
[75] Rome Statute art 21(2).

reflected in the OTP Policy on Cyber-Enabled Crimes Under the Rome Statute as well, which states:

> Thus, as a matter of law, genocide, crimes against humanity, war crimes and aggression, as well as offences against the administration of justice, can be committed or facilitated by cyber means, consistent with the established framework of international law. This is the key point that this Policy wishes to convey. This conclusion can be reached using ordinary, long-established means of interpretation, without impermissibly stretching existing criminal law by analogy or otherwise violating the *nullum crimen sine lege* principle.[76]

Moreover, while Article 22(b) represents one area of the Rome Statute that takes a stricter approach to limiting the discretion of prosecutors and judges, there are several other provisions that *do* allow for flexibility, such as more 'open ended' crimes like 'other inhumane acts', and the fact that gravity is left undefined and therefore subject to interpretation on a case-by-case basis. It could therefore be argued that while, of course, Rome Statute crimes cannot be radically analogised to encompass any type of harm, there are still provisions which indicate that the drafters did not intend for a static, conservative Court, and therefore that there is still room to accommodate novel harm.

In addition, a related theory that may encompass more 'novel' digital harms is DeGuzman's 'human dignity theory of international criminality', which argues that as all humans have an interest in preventing harms to human dignity, the global community has legitimate authority to prescribe rules of conduct (including criminal laws) to protect dignity.[77] DeGuzman links this theory to the gravity requirement for ICL, which will be considered in chapter six,[78] but overall argues that this approach favours flexible ICL norms that may evolve over time and accommodate new ways to protect human dignity.[79]

Yet, though the broadness of harm prevention allows for a progressive expansion of ICL, as noted by Keenan, approaches that focus on harm can also be subjective and inherently vulnerable to abuse or misuse.[80] For example, Keenan recalls that when the ICTY analysed the meaning of 'other inhuman acts' in the *Kupreškić* case, the Chamber described its approach as 'identify[ing] a set of basic rights appertaining to human beings, the infringement of which may amount, depending on the accompanying circumstances, to a crime against humanity'.[81] Keenan argues that this broad approach can leave room for prosecutors' or others' assumptions about what constitutes a 'basic right' to influence their decisions, which could

[76] Office of the Prosecutor (n 57) [4], footnotes omitted.

[77] 'Global Prescriptive Authority' in MM deGuzman, *Shocking the Conscience of Humanity: Gravity and the Legitimacy of International Criminal Law* (OUP, 2020) 3.

[78] See ch 6, s II.A of this book.

[79] deGuzman (n 77).

[80] ibid 428.

[81] ibid; *Prosecutor v Kupreškić et al* (Judgment) IT-95-16-T, Trial Chamber (14 January 2000) ('*Kupreškić et al* Trial Judgment').

leave out considerations of minority groups.[82] Hörnle has also cautioned against broad approaches in relation to protecting dignity, who emphasises that for criminalisation purposes, harms to dignity must be characterised narrowly as 'severe humiliation' to avoid being too restrictive, especially with regard to speech.[83] This is because if all degrees of humiliation were subject to criminalisation, it would result in individuals facing criminal charges for acts that did not cause a level of harm worthy of restricting their freedom of expression. These considerations are important, as reflected by the earlier discussion of intent for sharing content for example, since criminalisation should not be so broad to encompass all forms of harm, both in the interests of preserving limited resources at international courts and in protecting the right to freedom of expression. However, these concerns can likely be overcome by the gravity threshold for international crimes, which will be considered in chapter six.

B. Punishment

A second reason for criminalising digital harm is that the harm warrants punishment. Punishment is a core purpose of ICL, as reflected in the Preamble of the Rome Statute, which affirms 'that the most serious crimes of concern to the international community as a whole must not go unpunished' and states that the States Parties are 'determined to put an end to impunity … and thus contribute to the prevention of such crimes'.[84] These statements reflect one of the key purposes of the ICC, which is to investigate, prosecute, and punish individuals for international crimes when it would not be possible to do so otherwise.[85]

There are two main groups of theories for why punishment is desirable – first, that the consequences of punishment are desirable outcomes for prosecuting digital harms (in line with consequentialist theories of punishment, such as deterrence, incapacitation, or rehabilitation), and second, that those who perpetrate digital harms deserve to be punished (non-consequentialist theories, namely retribution).[86] With regard to the former, consequentialist theories of punishment traditionally include those of deterrence, prevention, incapacitation, re-education, and rehabilitation.[87] However, not all of these traditional theories translate easily to an ICL context.[88] For example, incapacitation is concerned with physically impris-

[82] ibid.

[83] T Hörnle, 'Criminalizing Behaviour to Protect Human Dignity' (2012) 6 *Criminal Law and Philosophy* 307.

[84] Rome Statute, Preamble.

[85] This is in line with the principle of complementary of the ICC, which means that it is a 'court of last resort', to be used when national jurisdictions are unwilling or unable to prosecute; Rome Statute, Preamble and art 1; see also C Stahn and MM El Zeidy (eds), *The International Criminal Court and Complementarity: From Theory to Practice* (CUP, 2011).

[86] A Coco, *The Defence of Mistake of Law in International Criminal Law* (OUP, 2022) 197.

[87] ibid.

[88] ibid.

oning or restricting an offender so that they cannot commit further crimes. When applied to ICL, it could be argued that because ICL is concerned mainly with high ranking officials with the capacity to command and commit international crimes, when they are taken out of circulation, there may be a possibility of reducing the ability of their forces to continue committing crimes or fighting. Conversely, it is also possible that since most offenders prosecuted by ICCTs are only arrested and transferred into custody after the conflict has ended or once they lose their power, incapacitation would not be as relevant for ICL. This was the case for Nazi perpetrators who were no longer in their roles that enabled them to perpetrate crimes at the time of the Nuremberg Trials, and for the former President of Serbia, Slobodan Milošević, who was not arrested and transferred to ICTY custody until six months after his fall from power.[89]

Further, considering the theory of rehabilitation, as observed by Riegler, in an ICL context, there can be challenges such as those relating to language or cultural barriers, and the fact that those convicted of international crimes might not benefit from more traditional rehabilitative programmes.[90] This is because perpetrators of international crimes can differ from 'ordinary' criminals in certain ways – they are many times in a high position of power and present as 'non-deviant and well-adjusted citizens before the commission of crimes'.[91] Nevertheless, rehabilitation, along with deterrence, are two consequentialist theories of punishment that have been explicitly recognised by ICCTs.[92] Rehabilitation has been briefly discussed by ICTR, ICTY, and ICC Chambers in regard to sentencing,[93] but seems to have trivial status as a reason for punishment at international courts, especially in comparison with deterrence.[94] Deterrence signifies that acts are criminalised to prevent (or to 'deter') people from committing them. Deterrence has a long history in domestic criminal law, and can be classified as either 'personal', meaning that punishment is designed to personally deter the specific individual from committing future crimes, or 'general', meaning that the public will be deterred from committing crimes due to the threat of punishment.[95]

[89] Human Rights Watch, 'Weighing the Evidence: Lessons from the Slobodan Milosevic Trial' (13 December 2006) www.hrw.org/report/2006/12/13/weighing-evidence/lessons-slobodan-milosevic-trial.

[90] E Riegler, 'Rehabilitating Enemies of Mankind: An Exploration of the Concept of Rehabilitation as a Sentencing Aim at the ICTY and ICC' (2020) 20 *International Criminal Law Review* 701–27, 708–09.

[91] ibid.

[92] Coco (n 86) 198.

[93] At the ICTY, rehabilitation has been recognised in cases such as *Blaškić*, *Kordić & Čerkez*, *Kunerac et al.*, *Obrenović*, *Čelebići* and *Tolimir*, and in *Katanga* at the ICC; Riegler (n 90). Notably, in the *Delalić et al* Appeal Judgement, the Appeals Chamber stated that rehabilitation 'should be considered as a relevant factor' but 'not one which should be given undue weight'; *Prosecutor v Delalić et al* (Judgment) IT-96-21-A, Appeals Chamber (20 February 2001) [806]. This was referenced by the Appeals Chamber in *Nahimana et al* at the ICTR; *Prosecutor v Nahimana, Barayagwiza and Ngeze* (Judgment) ICTR-99-52-A, Appeals Chamber (28 November 2007) ('*Nahimana et* al Appeal Judgment') [1057].

[94] Riegler (n 90) 727.

[95] J Herring, *Criminal Law: Text, Cases, and Materials* (10th edn, OUP, 2022) 58.

In the context of ICL, personal deterrence does not translate as easily given that many of those convicted of international crimes are no longer in the position that enabled them to commit such acts and because trials are very long,[96] so there is less likelihood that someone who serves a prison sentence for an international crime would thereafter go on to reoffend. However, general deterrence has been mentioned by ICL Chambers as a purpose for punishment. For instance, in the case of *Katanga et al.*, the ICC Trial Chamber noted that one purpose for punishment is 'deterrence, the aim of which is to deflect those planning to commit similar crimes'.[97] Deterrence has also been recognised as a paramount reason for punishment both in the Preamble of the Rome Statute through its mention of being 'determined…to contribute to the prevention of such crimes' and in numerous other cases at the ICTR, ICTY, and ICC.[98] At the time of writing, five of the six ICC sentencing decisions have listed deterrence as a fundamental purpose of sentencing at the Court.[99] Expanding upon this, in *Al Mahdi*, the Trial Chamber wrote that '[i]n respect of deterrence, the Chamber considers that a sentence should be adequate to discourage a convicted person from recidivism (specific deterrence), as well as to ensure that those who would consider committing similar crimes will be dissuaded from doing so (general deterrence)'.[100] It is therefore clear that deterrence has a place as a prominent theory of punishment under ICL.

However, the ability of international prosecutions to deter international crimes can be questioned. Scholars such as Lee and Price have pointed out evidence of prosecutions at international tribunals not succeeding to deter future crime – for example, the massacre at Srebrenica occurred two years after the establishment of the ICTY.[101] Further, as summarised by Coco, it is difficult to imagine there being any deterrent effect at all regarding international crimes due to the fact that (1) for 'a hypothetical average perpetrator of international crimes, it would be harder to possess the cognitive ability to be influenced by international criminal law, as

[96] See C Davidson, 'Aging Out: Elderly Defendants and International Crimes' (2020) 61(1) *Virginia Journal of International Law* 1–53.

[97] *Prosecutor v Katanga et al* (Decision on Sentence pursuant to article 76 of the Statute), ICC-01/04 -01/07-3484-tENG, Trial Chamber II (23 May 2014) 38.

[98] Rome Statute; see *Prosecutor v Katanga et al* (Decision on Sentence pursuant to article 76 of the Statute), ICC-01/04-01/07-3484-tENG, Trial Chamber II (23 May 2014) ('*Katanga et al* Sentencing Judgment') [38]; *Prosecutor v Bemba,* (Decision on Sentence pursuant to Article 76 of the Statute) ICC-01/05-01/08-3399, Trial Chamber III (21 June 2016) ('*Bemba* Sentencing Judgment') [11]; *Delalić et al* Trial Judgment (n 26) [1234], *Prosecutor v Češić* (Sentencing Judgment) IT-95-10/1-S, Trial Chamber (11 March 2004) [25]; *Prosecutor v Šainović et al* (Judgment) IT-05-87, Trial Chamber II (26 February 2009) [1146]; and *Prosecutor v Akayesu* (Sentencing Judgment) ICTR-96-04, Trial Chamber (2 October 1998) [19]; Coco (n 86) 208.

[99] See *Katanga et al* Sentencing Judgment (n 98), *Bemba et al* Sentencing Judgment (n 98), *Prosecutor v Ongwen* (Sentencing Judgment) ICC-02/04-01/15-1819-Red, Trial Chamber IX (6 May 2021) ('*Ongwen* Sentencing Judgment'); *Prosecutor v Al Mahdi* (Judgment and Sentence) ICC-01/12-01/15-171, Trial Chamber VIII (27 September 2016) ('*Al Mahdi* Judgment') and *Prosecutor v Ntaganda* (Sentencing Judgment) ICC-01/04-02/06, Trial Chamber VI (7 November 2019) ('*Ntaganda* Sentencing Judgment').

[100] *Al Mahdi* Judgment (n 99) [67].

[101] J Lee and R Price, 'International Tribunals and the Criminalization of International Violence' in R Price and M Zacher (eds), *The United Nations and Global Security* (Springer, 2004) 129.

international norms would not necessarily be those to which they are accustomed and exposed', and (2) 'international crimes often occur in situations where the ordinary ranking of social values is turned upside down, and where criminal conduct might not even be deviant when compared to the majority's behaviour'.[102] This could reasonably be applied to digital harm, especially with regard to the second point, in the sense that if seemingly many other users are posting graphic and violent images of international crimes or sharing misinformation, the perpetrator might assume that this is 'normal' behaviour that they would never be punished for participating in and would not be deterred from such conduct.[103] Or, it could be possible that due to the ability to remain anonymous online, perpetrators of digital harm may not be deterred because they may not believe there is any chance of being identified.

Nonetheless, due to the impossibility of being able to isolate variables that could affect why perpetrators commit crimes, it cannot be determined with certainty that deterrence does or does not work in an ICL context. Moreover, just because international crimes continue to occur does not mean that other crimes have not been deterred, which is also difficult to measure. In terms of digital harm, it is difficult to see how these challenges related to deterrence would be any different, since it still would be impossible to determine whether a digital act being criminalised would be the exact factor that led to any potential decrease in harmful activity. On this note, v H Holtermann argues that this criticism of deterrence is not compelling, emphasising that just because we cannot be certain about whether punishment for international crimes has a deterrent effect, that it does not mean that it does not actually deter crime or that punishment would be unwarranted.[104] Further, he uses the 'presumption of instrumental rationality' (meaning that humans are rational actors) along with the fact that punishment induces suffering on human beings to argue that it is prima facie reasonable to believe that people are deterred from crime when there is a threat of punishment.[105]

However, it is important to consider that the instantaneousness of the internet can possibly affect the rationality of some perpetrators of digital harm. As hypothesised by Brown, the online environment encourages 'gut reactions' and 'unconsidered judgments' due to the ability of the user to be able to instantly share

[102] Coco (n 86) 210, footnotes omitted. See also I Tallgren, 'The Sensibility and Sense of International Criminal Law' (2002) 13 *European Journal of International Law* 561, 568 and M Drumbl, *Atrocity, Punishment and International Law* (CUP, 2007) 8, 23–44.

[103] It has also been found that punishment does not deter perpetrators of cybercrime in the domestic context, such as hackers, because they commonly feel that there is a low likelihood of punishment occurring; see R Young, L Zhang and VR Prybutok, 'Hacking into the Minds of Hackers' (2007) 24 *Information Systems Management* 281–87; G Kirwan and A Power, *The Psychology of Cyber Crime: Concepts and Principles* (IGI Global, 2011) 66.

[104] J v H Holtermann, 'A "Slice of Cheese": a Deterrence-Based Argument for the International Criminal Court' (2010) 11 *Human Rights Review* 289–315, 292–95; see also J v H Holtermann, '"Can I Be Brought before the ICC?": Deterrence of Mass Atrocities between Jus in Bello and Jus ad Bellum' in F Jeßberger and J Geneuss (eds), *Why Punish Perpetrators of Mass Atrocities? Purposes of Punishment in International Criminal Law* (CUP, 2020) 137–60.

[105] v H Holtermann, '"A Slice of Cheese"' (n 104) 295.

speech on social media, and while this is not to say that online hate speech is never well-thought out, it is more likely in an online space that perpetrators are not considering rationally the consequences of their actions.[106] If this is the case, then the argument that punishment deters perpetrators because they are rational beings would not stand as strongly for those who inflict some types of digital harm. Overall, Brown's argument is not entirely convincing, as 'gut reactions' such as murder in a fit of rage or saying something hateful occur in the offline context, and at present there does not seem to be sufficient evidence that the instantaneous nature of the internet makes people any less rational than in the physical world.

In the case of digital harm committed against a population by those in high positions of power at technology companies, deterrence might also not work if those individuals have no actual concern of being prosecuted at a court like the ICC due to jurisdictional issues. For instance, if a US-based company illegally harvested data akin to what happened in the Facebook-Cambridge Analytica data scandal,[107] and used that data to assist in suppressing or committing genocide against a particular group (such as what has been previously discussed in chapter four in relation to the situation in Xinjiang),[108] it may seem too impossible to bring executives of the company (who are US nationals) to the ICC. This is because the US (where most current big social media and tech companies are based) is not a party to the Rome Statute, and in order for non-State Party nationals to be prosecuted before the Court, they must have committed acts falling within the jurisdiction of the Court on the territory of a State Party.[109] Yet, if the harms affect victims on State Party territory, there is still space to argue that the Court should have jurisdiction,[110] and further, it is possible that an attempted prosecution of a company executive would be bad for business and could serve as a deterrent regardless of whether it is successful. Therefore, while it is important to consider whether punishment is too distant a possibility to act as a deterrent for some perpetrators of digital harm, it could still be possible that the criminalisation of such harms would cause those individuals to change their behaviour.

[106] A Brown, 'What Is So Special About Online (as Compared to Offline) Hate Speech?' (2017) 18 *Ethnicities* 297–326.

[107] N Confessore, 'Cambridge Analytica and Facebook: The Scandal and the Fallout So Far' (New York Times, 4 April 2018) www.nytimes.com/2018/04/04/us/politics/cambridge-analytica-scandal-fallout.html.

[108] See ch 4, ss III.A and ch 7, s III of this book.

[109] Rome Statute art 12(2).

[110] Jurisdiction will be explained in more detail in ch 6, s II.B of this book, however the jurisdiction of a cyber offence can be determined by many different factors, such as the nationality or location of the perpetrator, the location of the technology company, or the nationality or location of the victims, as the digital space does not have tangible boundaries. See for instance A Perloff-Giles, 'Transnational Cyber Offenses: Overcoming Jurisdictional Challenges' (2018) 43 *Yale Journal of International Law* 191–226; K Pipyros, L Mitrou, D Gritzalis, and T Apostolopoulos, 'Cyberoperations and International Humanitarian Law: A Review of Obstacles in Applying International Law Rules in Cyber Warfare' (2016) 24 *Information and Computer Security* 38–52; Oxford Institute for Ethics, Law and Armed Conflict, 'The Oxford Process on International Protections in Cyberspace: A Compendium' (2022) www.elac.ox.ac.uk/wp-content/uploads/2022/10/Oxford-Process-Compendium-Digital.pdf.

However, aside from deterrence, punishment could also be an arguably desirable outcome of criminalisation of digital harm for non-consequentialist reasons. Non-consequentialist theories of punishment are most associated with the theory of retribution.[111] Retribution is centred around punishment as a form of vengeance – in literal terms, it means 'payback'.[112] In this sense, perpetrators of crimes are punished for their actions not to deter future crime or to send a message to broader society, but because it is what they deserve. This is a debated theory of punishment, as some argue that retributive justice is 'primitive' and constitutes a form of 'state-sanctioned revenge' that could be 'overly sympathetic to victims and less protective of the accused'.[113] Conversely, retribution could also be viewed as a testament to personal autonomy, as it rests on the assumption that individuals are autonomous and morally free, and fully responsible when deciding to commit a crime.[114] In this sense, retribution could instead be seen as a fair process linked with intentional wrongdoing. However, concerning international crimes, which many times take place during armed conflict and where there may be a command structure or individuals acting under duress, it is less convincing that all individuals are completely autonomous. Nevertheless, as will be discussed in the subsequent paragraphs, retribution has been recognised as an important theory in ICL jurisprudence.

In the criminal law context, retributive justice has been defined in various ways, but is generally committed to the following three principles: (1) that those who commit certain wrongful acts morally deserve to suffer a proportionate punishment; (2) that it is intrinsically morally good if a legitimate punisher allocates the punishment; and (3) that it is morally impermissible to intentionally punish the innocent or to inflict disproportionately large punishments on wrongdoers.[115] Retribution as a purpose of punishment, along with its emphasis on the proportionality of sentencing, has also been embraced by ICL,[116] dating back to the Nuremberg Trials. As noted by Finch in his 1946 address before the Section of International and Comparative Law of the American Bar Association, the Nuremberg Trials were (at least, in part) motivated by a desire for retribution 'for the shocking crimes and atrocities committed by the enemy' that was 'made imperative by the overwhelming demands emanating from the public conscience throughout the civilized world'.[117] During more recent international

[111] Coco (n 86) 197.

[112] 'Retribution' in *Merriam-Webster Dictionary* (Online) www.merriam-webster.com/dictionary/retribution.

[113] C Stahn, *Justice as Message: Expressivist Foundations of International Criminal Justice* (OUP, 2020) 406.

[114] GP Fletcher, 'Political Theory and Criminal Law' (2006) 25 *Criminal Justice Ethics* 18, 22.

[115] 'Retributive Justice' (Stanford Encyclopedia of Philosophy, 31 July 2020) plato.stanford.edu/entries/justice-retributive/.

[116] Coco (n 86) 200.

[117] G Finch, 'The Nuremberg Trial and International Law: Revised, enlarged, and annotated version of an address delivered at Atlantic City, N. J., Oct. 29, 1946, before the Section of International and Comparative Law of the American Bar Association, as Chairman of the Committee on Punishment of War Criminals' (2017) 41 *American Journal of International Law* 1.

trials, the ICTY Trial Chamber stated in *Jokić* that '[a]s a form of retribution, punishment expresses society's condemnation of a criminal act and of the person who committed it and should be proportional to the seriousness of the crimes'.[118] Further, references to proportionality between the sentence and the severity of the crime are included in the Rome Statute (Articles 78(1) and 83(3)) and the ICC Rules of Procedure and Evidence (Rule 145(1)).[119] Proportionality of punishment is especially important to ICL, as evidenced by, for example, the defence of duress – in a context of armed conflict where many perpetrators might be acting under duress or under superior orders, proportionality is necessary to ensure morally just punishments.[120]

In addition, in 2005, Drumbl noted that the ICTY had

> issued judgments that cite retribution and general deterrence as 'equally important', judgments that cite retribution as the 'primary objective' and deterrence as a 'further hope', warning deterrence 'should not be given undue prominence', and judgments that flatly state 'deterrence probably is the most important factor in the assessment of appropriate sentences'.[121]

The inconsistencies of these quotes suggest that the Tribunal's approach to considering theories of deterrence and retributivism is flexible and one left to the discretion of the Chamber. Since then, other courts such as the ICC have also cited to the same concepts in their sentencing decisions – in *Ntaganda*, Trial Chamber VI stated that it considered 'that the Preamble [of the Rome Statute] establishes retribution and deterrence as the primary objectives of punishment at the Court'.[122] This statement was confirmed also by the Trial Chambers in *Katanga et al.*, *Bemba*, and *Al Mahdi*.[123] While the differences in how ICL Chambers have interpreted how deterrence and retributivism should (or should not) be applied could also signify a lack of certainty, the few sentencing decisions issued since then at the ICC suggest that as time has progressed, both theories have become solidified in their importance.[124]

[118] *Prosecutor v Jokić* (Sentencing Judgment) IT-01-42/1-S, Trial Chamber I (18 March 2004) [31]–[32]. This case concerned war crimes charges against the commander of the 9th Military Naval Sector of the Yugoslav navy.

[119] Rome Statute; ICC Rules of Procedure and Evidence; Coco (n 86) 200.

[120] M Kremnitzer, 'An Argument for Retributivism in International Criminal Law' in F Jeßberger and J Geneuss (eds), *Why Punish Perpetrators of Mass Atrocities? Purposes of Punishment in International Criminal Law* (CUP, 2020) 161–75.

[121] M Drumbl, 'Collective Violence and Individual Punishment: The Criminality of Mass Atrocity' (2005) 99 *Northwestern University Law Review* 539, 560–61, footnotes omitted. These quotes came from the ICTY Trial Chamber judgments in *Prosecutor v Stakić* (Judgment) IT-97-24, Trial Chamber II (31 July 2003) [900]; *Prosecutor v Nikolić* (Judgment) IT-94-2 (18 December 2003) [59], [90]; and *Delalić et al* Trial Judgment (n 26) [1234].

[122] *Ntaganda* Sentencing Judgment (n 99) [9].

[123] ibid; *Al Mahdi* Judgment (n 99) [66]; *Katanga et al* Sentencing Judgment (n 98) [37]–[38]; and *Bemba* Sentencing Judgment (n 98) [10].

[124] *Prosecutor v Lubanga* (Decision on Sentence pursuant to Article 76 of the Statute) ICC-01/04-01/06-2901, Trial Chamber I (13 July 2012); *Katanga et al* Sentencing Judgment (n 98); *Al Mahdi*

C. Expressivism

A third reason to criminalise digital harm under ICL could be to send a message about the type of conduct that should be condemned as an international crime. Expressivist theory is rooted in the idea that the law can be symbolic or meaningful,[125] and can send a message about the values of those who enact it. Through an expressivist lens, one could argue that the reason something is characterised as a crime is not necessarily to deter it from happening or because there is a need for retribution, but because of a desire to express that the conduct goes against the values of a particular society. In other words, expressivist theory 'tends to see criminal law as an instrument to transmit values and change attitudes',[126] which could result in certain acts being deterred and others being promoted.

Stahn conceptualises expressivist theory in the criminal justice context as a 'communicative cycle' of three layers of communication: the criminal norm (which contains a normative statement), the crime itself (which can be read as a message), and trial and punishment (which seek to answer such messages).[127] The first layer – criminal norms – provide authorisation for the exercise of criminal powers and the infliction of punishment, but also entail value judgments, or 'messages about behaviours that should be avoided and correspondingly that a sanction will be applied in case of violation'.[128] The second layer is the crime itself as an expression of objective, defiance, or negligence towards the criminal norm.[129] The third layer of the communicative cycle is trial and punishment, which provide (to some extent) a reaction to the message of the crime.[130] Within this third layer, trials carry a range of messages, including 'speaking' to citizens as members of the normative community, reinforcing beliefs in the validity of norms, and articulating the social meaning of the crime 'in the language of the law' and identifying the consequences of it.[131] Further, punishment is 'deemed to satisfy public expectations, express wrongdoing, and induce future compliance'.[132]

Judgment (n 99); *Bemba* Sentencing Judgment (n 99); *Prosecutor v Bemba et al* (Decision on Sentence pursuant to Article 76 of the Statute) ICC-01/05-01/13, Trial Chamber VII (22 March 2017); *Prosecutor v Bemba et al* (Decision Re-sentencing Mr Jean-Pierre Bemba Gombo, Mr Aimé Kilolo Musamba and Mr Jean-Jacques Mangenda Kabongo) ICC-01/05-01/13, Trial Chamber VII (17 September 2018); *Ntaganda* Sentencing Judgment (n 99); *Ongwen* Sentencing Judgment (n 99); *Prosecutor v Ongwen*, (Judgment on the appeal of Mr Dominic Ongwen against the decision of Trial Chamber IX of 6 May 2021 entitled "Sentence") ICC-02/04-01/15-2023, Appeals Chamber (15 December 2022).

[125] MD Adler, 'Expressive Theories of Law: A Skeptical Overview' (2000) 148 *UPenn Law Review* 1363, 1364.

[126] KJ Fisher, *Moral Accountability and International Criminal Law, Holding Agents of Atrocity Accountable to the World* (Routledge, 2011) 49–65, 59; Stahn (n 113) 20.

[127] Stahn (n 113) 21.

[128] ibid 22.

[129] ibid 24.

[130] ibid 25.

[131] ibid.

[132] ibid.

Expressivism has been present in ICL dating back to the aftermath of the Holocaust. As noted by Amann, during the Nuremburg Trials, '[c]ondemnation, the process of compiling a record of evil and expressing repulsion, received as much attention as punishment'.[133] This was also shown in the IMT's 1946 judgment, when it described pre-war attacks on German Jews that 'must not be forgotten' even while ruling that those attacks fell outside its jurisdiction.[134] This message has been reflected in later ICL instruments, such as in the Preamble of the Rome Statute, which states that 'millions of children, women and men have been victims of unimaginable atrocities that deeply shock the conscience of humanity',[135] demonstrating that the crimes falling under the Court's jurisdiction are those that are particularly serious and therefore deserving of strong condemnation by the international community.

Stahn argues that expressivist practices have a larger space in international criminal justice than traditionally assumed.[136] For instance, ICCTs have established outreach projects to 'communicate judicial narratives', publicise outcomes of proceedings, and 'speak more directly to victims and local communities', which spreads information about and works to publicly condemn the crimes being prosecuted.[137] In addition, victims have a voice in proceedings, and images, press releases, broadcastings of proceedings, and social media are used to relay trials to audiences and present them in more accessible formats.[138] All of these practices show that, at the very least, ICCTs understand the importance of the expressive functions of a criminal court and wish to catch up with the expressivist capacities of domestic courts, which have long implemented such practices. In addition, these expressivist practices serve what Stahn classifies as two broader social functions. First, this expressivism 'serves as a means to continuingly reaffirm the purposes and ambitions of the field, and to encourage engagement and commitment to it'.[139] Second, it makes ICL 'real and tangible', creating meaning, relating the law to audiences, and encouraging norm internalisation or compliance.[140]

Further, as emphasised by Demko, international punishment through international criminal trials not only signals condemnation for crimes or assigns responsibility for their perpetration, but can aid in the protection of the truth, of victims, and the rejection of collective guilt.[141] Regarding the protection of the truth, ICL proceedings 'make an important and necessary contribution' by

[133] DM Amann, 'Group Mentality, Expressivism, and Genocide' (2002) 2 *International Criminal Law Review* 93–143, 121.

[134] ibid; *The Trial of Major German War Criminals (Göring et al.)* (Judgment) (1 October 1946) [418].

[135] Rome Statute, Preamble.

[136] Stahn (n 113) 391.

[137] ibid 393.

[138] ibid.

[139] ibid 395.

[140] ibid.

[141] D Demko, 'An Expressive Theory of International Punishment for International Crimes' in F Jeßberger and J Geneuss (eds), *Why Punish Perpetrators of Mass Atrocities?: Purposes of Punishment in International Criminal Law* (CUP, 2020) 176–95, 193.

reviewing a historical event and clarifying the truth, which is needed for successful reconciliation processes.[142] Concerning the protection of victims and the rejection of collective guilt, Demko writes:

> By assigning to the offender the responsibility for the international crime the offender has committed, international punishment communicates not only to the convicted offender, but also to the victims of international crime and to all other human beings in a clear and unambiguous manner to whom – namely, to the convicted offender – individual reproachability (individual criminal responsibility) for the international crime is to be assigned. At the same time, international punishment communicates (first) that the suffering and the injuries of the victims are not the result of an accident or a misfortune, but rather a direct result of the international crime for which the offender is individually criminally responsible. International punishment thereby expresses the recognition of the victims of the international crime and their suffering and conveys to the victims of the international crime that they can trust in the international law and international criminal law that protect them.[143]

Taking this into account, the international criminalisation of digital harms could serve a variety of expressivist goals, from reassuring victims about the ICL process, to establishing a historical record, to sending a message to the international community that digital harms are deserving of condemnation and punishment. These functions are of a heightened importance for digital harm, as new technologies are rapidly evolving leading to new ways of inflicting harm, and criminalisation would demonstrate to the international community that these technologies should be approached with caution and further that ICL is able to catch up to accommodate the resulting harm.

For example, two prominent areas where technology is repeatedly being used and continuing to develop are new autonomous and AI weapons and online disinformation campaigns. In the case of the former, autonomous technologies can be used to commit core international crimes both inside and outside the context of armed conflict. In terms of armed conflict, there has been increasing use of autonomous and AI weapons by States, including (but not limited to) drones,[144] unmanned aerial vehicles,[145] AI-guided missiles that can switch targets mid-flight without human involvement,[146] and autonomous robots on the ground.[147] These technologies have potential benefits through minimising the number of injured or

[142] ibid 194.

[143] ibid, footnotes omitted.

[144] B Boutin, 'State Responsibility in Relation to Military Applications of Artificial Intelligence' (2023) 36 *Leiden Journal of International Law* 133–50.

[145] E Winter, 'The Compatibility of Autonomous Weapons with the Principles of International Humanitarian Law' (2022) 27 *Conflict & Security Law* 1–20, 6.

[146] ibid; T O'Connor, 'Russia's Military Challenges US and China By Building a Missile That Makes Its Own Decisions' (Newsweek, 20 July 2017) www.newsweek.com/russia-military-challenge-us-china-missile-own-decisions-639926.

[147] 'Robots could be used to support soldiers in combat' (BBC News, 28 January 2022) www.bbc.co.uk/news/uk-england-bristol-60145220.

killed human combatants or for avoiding human error caused by fatigue, revenge, or other biases, but they also carry significant risks. As observed by Deeks, Lubell, and Murray, algorithms may not be able to perform desired tasks well if there is not enough quality data available to learn from and make reliable predictions.[148] In addition, the authors emphasise the difficulty of encoding legal rules, such as the principle of distinction in armed conflict,[149] which could result in a war crime if the algorithm attacks a civilian by mistake.

Further, as argued by Swart, AI tools could also be used to commit other international crimes such as torture and genocide.[150] Concerning torture, Swart notes that it is foreseeable that algorithmic capabilities could be implemented into interrogation systems to perpetrate either physical or psychological torture.[151] 'Robot interrogators' have already been experimented with in the United States,[152] and run the risk of being tireless interrogators without experiencing empathy or feelings of mercy.[153] Regarding genocide, AI tools may exacerbate divisions between groups through aiding in the spread of hate speech and deepfakes online, and could be used to monitor oppressed groups such as through facial recognition software, which has already allegedly been implemented in Xinjiang to target the Uyghur population.[154]

While there have been campaigns to ban the use of autonomous weapons by organisations such as Human Rights Watch with the Campaign to Stop Killer Robots,[155] and many States,[156] these efforts have been unsuccessful so far as States such as the United States, the United Kingdom, China, Russia, Japan, India, Israel, and South Korea have continued to develop such technologies.[157] Similar calls have also been made to limit AI technology used for surveillance and spreading disinformation and to implement strategies to combat those challenges, such as ensuring that technology companies abide by business and human rights standards and requiring platforms to alert their audiences when they are exposed to AI-generated content.[158] The potential international criminalisation of the harms

[148] A Deeks, N Lubell, and D Murray, 'Machine Learning, Artificial Intelligence, and the Use of Force by States' (2019) 10 *Journal of National Security Law & Policy* 1–25, 12–14.

[149] ibid.

[150] M Swart, 'Constructing "Electronic Liability" for International Crimes: Transcending the Individual in International Criminal Law' (2023) 24 *German Law Journal* 589–602.

[151] ibid 592.

[152] J Pearson, 'The CIA Used Artificial Intelligence to Interrogate Its Own Agents in the 80s' (Vice, 22 September 2014), www.vice.com/en/article/qkvz85/the-cia-used-artificial-intelligence-to-interrogate-its-own-agents-in-the-80s.

[153] Swart (n 150) 592.

[154] ibid 593.

[155] Human Rights Watch, 'Stopping Killer Robots: Country Positions on Banning Fully Autonomous Weapons and Retaining Human Control' (10 August 2020) www.hrw.org/report/2020/08/10/stopping-killer-robots/country-positions-banning-fully-autonomous-weapons-and.

[156] '33 states call for urgent negotiation of new international law to limit autonomous weapons' (UN Action UK, 27 February 2023) una.org.uk/news/33-states-call-for-urgent-negotiation-of-new-international-law-to-limit-autonomy-in-weapons-systems.

[157] Winter (n 145) 5.

[158] 'Regulation essential to curb AI for surveillance, disinformation: rights experts' (UN News, 2 June 2023) news.un.org/en/story/2023/06/1137302.

that can result from these technologies (which are not already criminalised) could serve the expressivist function of sending a message that the international community does not tolerate them, which could put pressure on States who deploy new technologies to take steps to minimise any resulting damage. For instance, the ICC Prosecutor is reportedly investigating Russian drone attacks on power and other critical infrastructure in Ukraine.[159] If the OTP were to proceed with these efforts and charge an individual for directing these drone attacks, similarly to how a commander of an artillery battalion could be charged for directing an attack, or potentially even members of the company who produced and supplied the drones, it would send a strong message that the use of new technologies is on the radar of the ICC and will not go unpunished because the law is ready to catch up with new ways of inflicting harm.

Another area where technology is becoming more prominently used to cause harm and potentially international crimes is online disinformation campaigns. As discussed previously in chapter four,[160] it was determined by US authorities that Russia attempted to influence the results of the 2016 and 2020 Presidential Elections through disinformation aimed at denigrating President Biden and the Democratic Party, and supporting former President Trump.[161] This was done through a variety of methods, including 'troll farms', which are organised groups that come together with the purpose of affecting public opinion through generating disinformation on the internet.[162] Similar tactics were found to be used in the context of the 2019 European Parliament,[163] Portuguese,[164] and Indian elections.[165] Further, as AI capabilities have developed, it is likely that in subsequent elections, AI-generated disinformation including deepfake imagery could be used to sway opinions.[166] Considering that online disinformation campaigns directly undermine democracy (which can infringe upon fundamental rights such as self-determination) and are only becoming more prevalent and easier to run with new technologies, a desirable outcome of international criminalisation of digital harms such as online hate

[159] M Collett-White, 'ICC's top prosecutor in Ukraine to probe Russian attacks on power grid' (Reuters, 1 March 2023) www.reuters.com/world/europe/iccs-top-prosecutor-ukraine-probe-russian-attacks-power-grid-2023-02-28/#:~:text=ICC%20Prosecutor%20Karim%20Khan%20was,with%20no%20electricity%20or%20water.

[160] See ch 4, s III.D of this book.

[161] National Intelligence Council, 'Foreign Threats to the 2020 US Federal Elections' (10 March 2021) www.dni.gov/files/ODNI/documents/assessments/ICA-declass-16MAR21.pdf; S McCombie, A Uhlmann and S Morrison, 'The US 2016 Presidential Election & Russia's Troll Farms' (2019) 35 *Intelligence & National Security* 95–114.

[162] ibid.

[163] F Pierri, A Artoni, and S Ceri, 'Investigating Italian Disinformation Spreading on Twitter in the Context of 2019 European Elections' (2020) 15 *PLoS ONE* 1–23.

[164] JP Baptista and A Gradim, 'Online Disinformation on Facebook: The Spread of Fake News During the Portuguese 2019 Election' (2022) 30 *Journal of Contemporary European Studies* 297–312.

[165] A Das and R Schroeder, 'Online Disinformation in the Run-up to the Indian 2019 Election' (2021) 24 *Information, Communication & Society* 1762–78.

[166] D Milmo and A Hern, 'Elections in UK and US at risk from AI-driven disinformation, say experts' (The Guardian, 20 May 2023) www.theguardian.com/technology/2023/may/20/elections-in-uk-and-us-at-risk-from-ai-driven-disinformation-say-experts.

speech or disinformation as a means of incitement, persecution, or even the crime of aggression,[167] would be the recognition and condemnation of these acts. In line with one of expressivist practices' key social functions of reaffirming the purposes and ambitions of the field,[168] international criminalisation of digital harm would be critical to demonstrating that ICL is ready and able to catch up to accommodate new forms of harm.

III. Pathways to Criminalisation

A key question of criminalising digital harm under ICL is how the criminalisation should be implemented. As outlined in this book thus far, some digital harms may require the development of a new crime while others may fit well within existing ICL frameworks.

A. Developing a New Crime

In cases such as mass surveillance or using algorithms that are prejudicial to a particular group, the unique nature of the digital harm where technology can permeate every aspect of life might warrant the creation of a new crime because the technology is so central to the offence. For example, in relation to the ongoing situation in which AI surveillance tools are being implemented throughout South Africa and in the Occupied Palestinian Territory, the term 'digital apartheid' has been used in the media and by NGOs.[169] This term emphasises how the digital component drives the crime. In South Africa, the use of facial recognition cameras by police and private security forces that can be prone to bias both in their coding and by those who monitor them can disproportionately harm black individuals

[167] Whether an act committed in cyberspace can constitute an act of aggression under ICL is debated, as the Rome Statute requires the use of 'armed force' by one state against another, which may exclude purely digital acts like election-meddling via disinformation. This debate falls outside the scope of this book, but in my view, though online disinformation campaigns aimed at affecting the sovereignty of another state can constitute a violation of international law (such as infringement upon the right to self-determination), it would likely not constitute an act of aggression under the Rome Statute (which this book is concerned with) given the requirement of 'armed force'. For further reading, see CI Keitner, 'Foreign Election Interference and International Law' in JD Ohlin and DB Hollis (eds), *Defending Democracies: Combating Foreign Election Interference in a Digital Age* (OUP, 2021); MN Schmitt, '"Virtual" Disenfranchisement: Cyber Election Meddling in the Grey Zones of International Law' (2018) 19 *Chicago Journal of International Law* 30.

[168] Stahn (n 113) 395.

[169] K Hao and H Swart, 'South Africa's private surveillance machine is fuelling a digital apartheid' (MIT Technology Review, 19 April 2022) www.technologyreview.com/2022/04/19/1049996/south-africa-ai-surveillance-digital-apartheid/; Amnesty International, 'Automated Apartheid: How Facial Recognition Fragments, Segregates and Controls Palestinians in the OPT' (2 May 2023) www.amnesty.org/en/documents/mde15/6701/2023/en/; O Zahzah, 'Digital apartheid: Palestinians being silenced on social media' (13 May 2021, Aljazeera) www.aljazeera.com/opinions/2021/5/13/social-media-companies-are-trying-to-silence-palestinian-voices.

through false identifications and contribute to a divide between racial groups.[170] In the Occupied Palestinian Territory, similar technology has been allegedly used by Israeli authorities to keep Palestinians under strict observation and to subject them to discriminatory policing.[171] In addition to facial recognition technology, it has been alleged that social media platforms have unfairly censored pro-Palestine posts due to pressure from the Israeli government, resulting in a systemic erasure of Palestinian voices.[172] While the crime of apartheid is a crime against humanity under the Rome Statute,[173] adding 'digital apartheid' as its own new crime would better recognise the full scope of harm to victims and the unique, pervasive role technology can play in the offence.

Another example is 'cultural genocide', defined as 'the systematic destruction of traditions, values, language, and other elements that make one group of people distinct from another'.[174] Cultural genocide is not a crime under international law, as 'cultural groups' are not listed as protected groups under the Genocide Convention or under the Rome Statute.[175] However, it has been argued that the development of a new crime of cultural genocide would fill a gap in ICL frameworks that currently prevents international courts from prosecuting genocidal acts that are not related to the physical destruction of members of a targeted group.[176] This is relevant in the context of criminalising digital harm because digital means are often used to destroy elements of culture such as traditions, values, and languages, which are not currently encompassed within the definition of genocide. For instance, cultural genocide has been applied to the situation in Xinjiang, where digital means are allegedly used to suppress and eradicate the Uyghur culture.[177] For instance, AI facial recognition technology is used to identify individuals and assign them scores for factors such as ethnicity, religion, having a passport, having foreign contacts, or relatives in detention.[178] Depending on these scores (or sometimes if identified directly by police as having a long beard, not smoking or drinking, studying Arabic,

[170] Hao and Swart (n 169).

[171] Amnesty International (n 169).

[172] Zahzah (n 169).

[173] Rome Statute art 7(1)(j).

[174] E Novic, *The Concept of Cultural Genocide: An International Law Perspective* (OUP, 2016); A Tiemessen, 'Cultural Genocide in Law and Politics' (2023) *Oxford Research Encyclopedia of International Studies*.

[175] Genocide Convention; Rome Statute art 6. The list of protected groups includes 'national, ethnical, racial, or religious' groups.

[176] C Finnegan, 'The Uyghur Minority in China: A Case Study of Cultural Genocide, Minority Rights and the Insufficiency of the International Legal Framework in Preventing State-Imposed Extinction' (2020) 9 *Laws* 1–20, 3; S Negri, 'Cultural Genocide in International Law: Is the Time Ripe for a Change?' (2013) 5 *Transnational Dispute Management* 5.

[177] Finnegan (n 176); Human Rights Watch, 'China's Algorithms of Repression: Reverse Engineering a Xinjiang Police Mass Surveillance App' (1 May 2019) www.hrw.org/report/2019/05/01/chinas-algorithms-repression/reverse-engineering-xinjiang-police-mass.

[178] ibid; D Tobin, 'Genocidal processes: social death in Xinjiang' (2022) 45 *Ethnic and Racial Studies* 93–121, 105.

or praying outside mosques),[179] individuals will then be rated as 'safe', 'average', or 'unsafe', which constitutes 'average' Uyghurs as potential threats.[180] Being labelled as a threat by this system allows for the Chinese government to detain individuals in 're-education camps' under the guise of 'anti-terrorism',[181] where they are forced to abandon their religious beliefs, 'learn about religious extremism', and must speak Chinese instead of their native Uyghur language.[182] The result of this is well described by the term 'cultural genocide', because while the group may not be physically destroyed, the cultural traditions, values, and language that form the group's identity are being eradicated.

Establishing new crimes such as 'digital apartheid' or 'cultural genocide' could be a compelling solution for accommodating the digital harms encompassed by them under ICL, in part, because of the principle of fair labelling. The principle of fair labelling 'seeks to ensure that the definition of an offence would provide society with an accurate moral grasp of the defendant's wrongdoing' and that offences are categorised in a way that reflects different levels of wrongdoing and punishment.[183] In cases where the harm is significantly driven by the use of technology, it would be valuable for the label of the crime to reflect this for both the specific harm to victims to be fully recognised and to better show a distinction between the technology-facilitated offence and the 'traditional' crime (ie apartheid or genocide). Fair labelling can also serve the expressivist function of sending a message to future perpetrators that the digital harms do constitute international crimes that carry severe consequences.[184]

While it could be argued that it would be simpler to consider a new offence like 'digital apartheid' as merely another form of apartheid or falling under another existing offence like persecution,[185] in cases where technology is central to perpetrating the offence, there would be a risk of a partial or superficial treatment of serious crimes at international courts.[186] This was also the reasoning for why

[179] Finnegan (n 176) 9; A Ramzy and C Buckley, '"Absolutely No Mercy": Leaked Files Expose How China Organized Mass Detentions of Muslims' (The New York Times, 16 November 2019) https://www.nytimes.com/interactive/2019/11/16/world/asia/china-xinjiang-documents.html.

[180] Tobin (n 178) 105.

[181] ibid.

[182] Finnegan (n 176).

[183] HM Zawati and TA Doherty, 'Fair Labelling as a Common Legal Principle in Criminal Law' in HM Zawati (ed), *Fair Labelling and the Dilemma of Prosecuting Gender-Based Crimes at the International Criminal Tribunals* (OUP, 2014) 27.

[184] T de Souza Dias, 'Recharacterisation of Crimes and the Principle of Fair Labelling in International Criminal Law' (2018) 18 *International Criminal Law Review* 788–821, 789.

[185] The use of technology for mass surveillance purposes has been argued to constitute persecution, see for example N Turkel, 'High-Tech Surveillance for Religious Persecution: Technology Enabled and Facilitated Uyghur Genocide in China' (2022) 97 *Notre Dame Law Review Reflection* 310; LE Papa and T Hayajneh, 'A Survey of Defensive Measures for Digital Persecution in the Global South' (2020) 12 *Future Internet* 166.

[186] Zawati and Doherty (n 183) 113.

following the arrest of Radovan Karadžic at the ICTY, feminist legal scholars and human rights activists criticised the Prosecutor's decision to prosecute rape under the charge of sexual violence.[187] They argued that the distinct gender-based crimes merited distinct charges, otherwise rape would be prosecuted in an 'ambiguous way' that could 'undermin[e] gender justice, relegat[e] wartime rape once again to the margins of international criminal law, and subver[t] international criminal law's capacity to develop a deterrent to such heinous crimes'.[188] This is also a compelling reason to criminalise digital harm under a new offence as opposed to using existing frameworks, even where they may be able to encompass them. For instance, although 'digital apartheid' would be similar to apartheid as it would involve the separation of racial groups, the development of a distinct new crime which explicitly adds that the separation is through digital means would more greatly recognise the digital divide that is central to understanding the harm to victims, and therefore the label would better reflect the harm of the offence.

To establish a new crime for prosecution at the ICC, the Rome Statute would need to be amended in accordance with Articles 121 and 122 – in brief, this would require a State Party to propose an amendment, for the Assembly of States Parties to vote on whether to take up the proposal by a majority of those present, and then for the amendment to be adopted through a two-thirds majority of States Parties.[189] Proposed new crimes could be added as entirely new offences or through expanding existing crimes, such as adding to the list of crimes against humanity or war crimes under Articles 7 and 8, respectively. This was achieved in the case of starvation, where Switzerland proposed an amendment to Article 8 to add the starvation of civilians as a war crime.[190] The proposal was voted on at the Assembly of States Parties and adopted unanimously in 2019.[191]

Though possible, creating a new crime would be a difficult and long process subject to negotiations and voting on behalf of States Parties. For example, though it was already included in the original Rome Statute, the ICC did not have jurisdiction over the crime of aggression until 20 years after the adoption of the Statute due to deliberations over the definition and the conditions for the exercise of jurisdiction of the crime.[192] In addition, in 2021, an independent expert panel published a draft legal definition for 'ecocide' including a proposal to amend the

[187] ibid.
[188] ibid.
[189] Rome Statute arts 121(1), 121(2), and 121(3).
[190] 'A strong signal in the fight against famine during armed conflict' (Swiss Confederation Federal Department of Foreign Affairs, 19 May 2021) www.eda.admin.ch/eda/en/fdfa/fdfa/aktuell/newsuebersicht/2021/05/aushungern-kriegsverbrechen.html.
[191] ibid. However, the amendment still needs to be ratified by States in accordance with Article 121(5) once it is adopted by the Assembly of States Parties; Rome Statute art 121(5).
[192] D Akande, 'The International Criminal Court Gets Jurisdiction Over the Crime of Aggression' (EJIL:Talk!, 15 December 2017) www.ejiltalk.org/the-international-criminal-court-gets-jurisdiction-over-the-crime-of-aggression/; 'Draft resolution proposed by the Vice-Presidents of the Assembly Activation of the jurisdiction of the Court over the crime of aggression', ICC-ASP/16/L.10 (14 December 2017) www.ejiltalk.org/wp-content/uploads/2017/12/ICC-ASP-16-L10-ENG-CoA-resolution-14Dec17-1130.pdf.

Rome Statute with a new preambular paragraph, the addition of 'ecocide' under Article 5 ('Crimes within the jurisdiction of the Court'), and the addition of Article 8*ter* ('The core definition of Ecocide').[193] In September 2024, ecocide was formally introduced for consideration by the ICC member States of Vanuatu, Fiji, and Samoa, but as of the time of writing, an amendment to the Rome Statute has not progressed further.[194] Though the progress on ecocide may be considered relatively quick, its addition to the Rome Statute remains at a standstill with its fate still unknown. Thus, since amending the Rome Statute to adopt new crimes is an arduous route to take, where the digital harm can reasonably fit into existing crimes, this would be the most practical solution.

In addition, the principle of 'fair labelling' has been challenged by those who argue that the creation of more crimes might do more harm than good. For example, Cornford argues that fair labelling can lead to a 'highly differentiated' and complex criminal law that could 'create problems of inefficiency, inconsistency and unpredictability' and 'exacerbate the problems associated with charge bargaining'.[195] Though these concerns are valid, it is possible that they are less relevant in an ICL context, where there are generally less international crimes than in most domestic criminal codes and so the risk of an overcomplex framework is smaller. Cornford also assumes that the only justification of the fair labelling principle is 'to ensure that the blame expressed through criminal conviction is allocated justly'.[196] While this is *one* of the arguments in favour of fair labelling, it is not the only one – as discussed above, fair labelling can be justified in relation to its benefits to victims as well as the accused, and the value of labelling an offence to reflect the full scope of its harms should not be ignored. If applied to the international criminalisation of digital harm, fair labelling is critical for explaining why a new offence would be justified over trying to accommodate digital harms with existing crimes.

B. Prosecuting Under Existing Offences

It is also possible that digital harms could be encompassed through expanding interpretations of the existing Statute and Elements of Crimes. One way this could be done, as argued by Keenan, is for prosecutors to argue that novel harms should constitute a particular crime due to their similarity to the harms already addressed by that crime.[197] This would mean that digital harms would be compared to exist-

[193] 'Ecocide Definition, Commentary and Core Text' (Stop Ecocide, June 2021) www.stopecocide.earth/expert-drafting-panel.

[194] 'Mass destruction of nature reaches International Criminal Court (ICC) as Pacific island states propose recognition of "ecocide" as international crime' (Stop Ecocide International, 9 September 2024) www.stopecocide.earth/2024/mass-destruction-of-nature-reaches-international-criminal-court-icc-as-pacific-island-states-propose-recognition-of-ecocide-as-international-crime.

[195] A Cornford, 'Beyond Fair Labelling: Offence Differentiation in Criminal Law' (2022) 42 *Oxford Journal of Legal Studies* 985–1011, 987–88.

[196] ibid 987.

[197] Keenan (n 60).

ing harms (such as online hate speech and offline incitement, or sharing footage of crimes and outrages upon personal dignity or desecration of the dead) and the interpretation of certain crimes would be expanded to accommodate them. Yet, this could be too restrictive since the new harm would need to have a certain degree of similarity to the 'original' harms, and therefore those harms falling outside this scope would not be addressed.

As discussed in chapter four, the digital harms of posting footage of crimes online, online sexual violence, and online hate speech and disinformation could foreseeably fit within the current framework under pre-existing war crimes, crimes against humanity, and incitement to genocide.[198] To do this, ICL prosecutors and chambers would need to take a flexible approach and interpret existing definitions of crimes in a manner which encompasses the digital harm (such as how domestic courts have prosecuted sharing footage of crimes on social media as the war crime of outrages upon personal dignity).[199]

Further, internal policy documents such as the ICC OTP Policy on Cyber-Enabled Crimes Under the Rome Statute (the 'Policy'), launched in December 2025, provide a road map for prosecutors as to how to approach investigating, charging, and prosecuting individuals for such acts.[200] This new Policy represents a massive step towards accountability for 'cyber-enabled' crimes, which it defines as crimes committed or facilitated with the use of cyber means.[201] 'Cyber' is defined in the Policy as 'the range of activities involving information and communications technologies (also known as ICT, or loosely as digital technologies) or networks, including artificial intelligence'.[202]

The Policy outlines how Rome Statute crimes may be both committed and facilitated through cyber means.[203] Concerning genocide, the Policy states that all forms of genocide are susceptible to commission by cyber means, including killing members of a group, causing them serious bodily or mental harm, and inflicting on a group conditions of life calculated to bring about its physical destruction, in whole or in part.[204] It also specifies that 'there is no doubt that direct and public incitement of genocide can be committed by cyber means, for example, through postings on social media platforms'.[205] Regarding crimes against humanity and war crimes, the Policy states that acts facilitated or committed by cyber means

[198] See ch 4, s III of this book.

[199] See cases in The Netherlands and Finland discussed in ch 4, s IV.C of this book. Of course, should ICL prosecutors or chambers take a flexible approach to interpreting crimes, the rights of the accused would still need to be respected. Therefore, flexible approaches should not extend so far as to violate principles of legality such as nullum crimen sine lege (crimes must articulated in law to be crimes), lex praevia (ensuring foreseeability of prosecution for articulated crimes), and lex certa (guaranteeing certainty of the elements of the crime). See JL Corsi, 'An Argument for Strict Legality in International Criminal Law' (2018) 49 *Georgetown Journal of International Law* 1321–81.

[200] Office of the Prosecutor (n 57).

[201] ibid [19].

[202] ibid [18].

[203] ibid.

[204] ibid [55]–[56].

[205] ibid, [59].

can constitute crimes against humanity and war crimes provided the contextual elements are met.[206] While the crime of aggression and offences against the administration of justice are outside the scope of this book, the Policy details how they can be perpetrated through cyber means as well.

It also highlights practical considerations, such as challenges posed by institutional structures, strengthening expertise at the Court, issues during preliminary examinations and investigations (including accessing digital evidence), and challenges related to cooperation and complementarity.[207] Some of these practical considerations will be expanded upon in detail in the subsequent chapter of the book. While this Policy is limited to the ICC OTP, it represents a valuable step forward in achieving justice for victims of crimes perpetrated through digital technologies, and will provide helpful clarifications for its prosecutorial strategy for such harms going forward.

IV. Conclusion

This chapter answered the questions of why and how digital harm should be criminalised under ICL. Chapter four, section II focused on the reasons to criminalise digital harm, including to prevent harm, to punish perpetrators, and to send a message. Concerning preventing harm, I argue that due to the similarities between digital harms and the 'traditional' harm ICL has already sought to prevent, digital harm should also be able to be criminalised. Regarding punishment, it has been demonstrated through ICL jurisprudence that deterrence and retribution are two well-recognised reasons for international criminalisation, which could be applied to deter or proportionately punish perpetrators of digital harm with a nexus to the perpetration of international crimes. Further, in terms of sending a message, I argue that criminalising digital harm would serve the expressivist function of emphasising that digital harms are severe enough for international prosecution and are worthy of concern from the international community.

Criminalising digital harm (either as a new crime or through expanding interpretations of existing crimes) will not be an easy or quick process, but is feasible, and important for ensuring more tailored justice for victims. The next chapter will explore in greater detail the practical challenges of prosecuting digital harms at ICCTs, including jurisdictional issues, the internal obstacles ICCTs must overcome in a digital age, and cooperation between ICCTs and external entities. It will propose solutions for how to best ensure that digital harms can be successfully investigated and prosecuted at ICCTs and identify where any gaps left by criminalisation can be filled.

[206] ibid, [25]–[38].
[207] ibid.

6

Challenges of Adjudicating Digital Harm at International Criminal Courts and Tribunals

I. Introduction

The previous chapter made the case for why digital harms should be criminalised under international law and addressed the challenges of such criminalisation. The purpose of this chapter is to assess the issues that may arise if digital harms are criminalised and subject to adjudication by international criminal courts and tribunals (ICCTs).[1]

First, this chapter will consider questions of jurisdiction over digital harm,[2] which can in many instances take place in cyberspace. The legal framework for jurisdiction for ICCTs will be applied, with a focus on how jurisdiction for ICCTs may be established over acts committed in cyberspace, based upon personal, territorial, and/or universal jurisdiction. Next, challenges that ICCTs will need to address internally should digital harms be criminalised under international criminal law (ICL) will be evaluated, including the potential anonymity of the perpetrator(s), challenges raised by reliance on digital evidence, security, and technological expertise. Following this, the chapter will explore the challenges ICCTs may face regarding external actors, focusing on cooperation with States, corporations, and civil society organisations (CSOs) and third-party investigators.

[1] The ICCTs normally analysed in this book are those established by treaties or UN resolutions, but this does not preclude its application to other existing or future ICCTs that may be established through other means (such as agreements between individual States and the UN). See also GA Knoops, 'International Criminal Tribunals: Distinctions and Main Features' in GA Knoops, *An Introduction to the Law of International Criminal Tribunals: A Comparative Study* (2nd revised edn, Brill, 2014) 1–26.

[2] 'Jurisdiction' refers to 'the competence to control and alter the legal relations of those subject to that competence through the creation and application of legal norms'; S Allen et al (eds), *The Oxford Handbook of Jurisdiction in International Law* (OUP, 2019) 4. Concerning ICL, and more specifically ICCTs, jurisdiction can have multiple bases and is defined in the framework establishing the ICCT – these will be explained in the subsequent section.

II. Admissibility Challenges

This section will outline two of the main admissibility criteria for cases at the International Criminal Court (ICC): gravity and jurisdiction. While other requirements for admissibility exist under Article 17 of the Rome Statute relating to issues around complementarity and if the accused has already been tried,[3] gravity and jurisdiction are two with unique considerations in the context of digital harms, and have therefore been selected for discussion in more detail.

A. Gravity

A first issue to consider as a potential obstacle to criminalisation of digital harm is whether such harms would be considered grave enough to constitute international crimes and for eventual prosecution by an ICCT. Gravity is explicitly mentioned in the Rome Statute and is considered by the Prosecutor at the situation-selection stage as well as the case-selection stage.[4] Article 17 establishes a 'gravity threshold' for the Court, as a case shall be determined as inadmissible where it 'is not of sufficient gravity to justify further action by the Court'.[5] Therefore, gravity is a relevant challenge to both criminalisation (as international crimes should have a certain seriousness) and prosecution (as a criteria for admissibility) under ICL.[6] However, the term 'gravity' is not defined in the Statute. The definition of gravity has also been widely discussed in the literature,[7] and certain key points relevant to the criminalisation of digital harm are highlighted here.

First, in general, gravity is roughly synonymous with the 'grossness' or 'seriousness' of a crime – it is frequently used interchangeably with these terms in various treaties, judicial decisions, human rights reports, and resolutions of UN bodies.[8]

[3] See Rome Statute art 17.

[4] R Cryer, H Friman, D Robinson and E Wilmshurst (eds), *An Introduction to International Criminal Law and Procedure* (2nd edn, CUP, 2012) 160.

[5] Rome Statute art 17(1)(d).

[6] For this reason, gravity is considered in this chapter as it represents a challenge to criminalising digital harms, but could also be considered a challenge to *prosecuting* digital harms at ICCTs, which is addressed in the next chapter. The discussion here will not be repeated again in the next chapter, but it should be noted that the analysis could also apply at the admissibility stage at trial once the digital harm is criminalised.

[7] See for instance M M deGuzman, *Shocking the Conscience of Humanity: Gravity and the Legitimacy of International Criminal Law* (OUP, 2020); R Lopez, 'The Law of Gravity' (2020) 58 *Columbia Journal of Transnational Law* 567–614; A Pues, 'Discretion and the Gravity of Situations at the International Criminal Court' (2017) 17 *International Criminal Law Review* 960–84; S Ford, 'Understanding Crime Gravity: Exploring the Views of International Criminal Law Experts' (2019) 27 *William & Mary Bill of Rights Journal* 659–88.

[8] For example, the Optional Protocol of the Convention on the Elimination of All Forms of Discrimination Against Women (CEDAW) allows the UN Committee on the Elimination of Discrimination against Women to initiate an investigation where it has received information of 'grave or systemic violations' by a state party (art 8). The UNGA resolution establishing the Human Rights Council (UNGA 60/251) also provides that the Council will address situations of 'violations of human

While all crimes that fall under the jurisdiction of the Rome Statute are grave, some may be considered more grave than others, and due to limited resources the ICC must focus on situations and cases above a certain gravity threshold. Importantly, as provided by the Appeals Chamber in the case of *Al Hassan*, the purpose of the gravity threshold is 'not to oblige the Court to choose only the most serious cases, but merely to oblige it not to prosecute cases of marginal gravity'.[9] What this threshold actually is has been debated, as some crimes could be 'more grave' based on how extreme the harm is to the victim(s), the number of victims, the nature of the violation, who the perpetrator is, or the intent of the perpetrator, amongst other factors.[10] In its 2016 Policy Paper on Case Selection and Prioritization, the Office of the Prosecutor (OTP) provided that its assessment of gravity 'includes both quantitative and qualitative considerations', and that the factors that guide this assessment 'include the scale, nature, manner of commission, and impact of the crimes'.[11] The OTP defined 'scale' as dependent on factors such as the number of victims, the extent of the damage caused (and 'in particular the bodily or psychological harm caused to the victims and their families'), and the geographical or temporal spread of the crimes.[12] The 'nature' of the crimes concerns the specific factual elements of the offence, and the 'manner of commission' refers to the 'means employed to execute the crime'.[13] Finally, 'impact' can be assessed in light of 'the increased vulnerability of victims, the terror subsequently instilled, or the social, economic and environmental damage inflicted on the affected communities'.[14]

If the gravity of digital harms is assessed according to the OTP's criteria, digital harms should meet the gravity threshold for prosecution at the ICC. Regarding the 'scale' of the crimes, both the number of victims and the geographical or temporal spread of the crime can be especially high in the context of digital harm.[15] For instance, using digital means to monitor a particular group can allow for the suppression of a vast amount of individuals both directly and indirectly (and, as stated in the OTP Policy Paper, the assessment of 'scale' can factor in both the number of direct and indirect victims).[16] An example is the current suspected

rights, including gross and systemic violations'. See also Lopez (n 7) at 569 and Geneva Academy, 'Briefing No. 6: What amounts to 'a serious violation of international human rights law'?: An analysis of practice and expert opinion for the purpose of the 2013 Arms Trade Treaty' (August 2014) 11-12.

[9] *Prosecutor v Al Hassan* (Judgment on the appeal of Mr Al Hassan against the decision of Pre-Trial Chamber I entitled 'Décision relative à l'exception d'irrecevabilité pour insuffisance de gravité de l'affaire soulevée par la défense') ICC-01/12-01/18 OA, Appeals Chamber (19 February 2020) [59].

[10] Lopez (n 7) 569.

[11] Office of the Prosecutor, Policy Paper on Case Selection and Prioritization (September 2016) [37].

[12] ibid [38].

[13] ibid [39]–[40].

[14] ibid [41].

[15] However, it is important to note that in *Abu Garda*, the Court found that the number of victims alone cannot be the sole basis for a gravity decision and that the 'qualitative dimension' of the crime should also be considered; *Prosecutor v Abu Garda* (Decision on the Confirmation of Charges) ICC-02/05-02/09, PTC I (8 February 2010) [31].

[16] Office of the Prosecutor (n 11).

genocide in Xinjiang, where it has been reported that as of 2018, the global camera manufacturer Hikvision was awarded government contracts to implement facial recognition cameras at the entrances of 'at least 967' Uyghur mosques.[17] While this is only one example from the complex situation in Xinjiang, in which the Chinese government has allegedly used a variety of digital tools to surveil and consequently detain members of the Uyghur population,[18] it illustrates the sheer number of individuals who would be subject to such surveillance on a daily basis. Moreover, even those who are not directly subjected to the facial recognition cameras can face harm to their right to express their religion, as knowing such cameras are in place that could register them in a database and potentially send them to a detention camp could have a chilling effect on their cultural practices, discouraging them from going to the mosque or participating in other religious activities.[19] This also has implications for the impact of the crimes, as the suppression of cultural practices can be considered a serious 'social damage' (as mentioned in the Policy Paper) on the community.[20]

In addition, technology also drives restrictions upon movement and daily life activities in Xinjiang. Uyghur residents are scared out of travelling or sometimes even prevented from doing so by authorities if their ID is 'flagged' in a digital system and they are consequently prevented from activities such as riding a bus or entering a hospital.[21] As reported by Amnesty International, there are cameras on nearly all street corners, lamp posts, and the thousands of 'convenience police stations' set up throughout the region.[22] Residents have also stated that they are required to scan their IDs or subjected to iris or facial scans to make purchases everywhere from butcher stops to gas stations, and any 'suspicious' purchase, such as a knife, needs to have a : code registered with it.[23] The implementation of these surveillance technologies into every aspect of life instils constant fear in the Uyghur population and a real threat of being sent to an internment camp without warning should they make a single 'mistake'.[24] Once sent to the internment camps, which many times happens following a surprise arrest in the middle of the night in their homes, detainees face very poor living conditions and are allegedly subjected to intense interrogations, torture, and ill-treatment.[25] They are also forced to abandon their cultural practices and instead be 'educated' on the 'evils' of Islam and praise the Chinese Communist Party.[26] Importantly, these physical and cultural

[17] J Bhuiyan, '"There's cameras everywhere": testimonies detail far-reaching surveillance of Uyghurs in China' (The Guardian, 30 September 2021) www.theguardian.com/world/2021/sep/30/uyghur-tribunal-testimony-surveillance-china.

[18] Amnesty International, '"Like We Were Enemies In A War": China's Mass Internment, Torture and Persecution of Muslims in Xinjiang' (2021) xinjiang.amnesty.org/.

[19] ibid.

[20] Office of the Prosecutor (n 11).

[21] ibid 42.

[22] ibid.

[23] ibid 43.

[24] ibid.

[25] ibid.

[26] ibid 9.

harms follow directly from digital surveillance that the Chinese government uses to justify Uyghur detention. There is no question as to the large scale and impact of the harms that would be assessed in a gravity determination, where digital methods are used to inflict harm with clear similarities to previous genocides already addressed throughout ICL's history. The situation in Xinjiang will be assessed in greater detail as a case study in chapter seven.[27]

Further, concerning the scale of online content-based digital harms, including hate speech, disinformation, online sexual violence, or the sharing of footage of crimes to social media platforms, as previously discussed in chapter three,[28] the geographical and temporal spread of the harm can be exacerbated by the use of technology, as the internet can reach virtually any place at any time, and is difficult to remove once in circulation. The online element also affects the impact of the crimes by increasing 'the vulnerability of the victims' and 'the terror subsequently instilled',[29] due to the added humiliation of the victims knowing they are being filmed and the footage being shared on the internet, and the terror that violent content can instil in any person who comes across it.

An example relating to sharing footage of crimes online is the video of the beheading of American journalist James Foley by an Islamic State (IS) group in 2014, which represents one of many execution videos filmed and posted online by IS affiliates and other terrorist organisations.[30] The video begins with a graphic in Arabic and English and a low-resolution video of former US President Barack Obama's speech announcing the authorisation of airstrikes and a humanitarian mission in Iraq. However, the resolution then changes to high definition with messages only in English when it shows Foley in orange overalls, kneeling next to a hooded militant,[31] demonstrating the desire to ensure that others could clearly see Foley's face and execution. Foley is forced to make a humiliating speech, calling upon his 'friends, family and loved ones' to rise against the US government, and is then heard saying he wishes he could see his family once again before he is violently beheaded.[32] The video was circulated widely on social media and by news outlets, and though platforms such as YouTube and Twitter (now X) tried to scrub the video from their websites,[33] it could never be fully erased from the internet. This example, which will be considered in more detail as a case study in chapter seven,[34] conveys the extremely grave harm that can result when footage of crimes is recorded and shared. Though executions are already a crime and will have horrific effects on the family, friends, and communities of the victims, their

[27] See ch 7, s III of this book.
[28] See ch 3 of this book.
[29] Office of the Prosecutor (n 11).
[30] L Jacinto, 'Brutal IS beheading video sparks social media pushback' (France 24, 8 August 2014) www.france24.com/en/20140820-iraq-syria-video-beheading-journalist-twitter-social-media.
[31] ibid.
[32] ibid; CJ Carter, 'Video shows ISIS beheading US journalist James Foley' (CNN, 20 August 2014) edition.cnn.com/2014/08/19/world/meast/isis-james-foley/index.html.
[33] ibid.
[34] See ch 7, s II of this book.

online dissemination exacerbates the harm in terms of its nature and scale – the victim is shown at their most vulnerable, their loved ones can see and hear the pain they experienced,[35] and innocent users can stumble across the material and face secondary trauma.

The factors of the nature and the manner of commission of the crimes are arguably where digital harms will be most different from traditionally recognised international crimes, as digital harms can be perpetrated with a degree of distance between the person committing the act and the victim(s). For these reasons, digital harms may not fit the historic 'mould' that comes to mind when considering situations where ICL has been used, such as for mass killings or other gross physical violence akin to that of the Holocaust or the Rwandan Genocide.[36] However, digital harms can still fulfil these criteria, as nothing in the Rome Statute states that the nature or manner of commission of the crimes needs to be directly physical. In fact, the Elements of Crimes provides that suffering may be inflicted to mental as well as physical health for genocide, torture (both as a crime against humanity and a war crime), inhuman treatment, cruel treatment, other inhumane acts, biological experiments, wilfully causing great suffering, mutilation, and medical or scientific experiments.[37] Further, for crimes against humanity not explicitly detailed such as 'other inhumane acts', the character ('the nature and gravity') of the act must be similar to other crimes listed under Article 7.[38] For war crimes, crimes must be of comparable gravity to other grave breaches of the Geneva Conventions.[39] These provisions allow for (and were presumably intended to allow for) new harms to be encompassed within the framework if they are similar enough in gravity to existing crimes. As discussed in chapters three and four, the severity of digital harms can be the same degree as the harms traditionally reflected in ICL, especially in terms of harms to dignity such as humiliating or degrading treatment.[40]

[35] For example, the father of Jun Lin, the man whose murder was filmed and circulated online, stated regarding his murder and the fact that the video remains online, 'It causes me fresh pain to know that my son's legacy is to be remembered as a victim. He not only suffered in his murder but will be humiliated for each time his name is mentioned and it hurts me deeply and will haunt me forever'; 'The Magnotta verdict: Read Jun Lin's father's impact statement' (The Globe and Mail, 23 December 2014) www.theglobeandmail.com/news/national/the-magnotta-verdict-read-jun-lins-fathers-impact-statement/article22189477/; MK Farmand Jr, 'Who Watches this Stuff?: Videos Depicting Actual Murder and the Need for a Federal Criminal Murder-Video Statute' (2016) 68 *Florida Law Review* 1915, 1923.

[36] Yet, it is important to note that ICL has been concerned with physical violence that is less extreme than genocide, even though these may be what typically is associated with ICL. For instance, individual or smaller groups of killings have been prosecuted at international courts, such as at the STL, which was created for a crime that resulted in the deaths of 22 individuals, including the former Lebanese prime minister. At the ICC, in the *Abu Garda* case, the OTP still proceeded with the arrest warrant regarding the killing of 12 peacekeepers (though the case has since been closed as the charges were never confirmed); 'Abu Garda Case' (ICC) www.icc-cpi.int/darfur/abugarda; 'About the Special Tribunal for Lebanon' (UNHCR RefWorld).

[37] Rome Statute Elements of Crimes arts 6(b), 7(1)(f), 7(1)(k), 8(2)(a)(ii), 8(2)(a)(iii), 8(2)(b)(x), 8(2)(c)(i), and 8(2)(e)(xi).

[38] Rome Statute Elements of Crimes art 7(1)(k).

[39] Rome Statute art 8.

[40] See chs 3 and 4 of this book.

The issue of gravity has also been addressed in relation to cyber operations at the ICC. At the time of writing, most scholars who have written on the subject agree that to meet the gravity threshold at the ICC, cyber operations would need to be linked to physical harm. For instance, Mačák and Nijs argue that most cyber incidents that have occurred to date would not have met the gravity threshold because the scale of the human suffering caused is not comparable to that brought on by 'kinetic' warfare (such as from bombs and missiles).[41] Yet, the authors point out that this does not mean cyber incidents on their own could never pass the gravity threshold as long as they eventually manifested in physical harms, such as cyber-attacks against critical infrastructure that damage the electricity supply, health care systems, water, or sanitation services.[42] This type of attack has already occurred in the conflict between Russia and Ukraine, where Russian government hackers took out three power grids between 2015 and 2022.[43] As noted by Freeman, Ghahremani, and Lombardo, these were not just cyber-attacks on power grids, but 'attacks on every home, office, hospital, and essential service running on that power'.[44]

The focus of literature on cyber-attacks and ICL has mostly been, as demonstrated above, centred on only on cyber warfare that leads to direct physical harm, but question remains as to whether cyber-attacks that do not have a physical consequence could reach the gravity threshold. Trahan has briefly discussed this possibility but argues that cyber-attacks that do not produce physical effects 'probably should *not* be considered as rising to the level of gravity of the Rome Statute, nor indeed should any other penetration of systems or critical infrastructure – at least where there is no proximately ensuing loss of life or serious physical destruction'.[45] Trahan supports this argument mainly through discussions of examples where there have been considerable amounts of physical deaths or destruction but those cases still did not meet the gravity threshold (and so no physical destruction at all would, in her view, likely never be grave enough under the Rome Statute).[46] However, this argument assumes that physical harm is the gravest form of harm, and does not engage in detail with the other forms of harm (such as mental harm) which have met the gravity requirement in ICL jurisprudence.[47]

[41] K Mačák and M Nijs, 'Hackers in the Hague? The Prospects of Prosecuting International Cyber Crimes Before the ICC' (Lawfare, 18 October 2023) www.lawfaremedia.org/article/hackers-in-the-hague-the-prospects-of-prosecuting-international-cyber-crimes-before-the-international-criminal-court.

[42] ibid.

[43] L Freeman, A Ghahremani, and S Lombardo, 'The Gravity of Russia's Cyberwarfare against Ukraine' (Opinio Juris, 19 April 2023) opiniojuris.org/2023/04/19/the-gravity-of-russias-cyberwar-against-ukraine/.

[44] ibid.

[45] J Trahan, 'The Criminalization of Cyber-operations Under the Rome Statute' (2021) 19(5) *Journal of International Criminal Justice* 1133–64, 1142–43.

[46] ibid.

[47] Serious mental harm has been addressed by the Court in relation to multiple Rome Statute crimes, including torture and inhumane treatment, sexual violence, conscripting child soldiers, outrages upon personal dignity, amongst others. In fact, not a single case prosecuted before the ICC to date has *not*

Further, in August 2023, the ICC Prosecutor announced that the OTP would begin investigating acts of cyberwarfare, noting that the front lines of armed conflict 'are no longer just physical', and that 'the digital front lines can give rise to damage and suffering comparable to what the founders of the ICC sought to prevent'.[48] The Prosecutor also mentioned that his Office would be 'mindful of the misuse of the internet to amplify hate speech and disinformation, which may facilitate or even directly lead to the occurrence of atrocities'.[49] Though the emphasis by the Prosecutor still currently remains on the digital harm leading to physical harm, it is clear from this announcement that the ICC already considers that the gravity of some digital harms could be high enough for investigation, which is a strong starting point for the potential criminalisation of digital harm (regardless of whether it has physical effects) under ICL in the future.

In addition, other forms of harm aside from direct physical violence have been recognised as meeting the gravity threshold in practice. For example, in the *Al Mahdi* case, the accused was convicted of the war crime of intentionally directing attacks against religious and historic buildings in Mali.[50] In its gravity assessment, the Chamber considered the level of planning of the attacks, along with the fact that they were committed with a 'discriminatory religious motive'.[51] The Chamber further noted that 'the fact that the targeted buildings were not only religious buildings but had also a symbolic and emotional value for the inhabitants of Timbuktu is relevant in assessing the gravity of the crime committed'.[52] Importantly, the Chamber also considered the gravity to be heightened based on the fact that the attacks were relayed in the media.[53] The *Al Mahdi* case was centred around the destruction of property as opposed to human lives and the impact the loss of the heritage sites had on the people of Mali, and is one of the few convictions secured by the ICC to date. It is therefore possible that should cases concerning digital harm be brought before the Court, regardless of whether those cases result in physical harm to persons, they could still be considered grave enough for selection and prosecution. This is because while digital harms may not always manifest physically, as outlined in chapter four,[54] they can cause serious psychological and

mentioned the mental harm caused by the alleged crimes – even in cases of individual killings or 'only' physical violence, family members are still subjected to mental suffering. In addition, even when cases have only focused on physical destruction of property, such as the destruction of cultural heritage sites in the *Al Mahdi* case, the main harm considered was not the harm to the buildings themselves but the (non-physical) emotional and cultural loss experienced by the community. See 'Defendants' (ICC) www.icc-cpi.int/defendants; *Prosecutor v Al Mahdi* (Judgment and Sentence) ICC-01/12-01/15-171, Trial Chamber VIII (27 September 2016) ('*Al Mahdi* Judgment').

[48] K Khan, 'Technology Will Not Exceed Our Humanity' (Digital Front Lines, 20 August 2023) digitalfrontlines.io/2023/08/20/technology-will-not-exceed-our-humanity/.

[49] ibid.

[50] 'Al Mahdi Case' (ICC) www.icc-cpi.int/mali/al-mahdi. This case was concerned with war crimes charges against a member of Ansar Eddine in Mali.

[51] *Al Mahdi* Judgment (n 47) [78]–[81].

[52] ibid [79].

[53] ibid [78].

[54] See ch 4 of this book.

moral harm, which have both already been deemed grave enough to result in convictions by the Court without any direct connection to bodily harm.[55]

It is also important to note that as mentioned previously in chapter four, digital harms that have not caused physical effects have already been considered grave enough for prosecution and conviction in domestic war crimes cases.[56] For example, in its assessment of whether a man sharing a photo of himself next to a crucified body on Facebook could constitute an assault on personal dignity, a Dutch court noted that the fact that the man posed next to the body and knowingly had the photo taken and shared demonstrated that 'the body of the deceased should be seen as a trophy and that he is superior to the deceased'.[57] This was further supported by the fact that the man not only posed next to the body of the victim, but made it his profile photo on Facebook, showing he was 'proud' of the image.[58] In addition, the Court noted that by posting the photo online, the man 'ensured that a large number of people were given the opportunity to take note of the photo'.[59] In the view of the Court, this 'humiliating and/or degrading' online behaviour was of 'such seriousness that it is automatically regarded as an assault on the personal dignity of the deceased'.[60] Similar logic was applied by courts in Finland in three other scenarios in which individuals posted graphic photos of victims to social media.[61] Each of these cases concerned an individual publishing photos of himself posing next to a decapitated victim on Facebook, and the Finnish courts ruled that the acts constituted an outrage upon personal dignity under both the Criminal Code of Finland and the ICC Statute.[62] It is thus foreseeable that similar digital harms (i.e. posting graphic footage of executions to social media) could already be accommodated by existing crimes under the Rome Statute, such as the war crime of outrages upon personal dignity, and meet the gravity threshold.

In addition, though multiple different types of crimes have been considered 'grave' enough for prosecution at the ICC as mentioned above, one thing they have in common is their gross assault on human dignity, whether it arises from genocidal killings, sexual assault, watching crimes committed towards others, or

[55] In *Al Mahdi*, the Trial Chamber frequently emphasised the 'emotional' and 'moral' harms to victims caused by the destruction of cultural heritage sites in both the Judgment and Sentence and the Reparations Order, and the case did not concern bodily harm to victims; *Al Mahdi* Judgment (n 47); *Prosecutor v Al Mahdi* (Reparations Order) ICC-01/12-01/15, Trial Chamber VIII (17 August 2017).

[56] See ch 4 of this book.

[57] ECLI:NL:GHDHA:2021:103.

[58] ibid.

[59] ibid.

[60] ibid.

[61] *Prosecutor v Ammar Jebbar-Salman* (Judgment) District Court of Pirkanmaa, R 16/1304 (18 March 2016); *Prosecutor v Hadi Habeeb Hilal* (Judgment) R 16/214, District Court of Kanta Häme (22 March 2016); M Heikkilä, 'The Criminalisation and Prosecution of International Core Crimes in Finland' (2020) 66 *Scandinavian Studies in Law* 457–77, 473–74.

[62] *Prosecutor v Ammar Jebbar-Salman* (Judgment) District Court of Pirkanmaa, R 16/1304 (18 March 2016); M. Heikkilä (n 61) 473.

the destruction of important religious sites.[63] As argued previously in this book,[64] the human dignity aspect is an integral part of digital harm and is comparable to many harms encompassed in existing ICL crimes. It is therefore useful to consider deGuzman's 'human dignity theory of international criminality', which argues that gravity should provide a low threshold that allows for a wide range of harms to human dignity to be encompassed, and further that only those crimes that 'harm dignity so minimally that they may not warrant criminal sanction' should be excluded.[65] If one accepts that protecting human dignity is a central goal of ICL, as was discussed earlier in this chapter, then it makes sense to include a measure of harm to human dignity in gravity determinations. While it could be argued that the lack of a strict definition of the gravity threshold could potentially lead to inconsistency that could undermine the legitimacy of international prosecutions, a flexible approach can allow for ICL to be expanded to encompass current digital along with other novel harms that inevitably will arise in the future.

This leads into a second key point, being that conceptions of what should be considered 'grave' enough to be prosecuted as an international crime have evolved, and may continue to evolve, over time. For instance, in the earliest stages of ICL, the first widely recognised crime falling under universal jurisdiction was piracy, namely because piracy is a crime that takes place outside the territory of any State.[66] As argued by deGuzman, piracy was mostly considered grave (if at all) only in the sense that it 'harmed humanity by discouraging travel by sea'.[67] DeGuzman points out that piracy, 'essentially maritime robbery', was 'never considered an "atrocity" crime in the sense often attributed to the core crimes' (i.e., one that 'shocks the conscience of humanity').[68] After the Second World War and the establishment of the International Military Tribunal (IMT), gravity became a more central idea in ICL and associated with the horrors akin to those of the Holocaust.[69] In subsequent years, at ICCTs such as the International Criminal Tribunal for Rwanda (ICTR) and International Criminal Tribunal for the former Yugoslavia (ICTY), and eventually the ICC, other crimes besides genocide and mass killings began to be considered as grave enough for international prosecution, including (but not limited to) sexual and gender based offences like rape and forced marriage,[70]

[63] G Le Moli, 'Human Dignity in International Criminal Law' in G Le Moli, *Human Dignity in International Law* (CUP, 2021); JB Heath, 'Human Dignity at Trial: Hard Cases and Broad Concepts in International Criminal Law' (2012) 44 *George Washington International Law Review* 317.

[64] See ch 4, ss III and IV of this book.

[65] deGuzman (n 7) 62.

[66] D Luban, 'Fairness to Rightness: Jurisdiction, Legality, and the Legitimacy of International Criminal Law' in S Besson and J Tasioulas (eds), *The Philosophy of International Law* (OUP, 2010) 570–71.

[67] deGuzman (n 7) 36.

[68] ibid.

[69] ibid.

[70] See, eg *Prosecutor v Furundžija*, *Prosecutor v Lubanga*, and *Prosecutor v Ntaganda*.

enlisting child soldiers,[71] individual murders,[72] and the destruction of property.[73] Further, these crimes have moved to the forefront of cases at the ICC, such as in the *Al Mahdi* case,[74] where the destruction of cultural sites was the sole focus of the case. This demonstrates that the concept of gravity can be flexible and evolve to accommodate new international crimes (or new modes of perpetrating existing crimes) as time progresses.

B. Jurisdiction

As argued in chapters three and four, digital harms can meet the gravity threshold and other substantive requirements to be prosecuted as core international crimes at ICCTs.[75] To be prosecuted, digital harms also need to satisfy the additional requirements for jurisdiction as set out by the mandates of ICCTs.[76] At the ICC, jurisdiction is established on the basis of Articles 12 and 13 of the Rome Statute.[77] Article 12 provides that the Court has jurisdiction when crimes under Article 5 occur either on the territory of a State Party or are committed by a national of a State Party, and further when a non-State Party accepts jurisdiction via a declaration lodged with the Registrar.[78] Article 13 establishes the three ways the ICC may then exercise its jurisdiction – (a) a State Party referral, (b) a UN Security Council referral, or (c) when the Prosecutor decides to initiate an investigation and the Court agrees to proceed with that investigation.[79] At ICCTs established by the UN Security Council ('ad hoc' tribunals such as the ICTR and ICTY), or tribunals established by an agreement between the UN and the relevant government (such as the Special Court for Sierra Leone), the exact requirements for jurisdiction will be outlined in the Security Council resolution or agreement establishing the tribunal, though jurisdiction is generally limited to the particular territory (ie 'the territory of the former Yugoslavia' for the ICTY).[80] Thus, while other doctrines of jurisdiction exist under international law,[81] the jurisdiction of ICCTs is typically restricted to those bases of jurisdiction set out in the resolution or agreement establishing the tribunal. For the ICC jurisdiction is based on the nationality of the accused (active personality) or the territory where the conduct took place (the

[71] See, eg *Prosecutor v Lubanga* and *Prosecutor v Ongwen*.
[72] See, eg *Prosecutor v Bemba* and *Prosecutor v Katanga et al*.
[73] See, eg *Prosecutor v Katanga et al* and *Prosecutor v Al Mahdi*.
[74] *Al Mahdi* Judgment (n 47).
[75] See ch 4 of this book.
[76] Jurisdiction represents just one criteria for admissibility at the ICC, as noted at the beginning of s II.
[77] Rome Statute arts 12 and 13.
[78] ibid art 12.
[79] ibi art 13.
[80] ICTY Statute; LN Sadat, 'Understanding the Complexities of International Criminal Tribunal Jurisdiction' in WA Schabas and N Bernaz (eds), *Routledge Handbook of International Criminal Law* (Routledge, 2011) 199.
[81] C Staker, 'Jurisdiction' in M Evans (ed), *International Law* (5th edn, OUP, 2018) 289.

territorial principle). In some cases, it may also be possible for an ICCT to exercise universal jurisdiction, which will be considered later in this section.[82]

i. Personal Jurisdiction

The ability to establish personal jurisdiction over individuals who are accused of perpetrating digital harms as opposed to 'traditional' ICL crimes is virtually the same. Once individuals are identified, the ICCT would meet the personal jurisdiction requirement if the alleged perpetrators are State Party nationals in the case of the ICC.[83] In contrast, most ad hoc tribunals only have jurisdiction over acts occurring in a particular country.[84] Non-State Party nationals cannot be prosecuted by the ICC using personal jurisdiction, and could only be prosecuted if the alleged conduct takes place on the territory of a State Party (ie territorial jurisdiction, which is considered below) and meets all other relevant admissibility requirements, or in the case of a referral from the United Nations Security Council (UNSC).[85] Consequently, at the ICC, there may be jurisdiction over digital harms occurring in the territories of non-States Parties if the persons accused of conduct causing such harms are nationals of a State Party, just as there may be jurisdiction over digital harms occurring on the territory of a State Party, regardless of whether the accused persons are nationals of a State Party.[86]

In practice, the ICC OTP has rarely proceeded with cases solely on the basis of the personal jurisdiction of alleged perpetrators,[87] and doing so would constitute what Stahn has argued would be a 'fundamental shift in prosecutorial policy'.[88] As noted by Zakerhossein, territorial jurisdiction is preferable to nationality-based jurisdiction because relying solely on nationality 'spreads the risk of one-sided prosecutions and non-cooperation of the territorial states where the ICC crimes have been committed'.[89] In addition, establishing jurisdiction through the nationality

[82] See s II.B.iii of this chapter.

[83] Rome Statute art 12.

[84] Note, however, that there may be challenges to determine who the alleged perpetrators are, given the ability to remain anonymous on the internet, which will be considered in a later section of this chapter.

[85] The issue of whether subjecting non-State Party nationals to the jurisdiction of the ICC without the consent of those States is contrary to international law is outside the scope of this book but has been debated by scholars. See D Akande, 'The Jurisdiction of the International Criminal Court over Nationals of Non Parties: Legal Basis and Limits' (2003) 1 *Journal of International Criminal Justice* 618–50; JA Skulow and RW Ash, 'The Issue of ICC Jurisdiction Over Nationals of Non-Consenting, Non-Party States to the Rome Statute: Refuting Professor Dapo Akande's Arguments' (2020) 16 *South Carolina Journal of International Law & Business* 1.

[86] This was also clarified in the Policy on Cyber-Enabled Crimes Under the Rome Statute, see Office of the Prosecutor, Policy on Cyber-Enabled Crimes Under the Rome Statute (December 2025) [46].

[87] MH Zakerhossein, 'To Bury a Situation Alive – A Critical Reading of the ICC Prosecutor's Statement on the Isis Situation' (2016) 16 *International Criminal Law Review* 616.

[88] C Stahn, 'Why the ICC Should Be Cautious to Use the Islamic State to Get Out of Africa: Part 2' (EJIL: Talk!, 4 December 2014) www.ejiltalk.org/why-the-icc-should-be-cautious-to-use-the-islamic-state-to-get-out-of-africa-part-2/.

[89] Zakerhossein (n 87) 618.

of the perpetrator, especially where the conduct occurs on non-State Party territory, can potentially lead to those most responsible for international crimes (i.e. in more senior command positions) evading accountability if prosecutions are only directed at those who are State Party nationals. This argument was the basis for the 2015 decision of former ICC Prosecutor Bensouda not to open a preliminary examination into crimes committed by ISIS.[90] In her statement, the Prosecutor noted that because Syria and Iraq were not States Parties to the Rome Statute, the Court had no territorial jurisdiction over the alleged crimes, but through personal jurisdiction, there would only be jurisdiction to pursue foreign fighters from States Parties as opposed to the ISIS leaders, who she argued were primarily from Iraq and Syria.[91] The Prosecutor therefore concluded that the prospects of the OTP 'investigating and prosecuting those most responsible, within the leadership of ISIS, appear limited' and that 'the jurisdictional basis for opening a preliminary examination into [the] situation is too narrow'.[92] In the context of the digital harms analysed in this book, especially those pertaining to non-State armed groups such as ISIS' use of the internet to spread propaganda and instil fear, or potentially the complicity of tech company executives in international crimes (who are often nationals of the United States – a non-State Party), Bensouda's argument on the insufficient gravity of cases focused solely on the conduct of State Party nationals on the territory of non-States Parties could be raised once again. Further, given that some digital harms may occur in cyberspace and not on State Party territory, it could be argued that what Bensouda classified as 'insufficient gravity' would be even weaker for digital harms.

However, the Prosecutor's decision concerning ISIS crimes has been criticised.[93] First, the argument that a 'weak' jurisdictional link would have bearing on the gravity assessment seems to conflate the concepts of gravity and jurisdiction. As explained earlier in this chapter, gravity is one part of the admissibility assessment for the ICC, and refers to the 'grossness' or 'seriousness' of the crimes in terms of their scale, nature, manner of commission, and impact.[94] The question of whether the Court has jurisdiction over a case, either through personal or territorial elements outlined in Article 12, is a separate one to gravity (and the other criteria for admissibility), so the argument that a case does not have sufficient gravity to be admissible because of the way jurisdiction will be established does not follow logically from the Rome Statute.

In addition, the Prosecutor argued that the use of personal jurisdiction would only allow for prosecution of lower level perpetrators, and so therefore the case was too limited to be admissible. As argued by Zakerhossein, the Prosecutor's logic

[90] 'Statement of the Prosecutor of the International Criminal Court, Fatou Bensouda, on the alleged crimes committed by ISIS' (ICC, 8 April 2015) www.icc-cpi.int/news/statement-prosecutor-international-criminal-court-fatou-bensouda-alleged-crimes-committed-isis.

[91] ibid.

[92] ibid.

[93] Zakerhossein (n 87) 627.

[94] See section II.A of this chapter; Office of the Prosecutor (n 11).

was inconsistent with the Rome Statute, as the 'big fish or most-responsible policy' is not a 'jurisdictional threshold and limit', but something that should be considered later on in admissibility determinations.[95] Moreover, the existence of a policy to focus on those in leadership positions does not mean that the ICC does not have jurisdiction over 'mid' or 'low' level perpetrators or that there will never be reason to find such cases sufficiently grave. As further noted by Zakerhossein, in the eyes of victims of international crimes, the prosecution of lower level accused persons may be desirable, as they are often the ones who directly perpetrate crimes.[96] This was recognised by the former ICTY Prosecutor, Carla Del Ponte, who stated that prosecution of 'middle level' perpetrators was important because 'for the local people, the victims and the survivors, it was these people who brought their world to an end, not the remote governmental architects of the overall policy of genocide'.[97] If the interests of victims are to be truly taken into account, it is arguable that the OTP's policy of focusing only or mainly on senior level perpetrators (and accordingly why using the personal jurisdiction of State Party nationals where the alleged crimes occurred on the territory of a non-State Party is underutilised) is not necessarily aligned with gravity considerations in all cases, and may not be the best route to achieving a measure of justice for international crimes. Given these two critiques of the Prosecutor's arguments with regard to the ISIS situation, it can be argued that crimes (including digital harms) should not be considered inadmissible at the ICC merely because of the way jurisdiction is established (personal or territorial) or because of what type of rank of perpetrator would be 'available' for prosecution given the jurisdictional basis. Further, a shift in practice towards relying upon the personal jurisdiction could also be beneficial given that it would likely be more straightforward basis of jurisdiction – as opposed to territorial jurisdiction – for allegations of digital harm. This is considered below.

ii. Territorial Jurisdiction

The other avenue for jurisdiction available under the Rome Statute, and applicable to other ICCTs, is based upon the territory in which the alleged conduct took place ('territorial jurisdiction'). When cases involve harms occurring mainly in cyberspace (such as through the sharing of degrading footage or hate speech on social media), ICCTs would need to frame those harms as being within the jurisdictional territorial boundaries of their mandates. This may be further complicated by the fact that internet crimes may be recognised as offences where the action and consequence of the action occur in different jurisdictions – for example, if hate speech is posted from someone on a device in State A, it could be viewed

[95] Zakerhossein (n 87) 627.
[96] ibid 629.
[97] ibid; 'Statement by the Prosecutor addressed to the UN Security Council' (ICTY, 27 November 2001) www.icty.org/en/press/address-prosecutor-international-criminal-tribunal-former-yugoslavia-carla-del-ponte-un.

and harm victims in State B.[98] Although, this challenge is not necessarily new for digital harms, as in a similar vein, a weapon could be fired from State A and land in and cause harm in State B, or a population could be transferred out of State A and complete the crime of forced deportation in State B – the way jurisdiction has been determined for these 'physical' examples by ICCTs will be considered later in this section. Further, this challenge will not arise in all cases of digital harms considered in this book, since some harms may still be committed in whole or in part on a physical territory (ie using surveillance cameras to monitor and suppress a minority group, or auctioning victims of sexual slavery via an online marketplace followed by their physical transfer), and therefore may be more easily linked to a particular territory.

The question of which jurisdiction applies to acts committed in cyberspace under international law has risen to prominence in literature in recent years,[99] and as demonstrated by the agreement of key non-binding instruments such as The Tallinn Manual 2.0 on the International Law Applicable to Cyber Operations ('The Tallinn Manual 2.0'), the Oxford Process on International Law Protections in Cyberspace, and the Cyber Law Toolkit.[100] It has been argued that jurisdiction in cyberspace can be established through the 'physical' components of a crime, such as where the alleged perpetrator or victims are located, where the harm manifested, or where the internet servers are located. This is because, as explained by Chaumette, 'cyberspace is often presented as a disembodied, universal space that tries to avoid any connecting territory', but there is 'always a connecting link', such as the State where the attacker's device is, where the target is, or where the central server is.[101] Regarding ICL, this logic has been recognised through ICC case law – for instance, concerning the situation in Bangladesh/Myanmar, the Pre-Trial Chamber found that to establish territorial jurisdiction, it was sufficient for only an element of the crime to be completed on the territory of a State Party.[102] If a

[98] J Werle and F Jeßberger, *Principles of International Criminal Law* (4th edn, OUP, 2020) 320, fn 702.

[99] See, eg N Tsagourias and R Buchan (eds), *Research Handbook on International law and Cyberspace* (Elgar, 2015); G Greco, 'Cyber-Attacks as Aggression Crimes in Cyberspace in the Context of International Criminal Law' (2020) 4 *European Journal of Political Science Studies* 40; H Lin, 'Cyber Conflict and International Humanitarian Law' (2012) 94 *International Review of the Red Cross* 886; MN Schmitt, 'Grey Zones in the International Law of Cyberspace' 42 *Yale International Law Journal Online* 1.

[100] M Schmitt (ed), *Tallinn Manual 2.0 on the International Law Applicable to Cyber Operations* (2nd edn, CUP, 2017) ('Tallinn Manual 2.0'); Oxford Institute for Ethics, Law and Armed Conflict, 'The Oxford Process on International Protections in Cyberspace: A Compendium' (2022); 'International Cyber Law in Practice: Interactive Toolkit ('Cyber Law Toolkit')' (CCDOE) cyberlaw.ccdcoe.org/wiki /Main_Page.

[101] A Chaumette, 'International Criminal Responsibility of Individuals in Case of Cyberattacks' (2018) 18 *International Criminal Law Review* 1, 4–5.

[102] Werle and Jeßberger (n 97) 320, fn 702; *Situation in the People's Republic of Bangladesh/Republic of the Union of Myanmar* (Decision on the 'Prosecution's Request for a Ruling on Jurisdiction under Article 19(3) of the Statute') ICC-RoC46(3)-01/18, PTC I (6 September 2018) [64] et seq; *Situation in the People's Republic of Bangladesh/Republic of the Union of Myanmar* (Decision Pursuant to Article 15 of the Rome Statute on the Authorisation of an Investigation into the Situation in the People's Republic of Bangladesh/Republic of the Union of Myanmar) ICC-01/19, PTC III (14 November 2019) ('*Bangladesh and Myanmar* Article 15 Decision') 19 et seq. In this case, the Pre-Trial Chamber found that the Court

similar approach was applied to digital harms, if any element of the crime can be determined to have occurred on the territory of a State Party, then regardless of the nationality of the alleged perpetrator, the ICC would have jurisdiction.[103] Indeed, the Policy on Cyber-Enabled Crimes Under the Rome Statute states that the OTP is of the view that the Court's territorial jurisdiction over cyber-enabled crimes would 'extend to both the territory of the State (or States) in which the criminal conduct began (subjective territoriality), and to that of the State (or States) in which it is completed (objective territoriality)'.[104]

However, there are different benefits and drawbacks depending on the 'link' which is focused on. The weakest case is likely to be the one that focuses on using the location of servers through which communications pass through as the basis to determine territorial jurisdiction, due to the possibility of practically any State becoming involved on a random basis. This is because routing is extremely random, as 'packets' of data are essentially bounced from router to router, with no one having control over them, until they reach their destination.[105] So, for webpages to be accessed in different places, there is a communication between multiple servers that allows data packets to travel through nodes around the world to ultimately reach the destination where they are downloaded.[106] As noted by Menthe, this is a random process that can result in 'jurisdictional mayhem',[107] and could subject individuals arbitrarily to jurisdictions of States where a server momentarily held some data. It is difficult to foresee this type of jurisdictional approach being used at ICCTs as a basis for a prosecution, especially given the already conservative approach to gravity taken in the previously mentioned ISIS example where the OTP decided not to pursue an investigation because the jurisdiction based on

---

did have territorial jurisdiction because the perpetrators allegedly forced the Rohingya population to cross the border from Myanmar (a Non-State Party) into Bangladesh (a State Party). Since the crime of deportation was completed when the victims fled to Bangladesh, the Pre-Trial Chamber concluded that 'part of the actus reus' occurred on the territory of Bangladesh, and that it therefore had a basis for territorial jurisdiction.

[103] Some scholars have argued that the prosecution of non-State Party nationals to the ICC (or any other ICCT) would be in violation of international law if there is no consent from the State, see M Morris, 'High Crimes and Misconceptions: The ICC and Non-Party States' (2001) 64 *Law and Contemporary Problems* 13; D Scheffer, 'Address at the Annual Meeting of the American Society of International Law, Washington DC, 26 March 1999, "International Criminal Court: The Challenge of Jurisdiction"' (US Department of State Archive). This point will be addressed further in s II.B.iii, but a direct reading of Article 12 of the Rome Statute does not preclude the Court from prosecuting non-Party nationals (see the analysis of Article 12 above). For a comprehensive rebuttal of these claims, see MP Scharf, 'The ICC's Jurisdiction Over the National of Non-Party States: A Critique of the US Position' (2001) *Case Western Faculty Publications* 257.

[104] Office of the Prosecutor (n 86) [43]. The Policy is generally quite liberal in its interpretation of jurisdiction over cyber conduct. It further states at [44] that this analysis 'equally covers situations in which the cyber conduct in question took pace in the territory of more than two States simultaneously'.

[105] Rus Shuler, 'How Does the Internet Work?' (Stanford, 2002) web.stanford.edu/class/msande91si/www-spr04/readings/week1/InternetWhitepaper.htm#:~:text=When%20a%20packet%20arrives%20at,is%20sent%20to%20that%20network.

[106] DC Menthe, 'Jurisdiction in Cyberspace: A Theory of International Spaces' (1998) 4 *Michigan Telecommunications and Technology Law Review* 79.

[107] ibid.

active personality would be 'too narrow'. Further, there could be fairness implications for this approach concerning defendants, since being randomly subjected to a jurisdiction that the alleged perpetrator had no real intention of ever encountering is arguably incompatible with the principles of legality and fair trial. The OTP Policy on Cyber-Enabled Crimes Under the Rome Statute agrees with this approach, as it states that 'the Office would not regard the mere transit of data through a State Party's territory as a sufficient basis to assert the Court's territorial jurisdiction'.[108]

If territorial jurisdiction is established through the location of the alleged perpetrator at the time the criminal act was committed, this would be fairer regarding defendants, as it would be clearer which jurisdiction they could be subjected to. This approach would also be in line with many domestic jurisdictions – for example, many States consider existing criminal law to be sufficient in addressing cybercrimes, and therefore treat the internet as an instrument of the offence, implying that the crime would be committed where the perpetrator uses that instrument.[109] In addition, in some jurisdictions such as the United Kingdom under its Computer Misuse Act, the location of the accused at the time of the commission of the offence is enough to establish jurisdiction.[110] However, relying upon the location of the alleged perpetrator could prove to be challenging, as the location could be extremely difficult to determine in a cyberspace context. This is because the alleged perpetrator could hide or fake their IP address using a virtual private network (VPN), or access information stored on a server in a different State and send out harmful content from a territory other than where they are physically based. In addition, if an ICCT's jurisdiction was confined to conduct occurring on State Party territory or by a State Party national such as at the ICC, there would be a considerable gap in jurisdiction if the digital harm was perpetrated by a non-State Party national not on State Party territory. This would exclude from ICC jurisdiction, for example, American, Russian, or Chinese nationals who perpetrate digital harms such as spreading hate speech or disinformation in non-State Party territory like the US, which has been previously discussed in relation to election-meddling,[111] unless a situation was referred by the UNSC (for which each of those States have veto powers). Thus, in some cases it may be less desirable in terms of having the strongest scope for possible prosecutions for ICL prosecutors to base jurisdiction on the location of the alleged perpetrators than for other scenarios (such as if the consequence

[108] Office of the Prosecutor (n 86) [45].

[109] M Vagias, 'The Territorial Jurisdiction of the ICC for Core Crimes Committed Through the Internet' (2016) 21 *Journal of Conflict & Security Law* 523, 530; As of 2016, this included Australia, Albania, Armenia, Austria, Belgium, Bosnia and Herzegovina, Bulgaria, China, Croatia, Czech Republic, Dominican Republic, Estonia, Finland, France, Germany, Italy, Japan, Lithuania, Mexico, Morocco, Romania, the Russian Federation, Senegal, Slovakia, Spain, FYR of Macedonia, Myanmar, Thailand, Turkey, United Arab Emirates, Vietnam, and Kosovo. See also 'Cybercrime Legislation: Country Profiles' (Council of Europe Portal, 2024) www.coe.int/en/web/cybercrime/country-profiles.

[110] ibid; Computer Misuse Act (1990).

[111] See ch 4 of this book.

occurred on a non-State Party territory but was perpetrated from a State Party territory).

A final 'connecting link' could be if territorial jurisdiction is established via the location where the consequences of the digital harm were felt (ie where victims experience harm). At the ICC (or another ICCT which has jurisdiction over a particular territory), this would require interpreting the 'conduct' requirement for jurisdiction as taking place where the harm is experienced. This interpretation is viable, as public international law and ICL accept the principle of ubiquity, meaning that a crime occurs in the place where the perpetrator acted or in the place where the proscribed harm was experienced.[112] This principle was considered by the Permanent Court of International Justice in the *Lotus* case, where the Court found that there was no rule of international law that prohibited Turkey from exercising jurisdiction over an offence that 'produced its effects' on a Turkish vessel, and that many States interpret criminal law in the sense that offences are regarded as having been committed on national territory if the 'constituent elements of the offence, and more especially its effects, have taken place there'.[113]

The ubiquity principle has also been applied in ICC cases such as for the situations in Afghanistan and Bangladesh/Myanmar.[114] When considering whether to authorise an investigation into the situation in Afghanistan, the Pre-Trial Chamber noted that

> [t]he Court has jurisdiction if the conduct was either completed in the territory of a State Party or if it was initiated in the territory of a State Party and continued in the territory of a non-State Party or vice versa.[115]

In its decision to authorise an investigation into the situation in Bangladesh/Myanmar, the Pre-Trial Chamber cited the ubiquity principle when it found that there was territorial jurisdiction because victims crossed into Bangladesh (a State Party) as a part of the actus reus of the crime of deportation, even if the crime was initially perpetrated in Myanmar (a non-State Party).[116] This would also be

[112] CL Blakesley, 'Finding Harmony Amidst Disagreement Over Extradition, Jurisdiction, The Role of Human Rights, and Issues of Extraterritoriality Under International Criminal Law' (1991) 24 *Vanderbilt Journal of Transnational Law* 15.

[113] *SS Lotus (France v Turkey)* (Judgment) PCIJ (7 September 1927) [55].

[114] Anonymous, 'Territorial Jurisdiction of the International Criminal Court over the Russian Leadership: Locus Delicti in Complicity Cases' (EJIL:Talk!, 24 March 2022) www.ejiltalk.org/territorial-jurisdiction-of-the-international-criminal-court-over-the-russian-leadership-locus-delicti-in-complicity-cases/. See, eg *Bangladesh and Myanmar* Article 15 Decision (n 102) [62]; *Situation in the Islamic Republic of Afghanistan* (Public redacted version of 'Request for authorisation of an investigation pursuant to article 15') ICC-02/17-7-Conf-Exp (20 November 2017) [47].

[115] Though the Pre-Trial Chamber ultimately decided not to authorise the investigation (which has since been reopened), the Chamber did not find that there were any issues with territorial jurisdiction, as all the alleged crimes were, by this definition, committed on State Party territory. *Situation in the Islamic Republic of Afghanistan* (Decision Pursuant to Article 15 of the Rome Statute on the Authorisation of an Investigation into the Situation in the Islamic Republic of Afghanistan) ICC-02/17-33, PTC II (12 April 2019) [50].

[116] *Bangladesh and Myanmar* Article 15 Decision (n 102) [53] and [62].

consistent with the approach of the Tallinn Manual 2.0, as Rule 9(b) provides that states have territorial jurisdiction over cyber activities originating in or completing on their territories.[117]

Although ICL judges will have to conduct an individual assessment based on the specific facts of the case, assessing territorial jurisdiction using the location of the effects of the crime would likely be beneficial for prosecutions of some cases of digital harm. This is because as outlined in chapters two, three, and four, digital harms always produce effects on victims in the offline environment, whether these effects are mental, physical, an infringement upon rights or some combination. As discussed in chapter four, since linking the digital harm to its real-world effects will be the best avenue to demonstrate other admissibility criteria are satisfied for ICCTs, such as the gravity requirement,[118] it makes sense to apply the same logic to establishing jurisdiction. This approach would also benefit prosecutors in certain instances because it would allow for potential prosecutions against nationals of non-States Parties or against those who perpetrate the crime remotely from the territory of a non-State Party but with transboundary effects in the territories of States Parties. For ICL prosecutors to be able to establish who perpetrated digital harms and where and how they manifested with such evidence, it will be critical for prosecutors to both improve their own technological capacities and to foster cooperation with other actors that can assist in investigations and prosecutions. These issues will be analysed in the subsequent sections.

This analysis of the different avenues of establishing territorial jurisdiction demonstrates that while there are some ways to define territorial jurisdiction for cyberspace (i.e. through the location where the act is committed, or location of where the harm manifests), none come without challenges. As argued by Svantesson, it is also possible that territoriality as a basis for jurisdiction, which has historically been favoured throughout public and private international law jurisprudence, may no longer serve as the best starting point for jurisdiction in a globalised and digital age,[119] and other pathways such as personal or universal jurisdiction may be better suited to account for crimes perpetrated through cyberspace. Yet, while this is a valuable point and other means of jurisdiction should be considered, it is at present difficult to foresee ICCTs moving completely away from their focus on territorial jurisdiction, particularly given that jurisdiction at most ad hoc ICCTs is limited territorially. Importantly, however, the basis for jurisdiction can be flexible within and between different ICCTs and does not have to be applied the same for all cases – this has been demonstrated through the previously mentioned jurisprudence at the ICC, where prosecutors have taken different approaches to establishing jurisdiction. Maintaining this degree of

[117] Rule 9 of The Tallinn Manual 2.0 provides that 'a State may exercise territorial jurisdiction over: (a) cyber infrastructure and persons engaged in cyber activities on its territory; (b) cyber activities originating in, or completed on, its territory; or (c) cyber activities having a substantial effect on its territory'; Tallinn Manual 2.0 (n 100).

[118] See s II.A of this chapter.

[119] D Svantesson, *Solving the Internet Jurisdiction Puzzle* (OUP, 2017) 57.

flexibility regarding jurisdiction will be helpful as new technologies develop and enable different modes of perpetration of international crimes remotely through cyberspace.

iii. Universal Jurisdiction

A final possible avenue for ICCT jurisdiction in cyberspace is universal jurisdiction. Scholars have argued that cyberspace is like other international spaces where universal jurisdiction has been applied, such as the high seas or outer space, where conduct may take place outside the territorial bounds of any State.[120] The nature of such 'international spaces', as classified by Menthe,[121] and the nature of the crimes, makes it so that all nations have an interest in punishing perpetrators for crimes committed in those areas. Universal jurisdiction has been expanded over time to accommodate jus cogens crimes (peremptory norms of general international law, for example genocide or slavery),[122] and has been exercised by certain States to prosecute ICL crimes domestically.[123] However, universal jurisdiction may be of limited use for most ICCTs because they are bound by the confines of their specific mandates and can only exercise jurisdiction in the ways recognised by the relevant UNSC Resolution, Agreement, or Statute.

Concerning the ICC, universal jurisdiction over core international crimes was proposed during negotiations but ultimately was not mentioned in the Rome Statute.[124] As a consequence, given the framework agreed upon, the only way the Court could exercise jurisdiction over crimes committed on non-State Party territory by non-State party nationals would be if the situation was referred by the UNSC or if a non-State Party accepted the jurisdiction of the Court on an ad hoc basis – this is directly set out in the wording of Articles 12 and 13 of the Rome Statute.[125] The argument has been made by the United States (who opposed universal jurisdiction for the ICC at the time it was created and never ratified the Rome Statute) that any exercise of ICC jurisdiction over a national or territory of a non-State Party without the State's consent would be in violation of the *Monetary Gold* principle established by the International Court of Justice (ICJ) as a 'general principle of international law',[126] and of the Vienna Convention of the Law

[120] BT Parker, 'Piracy on the Internet High Seas: Using Hostis Humani Generis to Combat Cybercriminals' (2022) 29 *George Mason Law Review* 593.

[121] Menthe (n 106) 72.

[122] ibid.

[123] M Langer and M Eason, 'The Quiet Expansion of Universal Jurisdiction' (2019) 30 *European Journal of International Law* 779–817.

[124] For example, Germany proposed that the Court should have universal jurisdiction over genocide, aggression, crimes against humanity, and war crimes, with this competence still being limited by the principle of complementarity. AS Galand, *UN Security Council Referrals to the International Criminal Court: Legal Nature, Effects and Limits* (Brill, 2019) 28–29.

[125] A Abass, 'The International Criminal Court and Universal Jurisdiction' (2006) 6 *International Criminal Law Review* 349; Rome Statute art 12.

[126] The *Monetary Gold* principle refers to the notion that courts and tribunals should not proceed on the merits of cases where a third party's legal interests would form the subject-matter of the decision,

of Treaties.[127] Those holding this position argue that to bind States to treaties they do not agree to would violate their sovereignty.[128]

Yet, as noted by Kirsch, the exercise of jurisdiction over non-Party nationals 'does not bind non-parties to the Statute. It simply confirms the recognised principle that individuals are subject to the substantive and procedural criminal laws applicable in the territories to which they travel, including laws arising from treaty obligations'.[129] For instance, as an analogy, a United States citizen travelling to the United Kingdom can still be held accountable for violating the law while they are visiting, and this does not mean that the United States has to agree to or be bound by the law of the United Kingdom. In a similar vein, if a State accepts jurisdiction and signs onto the Rome Statute, those who travel onto its territory, even if their country of nationality is not a State Party, could be held liable for Rome Statute crimes. This argument is true when applied to non-State Party nationals being subject to the ICC for crimes committed on State Party territory, but does not address the issue of cases referred by the UNSC that may not have any links to State Party territory or State Party nationals. However, UNSC referrals would be voted on and then enacted through binding resolutions upon all UN Member States, so if a referral were to progress through the voting process and pass onto the ICC, it would be a stretch to state that such a case would inappropriately infringe upon the sovereignty of a concerned State.

Moreover, if a case is referred to the ICC by the UNSC under its Chapter VII powers, it must be in the interests of maintaining international peace and security.[130] As argued by Galand, the link between ICL and international peace and security is a 'vexed one', as some acts of genocide, crimes against humanity, and war crimes may not necessarily constitute a threat to international peace and security while others will. This could mean that even where the ICC has been argued to have a form of 'universal jurisdiction' through the binding power of UNSC referrals,[131] these referrals are still more limited than true universal jurisdiction and will not encompass every international crime that meets other criteria for admissibility at the ICC. For cases of digital harm, while it is possible that certain cyber operations (such as election-meddling or disinformation campaigns) could be considered as threats to international peace and security worthy of a Chapter VII referral, thereby granting the ICC jurisdiction over crimes committed on non-State Party territory by non-State nationals, there still would not be a means

unless the third party agrees to their jurisdiction. This was established in the *Monetary Gold* case; *Case of the Monetary Gold Removed from Rome in 1943 (Italy v. France, United Kingdom & United States)* (Preliminary Question) ICJ Rep 1954 (15 June 1954). See also Z Mollengarden and N Zamir, 'The Monetary Gold Principle: Back to Basics' (2020) 115(1) *American Journal of International Law* 41–77.

[127] *Monetary Gold* case (n 126); Abass (n 125); Scheffer (n 103); Scharf (n 103) 98.

[128] ibid.

[129] ibid.

[130] Charter of the United Nations (adopted 26 June 1945, entered into force 24 October 1945), Chapter VII: Action with Respect to Threats to the Peace, Breaches of the Peace, and Acts of Aggression; Galand (n 124) 37.

[131] ibid.

for the ICC to exercise truly universal jurisdiction as is derived from customary international law.

It is also possible that a future ICCT could be formed based on universal jurisdiction that could be used to prosecute digital harms. For example, after the Second World War, the IMT was established by the United States, the United Kingdom, France, and the Soviet Union (and adhered to by other Allied Parties) to try individuals for international crimes committed in Germany and other occupied territories.[132] While the corresponding Tokyo Tribunal was created with the consent of the Japanese government, the Nuremberg IMT was established without any explicit consent from Germany.[133] The IMT is an example of an ICCT formed by a treaty between States (The London Agreement) to prosecute serious international crimes that would be of interest to all States. In addition, subsequent war crimes trials conducted under the authority of Control Council Law No. 10 ('CCL 10'), a law adopted by the Allied Control Council in Germany providing for the punishment of those who committed international crimes and giving effect to the Moscow Declaration, the London Agreement, and the IMT Charter, were based upon universal jurisdiction.[134] As explained by the United States CCL 10 Tribunal, the international crimes it was formed to adjudicate were acts 'universally recognized as criminal' and 'considered a grave matter of international concern and for some valid reason [could not] be left within the exclusive jurisdiction of the State that would have control over it under ordinary circumstances'.[135] Digital harms can constitute crimes that meet these same criteria, which has been established throughout earlier chapters – for example, filming and sharing a degrading video of someone being violently executed can constitute an outrage upon personal dignity,[136] which is a war crime universally recognised as criminal that should be subject to the jurisdiction of a new tribunal if a State is unwilling or unable to prosecute it. As previous ICCTs have been created through universal jurisdiction for international crimes perpetrated through 'traditional' means, the same should be possible for those crimes perpetrated through digital means.

It could also be possible that an ICCT is formed through a UN Resolution that would have (nearly universal) jurisdiction over all UN Member States. This has already been considered by a coalition of expert working groups in the Draft United Nations Treaty on an International Court or Tribunal for Cyberspace (hereafter 'Draft Treaty'), which incorporates the work of international and regional organisations that have created cybercrime instruments.[137] The Draft Treaty provides the potential court with the authority to prosecute 'the most serious international

[132] Scharf (n 103) 105.
[133] ibid 106.
[134] ibid; Control Council Law No. 10 (adopted 20 December 1945) www.legal-tools.org/doc/ffda62/.
[135] ibid 107.
[136] See also S Zarmsky, 'Scenario 31: Sharing degrading content' (Cyberlaw Toolkit, 19 September 2024) cyberlaw.ccdcoe.org/wiki/Scenario_31:_Sharing_degrading_content.
[137] S Schjolberg, 'Draft United Nations Treaty on an International Criminal Court or Tribunal for Cyberspace' (Cybercrime Law, June 2015) www.cybercrimelaw.net/documents/Draft_Treaty_text_on_International_Criminal_Tribunal_for_Cyberspace.pdf.

crimes in cyberspace', including acts committed against computer, information, or data systems, and other crimes such as the distribution of child pornography, identify theft, and 'other most serious crimes on social networks of global concern'.[138] Further, the Draft Treaty provides that the tribunal would have jurisdiction over the aforementioned serious crimes committed in cyberspace through its establishment by either the UN General Assembly or the UNSC.[139] Though at the time of writing, there have not been any developments with regard to the establishment of a Cyberspace Tribunal, as technology continues to advance and the world becomes more digitalised, it is a possibility for the future.

Although the development of a new tribunal for international crimes committed in cyberspace could be beneficial, it may also take many years of treaty negotiations to establish. An alternative method to create an ICCT with a basis of universal jurisdiction could be similar to the establishment of the Extraordinary African Chambers (EAC), which was created via an agreement between Senegal and the African Union to prosecute a particular individual who was located in Senegal for international crimes committed in Chad.[140] Though as noted by Williams, the EAC may be considered more of an 'internationalised' tribunal that is closer to a national court exercising jurisdiction over international crimes as opposed to an ICCT, it is still an example of the first international(ised) tribunal to operate exclusively on the basis of universal jurisdiction.[141] However, at present, until any future ICCTs are developed on the basis of universal jurisdiction or otherwise, the most relevant international court to consider for the prosecution of digital harms with a nexus to the perpetration of international crimes is the ICC.[142]

This section explored the different pathways to jurisdiction over digital harm at ICCTs, including personal, territorial, and universal jurisdiction, and the benefits and challenges associated with each. Regarding personal jurisdiction, though active personality could be a beneficial way to establish jurisdiction over digital harms given it is already included within the Rome Statute and may be more straightforward than trying to establish the alternative of territorial jurisdiction in cyberspace, there may be a reluctance of ICL prosecutors to pursue jurisdiction on this basis. Concerning territorial jurisdiction, when digital harms are perpetrated through cyberspace, the clearest avenue for jurisdiction would be to establish a physical link to the crime – whether the best 'link' to use is the location of the perpetrator or the location of the effects of the harm (ie the victims) will depend on the specific circumstances of each case. It is also possible that future ICCTs may be created based on universal jurisdiction to address digital harms, such as through the proposed International Tribunal for Cyberspace, or through

[138] ibid, arts 1–4.
[139] ibid, art 8.
[140] S Williams, 'The Extraordinary African Chambers in the Senegalese Courts: An African Solution to an African Problem?' (2013) 11 *Journal of International Criminal Justice* 1139.
[141] ibid.
[142] Of course, it is possible for domestic courts to prosecute digital harms as international crimes, but this is outside the scope of this book which focuses on ICCTs.

an agreement with a State and an international organisation similar to the EAC, but this could take a significant amount of time and resources. Overall, approaches to jurisdiction over digital harms need not and should not be uniform to account for the full spectrum of harms perpetrated through rapidly advancing technologies under ICL.

III. 'Internal' Challenges

This section explores the challenges that are likely to be faced by ICCTs internally when adjudicating cases involving digital harm. These include how to identify anonymous alleged perpetrators, how to authenticate and preserve online content, how to maintain secure storage of digital data, and how to ensure courtroom actors have the necessary technological expertise to investigate, prosecute, adjudicate, or defend in cases of digital harm.

A. Anonymity of Perpetrator(s)

First, the nature of cyberspace, where digital harms may be perpetrated (in whole or in part), allows for potential perpetrators to be anonymous or difficult to identify. This can affect the viability of prosecution of digital harms, as considered in chapter four,[143] since ICL prosecutors cannot proceed with cases without an identifiable alleged perpetrator and may refrain from prioritising cases where this could happen to avoid wasting time and resources. In addition, even if a suspect is identified, it could be impossible to determine where the digital harm was perpetrated from – for example, IP addresses of devices are often used to identify the origin and destination of online data, but these addresses can be fairly easily hidden or 'spoofed', meaning that the IP address is altered to show a different location than where the device actually is.[144] Further, determining who an alleged perpetrator is and where they are located can be even more difficult if the digital harm is committed through the Dark Web,[145] which is common for a variety of crimes including online marketplaces for human trafficking, sexual slavery or illegal arms sales,

[143] See ch 4 of this book.

[144] M Roscini, 'Cyber Operations Can Constitute War Crimes Under the ICC Jurisdiction Without Need to Amend the Rome Statute' (ICC Forum, 7 March 2022) iccforum.com/cyberwar#Roscini; SJ Shackelford and RB Andres, 'State Responsibility for Cyber Attacks: Competing Standards for a Growing Problem' (2011) 42 *Georgetown Journal of International Law* 971.

[145] The internet consists of three parts: the Surface Web, the Deep Web, and the Dark Web. The Surface Web is what is readily available to the public and can be accessed through mainstream search engines. The Deep Web is not accessible to the public (it is either password or paywall protected), and is mostly used for confidential purposes, such as online banking or web mail. The Dark Web is the part of the internet which is not accessible by browsers used to access the Surface or Deep Webs – it requires the use of a special browser such as TOR (or the Onion Router). S Kaur and S Randhawa, 'Dark Web: A Web of Crimes' (2020) 112 *Wireless Personal Communications* 2131–58.

live streaming torture, or locating potential perpetrators for hire.[146] Each of the above scenarios will require increasingly advanced levels of technical capacity and expertise for ICCT investigators to navigate, and will make it even more important for prosecutorial teams to cooperate with external actors to piece together digital clues to be able to identify and attribute individual criminal responsibility (which will be discussed in section IV).[147]

It is unlikely that ICCT prosecutors will be able to fully investigate digital harms on their own given that they do not possess their own law enforcement bodies with subpoena powers. A potential obstacle will be that since IP addresses are acquired by law enforcement domestically through issuing subpoenas to the relevant Internet Service Provider (ISP), ICCTs will not have this capability and will therefore need to rely on States Parties to request such information for them or for the ISP to share it voluntarily. In instances where States or ISPs do not cooperate and provide the IP address and location (which already is not a guarantee of locating an alleged perpetrator, as considered above), the only option ICCTs will have to try and identify perpetrators of digital harm on their own will be to train their staff or hire new staff with expertise in online open source investigations, where it may be possible to track down where a crime was committed. In cases where this is not possible, anonymous alleged perpetrators will not be able to be identified and investigations will simply not move forward. As more crimes can be perpetrated anonymously through the internet, ICCTs must continue to build their internal capacity to investigate such crimes to avoid total reliance on external partners to assist them, but should still strive for cooperation to have the best possible investigations, which will be considered in section IV.[148]

B. Challenges Raised by Digital Evidence

Second, the evidence that will be tendered by the Prosecutor to demonstrate digital harms may also be digital in nature. For instance, evidence of online hate speech or the sharing of footage of crimes online may consist of digital content (including text messages, photos, and/or videos), and evidence of mass surveillance or 'digital apartheid' could include data retrieved from facial recognition-enabled surveillance cameras.[149] Consequently, prosecutorial teams would need the technological capabilities to identify, process, authenticate, and preserve such evidence in a secure manner. As established by the ICC Trial Chamber in the *Bemba* case, the

[146] ibid; see also MR Shillito, 'Untangling the "Dark Web": An Emerging Technological Challenge for the Criminal Law' (2019) 28 *Information & Communications Technology Law* 186–207.

[147] See s IV of this chapter.

[148] ibid.

[149] 'Digital apartheid' refers to the use of digital technologies to facilitate the separation of society to suppress a particular group. For a longer description and examples, see ch 4, s IV.A of this book, and for an analysis of its potential as a new crime under ICL, see ch 5, s III.A.

probative value of evidence is determined by criteria such as its reliability, authenticity, and provenance.[150]

Due to the ease with which digital content can be manipulated, staged, or generated with artificial intelligence (such as 'deepfakes'), digital evidence can be more difficult to authenticate than traditional forms of evidence. For example, applications on mobile devices now make it easy to edit and alter imagery, and generative AI software is now widely (and often freely) available. An example of this is when in 2022, a purported video of President Zelenskyy telling his soldiers to surrender to Russia circulated online, but was later debunked and found to be a deepfake.[151] Additionally, digital content can easily be taken out of context and misattributed to the wrong events. This famously occurred in relation to a viral video referred to as 'Syrian Hero Boy' from 2014, which was alleged to show children amongst the rubble in Syria but was actually taken from a film set with actors in Malta.[152] As a result of these types of considerations, digital information, especially online open source information, can require an in-depth verification process and expert witness testimony from those experienced with such content.[153]

Multiple specialist CSOs and archival organisations exist (such as eyeWitness or The Syrian Archive) that can and already have assisted ICL prosecutors to ensure that digital evidence, especially that which came from online open sources, is authentic and preserved properly.[154] However it is important for ICCT prosecutorial teams to process and store evidence themselves to avoid having to rely on external partners, who also may not be bound to the same standards. Recognising these challenges, in its Strategic Plan June 2012–2015, the ICC Prosecutor observed that its office was 'facing an explosive growth in its access to digital data' and consequently was starting to focus on 'expanding its capabilities to collect different forms of scientific evidence' and 'its own expert capabilities in the field of voice communication, electronic data and cyber investigations'.[155] Since then, the OTP

[150] *Prosecutor v Bemba*, (Decision on the Prosecution's Application for Admission of Materials into Evidence Pursuant to Article 64(9) of the Rome Statute) ICC-01/05-01/08, T Ch III (8 October 2012) [7]; See also K Hellwig, 'The Potential and the Challenges of Digital Evidence in International Criminal Proceedings' (2022) 22 *International Criminal Law Review* 965-988; L Freeman, 'Digital Evidence and War Crimes Prosecutions: The Impact of Digital Technologies on International Criminal Investigations and Trials' (2018) 41 *Fordham International Law Journal* 283.

[151] Bobby Allyn, 'Deepfake video of Zelenskyy could be "tip of the iceberg" in info war, experts warn' (NPR, 16 March 2022) www.npr.org/2022/03/16/1087062648/deepfake-video-zelenskyy-experts-war-manipulation-ukraine-russia?t=1660657155956.

[152] Anne-Marie Tomchak and Charlotte McDonald, '#BBCTrending: Syrian "hero boy" video faked by Norwegian director' (BBC News, 14 November 2014) www.bbc.co.uk/news/blogs-trending-30057401.

[153] C Quilling, 'The Future of Digital Evidence Authentication at the International Criminal Court' (2022) *Journal of Public and International Affairs*; M Gillett and W Fan, 'Expert Evidence and Digital Open Source Information: Bringing Online Evidence to the Courtroom' (2023) 21 *Journal of International Criminal Justice* 661–93.

[154] See 'Welcome to Eyewitness' (Eyewitness) www.eyewitness.global/ or 'Syrian Archive' (Syrian Archive) syrianarchive.org/. See also M Burgis-Kasthala, 'Assembling Atrocity Archives for Syria: Assessing the Work of the CIJA and the IIIM' (2021) 19 *Journal of International Criminal Justice* 1193; K Hellwig (n 150) 981. Cooperation between ICCTs and CSOs and third parties will be considered in section IV.C.

[155] Office of the Prosecutor, Strategic Plan June 2012-2015, [44].

has seemingly made progress, using new techniques such as 3D reconstructions to present electronic evidence at trial,[156] developing its platform to submit open source material ('OTPLink'),[157] creating a Trust Fund for Advanced Technology and Specialized Capacity,[158] and implementing AI technologies to assist in processing large quantities of data during investigations.[159] OTPLink and the AI technologies mentioned form parts of the OTP's new evidence management platform 'Project Harmony', which utilises features such as rapid pattern identification, automatic translations, facial identification, image enrichment, targeted searches of source material, automated transcription, and video and image analytics.[160]

While these developments are valuable for increasing the efficiency of the OTP in obtaining, preserving, analysing, and reviewing evidence,[161] this progress does not come without risk. First, it is possible that opening a public platform for anyone to share information with the Prosecutor could create more work for staff, as evidence that was previously able to be submitted via formal Article 15 communications can now be transferred with the click of a button, with the same information potentially submitted by multiple people. In its 2023 Annual Report, the OTP reported that as of 5 October 2023 (approximately four months after the launch of OTPLink), the Office received over 10,000 submissions through the portal, with the total number of files reaching close to 45,000 (which has likely increased since the time of the report).[162]

This volume of potential evidence cannot efficiently be processed by OTP staff alone, which is why AI-powered tools have been introduced to filter through the information.[163] There is limited public information available about the exact AI tools being used by the OTP,[164] but it is important to consider that AI in general

[156] See, eg the platform developed by SITU Research for the OTP for the Mali cases: 'International Criminal Court: Case Against M. Al Mahdi' (SITU Research) icc-mali.situplatform.com/; S Zarmsky, 'Why Seeing Should Not Always Be Believing: Considerations Regarding the Use of Digital Reconstruction Technology in International Law' (2021) 19 *Journal of International Criminal Justice* 213.

[157] 'ICC Prosecutor Karim A.A. Khan KC announces launch of advanced evidence submission platform: OTPLink' (ICC, 24 May 2023) www.icc-cpi.int/news/icc-prosecutor-karim-aa-khan-kc-announces-launch-advanced-evidence-submission-platform-otplink.

[158] Office of the Prosecutor, Towards a More Just World Every Day: Annual Report of the Office of the Prosecutor – 2022 (1 December 2022) www.icc-cpi.int/sites/default/files/2022-12/2022-12-05-annual-report-of-the-office-of-the-prosecutor.pdf 26.

[159] K Khan, 'Innovation and Technology in Building Modern Investigations and Prosecutions at the ICC' in C Stahn and R Braga de Silva (eds), *The International Criminal Court in its Third Decade* (Brill, 2023) 101–21, 111.

[160] H Evans and M Hazim, 'Digital Evidence Collection at the Int'l Criminal Court: Promises and Pitfalls' (Just Security, 5 July 2023) www.justsecurity.org/87149/digital-evidence-collection-at-the-intl-criminal-court-promises-and-pitfalls/; 'ICC Office of the Prosecutor to launch modern evidence management platform' (YouTube, 8 February 2023) www.youtube.com/watch?v=rqt63ghnJSE.

[161] ibid.

[162] Office of the Prosecutor, Delivering Better Together: Office of the Prosecutor Annual Report 2023 (December 2023) 52.

[163] ibid.

[164] In its 2023 Annual Report, the OTP reported that it implemented an e-discovery software called RelativityOne to assist with evidence review and analysis. While no further specifics were given about the technology, the company's website provides that the software uses generative AI through a partnership with Microsoft Azure's OpenAI, see 'Relativity aiR' (Relativity) relativity.com/data-solutions/air/.

does not operate without bias. For example, algorithms that use facial recognition can be biased against certain ethnicities or genders,[165] or be influenced by limited datasets to learn from.[166] It is therefore possible that the technology the OTP employs to sift through digital information could possess certain biases that affect which information gets selected to be viewed by the Prosecution and which does not. The OTP also reported that it would be using machine learning, including facial and object recognition systems, that will 'learn and improve as information is added' and that translation accuracy will 'improve as OTP language experts regularly interact with and train the system'.[167] Though systems may learn from new information and improve over time as they interact with people, the risks of bias will also increase, as the information added to the systems may be partial to certain parts of the world or the selection of languages used by Court staff may improve the accuracy of some dialects over others through reinforcement loops.[168] This could result in skewed datasets for Court investigators to examine that would then influence which cases are able to progress and which are not.

C. Security

In addition to developing a new evidence submission portal and tools to analyse such evidence, the ICC OTP also moved all its investigative data to cloud storage in 2023. In its 2023 Annual Report, the OTP stated that the cloud-based 'eVault' 'allows for ingestion of electronic evidence that needs to be preserved; ensures digital preservation of evidence with systematic backups; allows for capturing and management of contextual information; and ensures a full audit trail'.[169] The eVault is a positive development for ensuring that digital evidence is preserved for admissibility purposes at trial, but as with the other new technologies previously discussed, it comes with risks. While more efficient, the use of cloud storage for evidence (as opposed to keeping physical copies in a locked storage space, or electronic copies on an external offline hard drive) is prone to cyber-attacks. The potential for evidence to be stolen or destroyed has always existed (ie through documents being physically stolen, or being destroyed through a flood or fire), but the risk of losing evidence may be greater when it is stored electronically. This is

[165] J Buolamwini and T Gebru, 'Gender Shades: Intersectional Accuracy Disparities in Commercial Gender Classification' (2018) 81 *Proceedings of Machine Learning Research* 77–91; R Heilweil, 'Why algorithms can be racist and sexist' (Vox, 18 February 2020) www.vox.com/recode/2020/2/18/21121286/algorithms-bias-discrimination-facial-recognition-transparency.

[166] S Akter et al, 'Algorithmic Bias in Data-driven Innovation in the Age of AI' (2021) 60 *International Journal of Information Management* 102387; R Richardson, J Schultz and K Crawford, 'Dirty Data, Bad Predictions: How Civil Rights Violations Impact Police Data, Predictive Policing Systems, and Justice' (2019) 94 *NYU Law Review* 192.

[167] Office of the Prosecutor, Policy on Complementarity and Cooperation (April 2024) [67].

[168] See for example J Stray, 'The AI Learns to Lie to Please You: Preventing Biased Feedback Loops in Machine-Assisted Intelligence Analysis' (2023) 2 *Analytics* 350–58.

[169] Office of the Prosecutor (n 167) [54].

because cyber systems can be infiltrated remotely and/or anonymously, so information could be wiped or stolen from any place with potentially limited means to identify and punish hackers. In addition, even if evidence is not completely wiped or stolen, it could be subject to remote manipulation to add or delete content in particular files.

This risk has already materialised in practice. In September 2023, the ICC announced that its network had been hacked in an act of attempted espionage,[170] and Dutch authorities reported that a 'large number of sensitive documents' had been stolen.[171] The Court did not reveal which information had been accessed by the 'unprecedented cyber-attack', but announced that as a result, it would be reinforcing its risk management framework and accelerating existing initiatives aimed at enhancing its digital security.[172] Given that ICCTs possess sensitive information about victims and witnesses that can put them at a security risk, it is especially important that such institutions have secure systems to protect them. For example, the 2023 cyber-attack caused witnesses in all 17 cases before the ICC to have to take 'urgent security precautions'.[173] If ICCTs opt to move their information storage to online cloud systems, it is imperative that those systems are as secure as possible, that staff are trained in best practices for maintaining security, and that the relevant procedures are already in place for when there may be breaches.

D. Technological Expertise

It is also important that ICCTs ensure that counsel and judges are trained in technologies that are increasingly used to perpetrate digital harm or could be useful in their investigation or prosecution. While the Prosecution and Defence Counsel can call expert witnesses to explain certain aspects in detail at trial, counsel and judges need to be able to understand and query digital evidence, how it needs to be processed and stored, and to assign it appropriate probative value. Initiatives have already taken place at and focused on the ICC. The ICC has held online training sessions for counsel on digital forensics and electronic evidence,[174] the Association of Defence Counsel on open source methodologies and using open source evidence in court,[175] and the ICC Bar Association on applying the principles for using digi-

[170] T Sterling and S van den Berg, 'War crimes tribunal ICC says it has been hacked' (Reuters, 19 September 2023) www.reuters.com/world/international-criminal-court-reports-cybersecurity-incident-2023-09-19/; 'Measures taken following the unprecedented cyber-attack on the ICC' (ICC, 20 October 2023) www.icc-cpi.int/news/measures-taken-following-unprecedented-cyber-attack-icc.

[171] P Cluskey, 'Cyber attack on International Criminal Court sparks witness security concerns' (Irish Times, 20 September 2023) www.irishtimes.com/world/europe/2023/09/20/cyber-attack-on-international-criminal-court-sparks-witness-security-concerns/.

[172] ICC (n 170).

[173] Cluskey (n 171).

[174] 'ICC concludes online Training for Counsel' (ICC, 16 December 2022) www.icc-cpi.int/news/icc-concludes-online-training-counsel.

[175] 'Open Source Evidence Webinar Series' (ADC-ICT, 2023) perma.cc/PBD5-8NHL.

tally derived evidence from the Leiden Guidelines, which establish standards for the use of digital evidence at ICCTs.[176] It is also clear from the aforementioned initiatives that OTP staff are being trained and/or hired to deal with digital technologies. Further, it is essential that judges are also educated about how to assess digital evidence and devices – while no trainings have been publicly reported for ICC Chambers on this topic, there have been developments like 'Evaluating digital open source imagery: A guide for judges and fact-finders',[177] launched in 2024, that can be used to increase technological literacy.

Technological literacy is especially important in the context of criminal law, where those accused have the right to a fair trial.[178] This is, in part, because to ensure equality of arms, defence counsel should have the same levels of expertise and abilities to recreate analyses of digital materials, or be able to hire experts if they cannot do this themselves. Further, while digital evidence can be valuable, it is also extremely convincing, even when it may not show what it is suggested to depict. As an example, once one sees a realistic video of an individual committing an alleged war crime, it can be difficult to maintain a neutral eye throughout the rest of the investigation or to remember to question whether the video may have been altered or 'deep-faked'. This 'seeing is believing effect' takes place when courtroom actors place undue reliance on scientific or technological evidence that they may not be able to properly assess the faults of.[179] This can occur at all phases of international criminal proceedings. For instance, as online content may be the starting point for many investigations (such as when a user posts a video of an alleged war crime),[180] it is important that investigators and counsel on prosecutorial teams are knowledgeable enough to question the material so that it does not unduly prejudice investigations against an accused if it is not reliable. In addition to having the capacity and experts to verify digital evidence as discussed in section III.B,[181] OTP staff should operate with the knowledge that digital content may not be authentic and view it with a critical eye to avoid overlooking potential fake information or exculpatory material.[182] During the trial phase, all counsel (including counsel for victims and defence) and judges should be aware of the biases that may exist within digital evidence itself (such as potential errors in digital reconstructions, or

[176] 'An Introduction to the Leiden Guidelines on the Use of Digitally Derived Evidence in International Criminal Courts and Tribunals: its practicable application at the ICC' (ICCBA, 27 January 2024) perma.cc/99DZ-DAGP.

[177] 'Evaluating digital open source imagery: A guide for judges and fact-finders' (2024) www.trueproject.co.uk/osguide.

[178] The right to a fair trial is a universally recognised right. In the context of the ICC, it is enshrined in Article 67 of the Rome Statute ('Rights of the accused'). See also Y McDermott, The Right to a Fair Trial in Practice in International Criminal Trials in Y McDermott, *Fairness in International Criminal Trials* (OUP, 2016) 41–104.

[179] Zarmsky (n 156).

[180] Hellwig (n 150) 977.

[181] See s III.B of this chapter.

[182] See also S Zarmsky and J Mionki, 'Defence Perspectives on Digital Evidence: Insights from the ICC' in S Dubberley, A Koenig, D Murray, and Y McDermott (eds) *Digital Witness: Using Open Source Information for Human Rights Investigation, Documentation, and Accountability* (2nd edn, OUP, 2026).

prejudices that may have influenced the collection of open source material)[183] and how their own views may affect how they are swayed by the evidence.

IV. 'External' Challenges

This section will evaluate the 'external' challenges ICL prosecutors must overcome to effectively prosecute digital harm, including cooperation with States, companies, and third party investigators and CSOs. It will focus on elements of cooperation that may be especially important or pose challenges for prosecuting digital harm should it be criminalised at the international level.

Cooperation is essential for ICCTs to function because ICCTs cannot themselves implement decisions such as arrest warrants on the territory of States.[184] States are obligated to cooperate with ICCTs, stemming from their ratification of treaties (such as the Rome Statute for the ICC) or by virtue of the UN Charter in the case of UNSC-mandated tribunals.[185] Other entities, such as private companies or CSOs, may voluntarily cooperate with ICCTs or enter into their own cooperation agreements with courts. Concerning States, tribunals created via a Chapter VII UNSC resolution require cooperation from all Member States of the UN, whereas the cooperation regimes for other UN-mandated tribunals, such as the Special Court for Sierra Leone (SCSL), the Extraordinary Chambers in the Courts of Cambodia (ECCC), and the Special Tribunal for Lebanon (STL) are more limited in scope.[186] Each of these tribunals was established by an agreement between the concerned State (i.e. Sierra Leone, Cambodia, or Lebanon) and the United Nations, requiring cooperation from both the State and the UN with the respective tribunal, along with the host State, and while all UN Member States are encouraged to cooperate, there is no obligation to do so unlike UNSC-mandated tribunals such as the ICTY and ICTR.[187] The Rules of Procedure and Evidence (RPE) of the SCSL, ECCC, and STL all draw upon the constituent agreements establishing those tribunals and allow the respective tribunal to invite any State to provide assistance on the basis of an ad hoc agreement. The agreement would then determine the basis for and terms of those States' obligations to cooperate.[188]

[183] ibid; Zarmsky (n 156).

[184] R Cryer et al, 'State Cooperation with the International Courts and Tribunals' in R Cryer, H Friman, D Robinson and E Wilmshurst (eds), *An Introduction to International Criminal Law and Procedure* (2nd edn, CUP, 2012) 509.

[185] ibid 510.

[186] DA Mundis, 'The Cooperation Regime of the Special Tribunal for Lebanon', IRMCT Compendium Documents 1.

[187] Agreement Between the United Nations and the Government of Sierra Leone on the Establishment of A Special Court for Sierra Leone (adopted 16 January 2002); Statute of the Special Tribunal for Lebanon, S/RES/1757 (2007); Agreement Between the United Nations and the Royal Government of Cambodia Concerning the Prosecution Under Cambodian Law of Crimes Committee During the Period of Democratic Kampuchea (adopted 6 June 2003).

[188] Residual Special Court for Sierra Leone, Rules of Procedure and Evidence (last amended 16 December 2021); Extraordinary Chambers in the Courts of Cambodia, Internal Rules (Rev. 10) (last

In addition, the STL RPE provides that the Prosecutor and Head of the Defence Office may 'seek cooperation in a manner consistent with the Statute from any State, entity or person to assist with investigations and prosecutions'.[189]

At the ICC, Article 86 of the Rome Statute provides that States Parties have a general obligation to cooperate fully with the Court with respect to its investigations and prosecutions.[190] Further, Article 87 provides the Court with the power to request cooperation from a State Party, or a non-State Party by way of an ad hoc agreement, or an intergovernmental organisation.[191] As noted by Cryer et al., the ICC cooperation framework is closer to inter-State 'horizontal' cooperation than UN-mandated tribunals, as its regime is based on requests instead of orders, grounds for postponement or refusal exist, and the scope for on-site investigations and compelling witnesses to testify is limited (although there is an obligation for States Parties to cooperate).[192] It is for this reason that the ICC cooperation framework has been criticised.[193] Nevertheless, there are specific ways in which States (whether they are States Parties or non-States Parties) and other entities can improve their cooperation with the ICC and other tribunals to facilitate the prosecution of digital harm. These will be considered in the following subsections.

A. Cooperation with States

Cooperation with States is essential for ICCTs in apprehending and detaining alleged perpetrators, as such courts and tribunals do not have their own law enforcement capacities to carry out arrests and they also rely on national prison services to enforce sentences.[194] Article 93 of the Rome Statute lists a number of additional forms of cooperation that States Parties are obligated to comply with – in the context of prosecuting digital harm, important considerations arise for the taking and production of evidence,[195] the examination of places or sites,[196] the protection of victims and witnesses, and the preservation of evidence,[197] which are each considered in detail in this section.

amended 27 October 2022); Special Tribunal for Lebanon, Rules of Procedure and Evidence (last amended 10 April 2019).

[189] Special Tribunal for Lebanon Rules of Procedure and Evidence, Rules 14 and 15.

[190] Rome Statute art 86.

[191] ibid art 87.

[192] Cryer et al (n 184).

[193] ibid; B Swart, 'General Problems' in A Cassese, P Gaeta, and J Jones (eds), *The Rome Statute of the International Criminal Court: A Commentary* (OUP, 2002); H Kaul and C Kreß, 'Jurisdiction and Cooperation in the Statute of the International Criminal Court: Principles and Compromises' (1999) 2 *Yearbook of International Humanitarian Law* 143, 158–61.

[194] R Cryer, D Robinson, and S Vasiliev, *An Introduction to International Criminal Law and Procedure* (4th edn, CUP, 2019) 163.

[195] Rome Statute art 93(1)(b).

[196] Rome Statute art 93(1)(g).

[197] Rome Statute art 93(1)(j).

Regarding the production of evidence, at the ICC, States Parties (and others who sign on to an ad hoc agreement where the parties to the agreement agree to this form of cooperation) would be obligated to hand over evidence of digital harm to the Court, which would likely consist of (in addition to other 'traditional' forms of evidence such as witness testimony) digital information or devices. As stated above, at ICCTs mandated by the UNSC, States' obligations to cooperate (including through sharing information) would derive from the UNSC resolution establishing the ICCT, in accordance with the UN Charter. However, as noted by Freeman, States may seek to hide behind their 'national security privilege' as an excuse not to do so.[198] This problem is not new, as historically, the ICC has struggled with non-cooperation for a variety of reasons,[199] and solutions remain limited. For instance, if a State Party fails to comply with a request to cooperate, the Court may refer the matter to the Assembly of States Parties (ASP), but the ASP has no significant powers of enforcement and relies mainly on public expressions of concern.[200] In addition, when cases are referred to the ICC Prosecutor by the UNSC (as was done with the situations in Darfur and Libya), the Court may refer instances of non-cooperation to the UNSC, but at present the UNSC has refrained from taking significant action in response to such reports.[201] It is for this reason that the ICC's cooperation framework, especially in relation to the disclosure of evidence, has been criticised as being too deferential to States Parties.[202]

State cooperation is more difficult when the State is not legally bound to comply with the ICCT. For example, in 2023, the United States announced that it would not share evidence of possible Russian war crimes in Ukraine with the ICC, even though US Congress had modified its longstanding restrictions on assisting the Court with its investigations in Ukraine the year before.[203] Although

[198] L Freeman, 'Law in Conflict: The Technological Transformation of War and Its Consequences for the International Criminal Court' (2019) 51 *NYU Journal of International Law and Politics* 807, 867. However, in many cases, national security concerns are not a valid excuse for non-cooperation, even if States try to use them. In practice, because the ICC has no enforcement mechanism for non-cooperation, the decision of whether national security privilege can be used is essentially solely in the hands of States. Article 93(4) of the Rome Statute provides that 'a State Party may deny a request for assistance, in whole or in part, only if the request concerns the production of any documents or disclosure of evidence which relates to its national security'. Article 72(6) requires a State to give 'specific reasons' for withholding information, unless doing so would result in prejudice to its national security interests. As argued by Zemach, a combined reading of these two Articles suggests that States who invoke the national security exemption must demonstrate 'reasonableness and good faith' in explanations pursuant to Article 72. See A Zemach, 'National Security Evidence: Enhancing Fairness in View of the Non-Disclosure Regime of the Rome Statute' (2014) 47(3) *Israel Law Review* 331–59, 336.

[199] Cryer, Robinson, and Vasiliev (n 194); F Baetens, 'Multiple Avenues for State Cooperation with the International Criminal Court – Part One' (EJIL: Talk!, 11 March 2020) www.ejiltalk.org/multiple-avenues-for-state-cooperation-with-the-international-criminal-court-part-one/.

[200] Cryer, Robinson, and Vasiliev (n 194) 163–64.

[201] ibid.

[202] J Katz Cogan, 'The Problem of Obtaining Evidence for International Criminal Courts' (2000) 22 *Human Rights Quarterly* 404, 425.

[203] C Savage, 'Pentagon Blocks Sharing Evidence of Possible Russian War Crimes With Hague Court' (The New York Times, 8 March 2023) www.nytimes.com/2023/03/08/us/politics/pentagon-war-crimes-hague.html.

in this situation, given that the United States is not a party to the Rome Statute, there is no legal obligation for it to cooperate with the Court and therefore the Court has no means to compel it to do so. Yet, the US may voluntarily choose to cooperate with ICCTs, which occurred during the ICTY trials when the United States provided satellite imagery of Srebrenica that showed mass grave sites.[204] Additionally, during the case of *Nahimana et al.* at the ICTR, recordings of radio broadcasts were provided by the US State Department and the Rwandese Patriotic Front Secretariat in Rwanda.[205] However, in these cases, these States were bound to cooperate with the ICTR through the UN Security Council Resolution establishing the Tribunal,[206] which is not the case for the ICC. Therefore, depending on the type of ICCT, cooperation may be easier or harder to obtain from States.

Moving on to the specific methods of cooperation that will be important for prosecuting digital harm, potentially the most important way for States to assist the prosecutors of ICCTs is by sharing evidence. This was emphasised in the ICC OTP's Policy on Complementary and Cooperation of April 2024, in which the OTP highlighted the importance of receiving from national authorities and other actors such as private companies, digital information such as intercepted communications, financial data, satellite imagery, electronic devices, and video and audio files.[207] In the context of digital evidence, it is also important for States to ensure that the information is preserved properly and comes with an established chain of custody. This is because, as explained in section III.B,[208] preservation and provenance are key elements to ensure that evidence retains its probative value in international criminal trials, which may be especially difficult for digital evidence. As the evidentiary standards for ICCTs may differ from those of national jurisdictions, it is important that States are aware of those potential differences and collect and store digital information in a manner that is timely but still upholds the standards used by international courts. While at the time of writing, there are no official standards that cater specifically to digital evidence at any ICCT,[209] the Berkeley Protocol on Digital Open Source Investigations and the Leiden Guidelines on the

[204] M Tran, 'Spy pictures "show Bosnia massacre"' (The Guardian, 11 August 1995) www.theguardian.com/world/1995/aug/11/warcrimes.marktran; American Society of International Law, 'Task Force Report on Policy Options for US Engagement with the ICC' (2021) www.asil-us-icc-task-force.org/uploads/2021-ASIL-Task-Force-Report-on-US-ICC-Engagement-FINAL.pdf, 2. Although as the United States has a veto power as a permanent member of the UNSC, it is unlikely to be subject to sanctions, meaning this cooperation was voluntary in a situation where the United States favoured the prosecutions – the situation may not be the same where the United States does not support the prosecutions.

[205] 'Rwanda Tribunal Admits Alleged Recordings from 'Hate Radio' as Exhibits' (JusticeInfo, 8 March 2002) www.justiceinfo.net/en/17126-en-en-rwanda-tribunal-admits-alleged-recordings-from-qhate-radioq-as-exhibits78927892.html.

[206] UNSC Res 955 (8 November 1994) UN Doc S/Res/955; MN Shaw, 'The International Criminal Court - Some Procedural and Evidential Issues' (1998) 3 *Journal of Armed Conflict Law* 65, 79.

[207] Office of the Prosecutor (n 167) [70].

[208] See s III.B of this chapter.

[209] Of course, digital evidence must comply with the usual standards and procedures of evidence at ICCTs, but there are no standards that have been specifically developed or updated in light of the new challenges posed by digital (including open source) evidence.

Use of Digitally Derived Evidence, have aimed to fill this gap, and highlight the importance of keeping the metadata intact (where possible), submitting videos in their entirety as opposed to excerpts, using a hash system to keep a record of provenance, taking screenshots as a back-up copy, and having corroborative witness testimony.[210]

In addition to such external guidelines, it would be useful for ICCTs to adopt their own standards to preserve, store and safeguard digital information, as this would help to clarify what ICCTs require for digital information to be considered as probative evidence in a trial and would encourage the relevant evidentiary considerations (such as information being in its original form, or having a clear chain of custody) to be met by those seeking to share information with ICCTs. Additionally, Article 88 of the Rome Statute requires that States Parties ensure procedures exist under their domestic laws to enable them to cooperate with the ICC's investigative and evidentiary matters.[211] In line with this, it is also important that States Parties ensure their own procedures account for the unique nature of collecting and preserving digital evidence and that those standards align with those of ICCTs.

In line with their cooperation responsibilities, States would need to ensure the protection of victims and witnesses located in their territories. In the context of digital harm, especially crimes such as online sexual violence or the distribution of footage of crimes, the evidence will likely contain identifiable information of victims in vulnerable situations. When handling such evidence, States (and also companies and other entities such as CSOs) should make sure that relevant safeguards are in place to avoid causing further harm, including limiting access to the content to only those who require it, transferring the data as soon as possible to a storage destination and encrypting the information,[212] and using codes to protect the names of sources.[213]

Finally, though it is not mentioned in the cooperation framework outlined in Part 9 of the Rome Statute, an important form of cooperation from States Parties in relation to digital harm will also be financial contributions. The ICC relies heavily on funding from States Parties, who decide annually on the Court's budget at meetings of the ASP.[214] As provided by Article 116, the Court may also receive voluntary contributions from governments (amongst other sources) as additional

[210] OHCHR and Human Rights Center at the University of California, Berkeley, School of Law, 'Berkeley Protocol on Digital Open Source Investigations: A Practical Guide on the Effective Use of Digital Open Source Information in Investigating Violations of International Criminal, Human Rights and Humanitarian Law' (3 January 2022); 'Leiden Guidelines on the Use of Digitally Derived Evidence' (2022).

[211] Rome Statute art 88; See also V Oosterveld, M Perry, and J McManus, 'The Cooperation of States With the International Criminal Court' (2001) 25 *Fordham International Law Journal* 767.

[212] Eurojust and ICC, 'Documenting international crimes and human rights violations for accountability purposes: Guidelines for civil society organisations' (September 2022) www.icc-cpi.int/sites/default/files/2022-09/2_Eurojust_ICC_CSOs_Guidelines_2-EN.pdf, 29.

[213] ibid 39.

[214] 'Assembly of States Parties' (ICC) www.icc-cpi.int/asp.

funds.[215] The OTP has reported that multiple States Parties have already made significant voluntary contributions to allow it to invest in strengthening its technological capacity,[216] but more funding will likely be necessary to ensure that other organs, such as the Registry and Chambers, can benefit from new digital infrastructure and trainings for staff and for external counsel representing accused persons, victims, or States.[217]

Overall, ensuring State cooperation with ICCTs to effectively prosecute and adjudicate digital harms if they are criminalised would be a difficult obstacle to overcome – in cases of UNSC-mandated tribunals like the ICTY or ICTR where there is a binding duty on all States to comply with requests emanating from those tribunals, cooperation may be easier to achieve. However, ICCTs must rely on the willingness of States to cooperate.

B. Cooperation with Companies

In addition to cooperation with States, cooperation with technology companies will play a key role in enabling ICL prosecutors to effectively prosecute digital harms. This is because, for instance, companies like social media platforms will have access to user data and content that has been removed for violation of policies against hateful speech or graphic imagery, which will be crucial for investigations of digital harms like hate speech, sharing footage of crimes online, and online sexual violence. Also, should ICL prosecutors investigate digital harms perpetrated through novel technologies, their teams will need the expertise to process and understand such devices, that could be provided by those working for the relevant companies who develop the software.

ICCTs have collaborated with technology companies in the past and continue to do so. For instance, dating back to the Nuremberg Trials, IBM partnered with the Nuremberg IMT to provide a new system of microphones and headsets that could transmit language interpretation in real time.[218] Additionally, the

[215] Rome Statute art 116.

[216] Office of the Prosecutor (n 167) [65].

[217] It is also important to note that while financial contributions to the OTP and other Court organs will be valuable in assisting the ICC in obtaining justice for digital harms, the resources allocated to defence counsel should not be overlooked. The Defence receive only a small percentage of the budget of the OTP and as such may not have the same time and financial resources to properly query digital evidence. To avoid exacerbating existing issues with inequality of arms between the defence and prosecution, it would be beneficial for States Parties to consider increasing the budget of the Defence during ASP negotiations and/or provide contributions to be used for Defence capacity-building as well. See Zarmsky and Mionki (n 182); S Zarmsky and J Mionki, 'Out in the Open: Fair Trial Rights and Open Source Evidence at the ICC' (OpinioJuris, 10 February 2023) opiniojuris.org/2023/02/10/symposium-on-fairness-equality-and-diversity-in-open-source-investigations-out-in-the-open-fair-trial-rights-and-open-source-evidence-at-the-icc/.

[218] Freeman (n 150) 300; N Porzucki, 'How the Nuremberg Trials changed interpretation forever' (The World, 29 September 2014) theworld.org/stories/2014-09-29/how-do-all-those-leaders-un-communicate-all-those-languages.

Prosecution case at the STL was based almost entirely on telecommunications records provided by two major Lebanese companies, Alfa and Touch.[219] The ICC has been reportedly meeting with technology companies since 2014,[220] and in its 2023–2025 Strategic Plan, the OTP mentioned that it would be working with 'key partners' 'including social media companies'.[221] Further, at a side event at the UN General Assembly in late 2023, the ICC Prosecutor and Microsoft Vice Chair and President announced their new partnership in 'using AI to pursue justice'.[222] The OTP has reported that with its partners at Microsoft and Accenture Avanade, it has developed 'cutting-edge solutions for the analysis of large volumes of digital data'.[223] These facts demonstrate that cooperation between ICCTs and technology companies has become increasingly important, and as new digital harms develop, the need for cooperation will continue to grow. This section considers how cooperation between ICCTs and private companies can be best achieved, through both binding and non-binding legal mechanisms.

i. Binding Mechanisms

The cooperation framework outlined in the Rome Statute does not provide for cooperation with private entities, and at present, there is no binding mechanism that could be used to compel companies to cooperate either with the ICC or other ICCTs. Technology companies also appear to be reluctant to share or disclose data,[224] and examples like Meta's unwillingness to cooperate with the ICJ in *The Gambia v Myanmar* case may predict how similar companies may respond to requests to cooperate coming from other international courts.[225] Legal obligations for companies to cooperate with ICCTs could be generated if the States where those companies are headquartered or carry out the bulk of their operations introduce laws that require ICCTs to so cooperate, or if the companies sign binding cooperation agreements with ICCTs. For instance, States Parties to the ICC are effectively required by Article 88 to undertake such steps – the provision requires States Parties to 'ensure that there are procedures available under their national law for all of the forms of cooperation which are specified under this Part', which could be interpreted as including

[219] J Hendry, 'Special Tribunal for Lebanon and telecommunications evidence' (Global Justice Journal, 22 September 2020) globaljustice.queenslaw.ca/news/special-tribunal-for-lebanon-and-telecommunications-evidence.

[220] A Koenig, 'The International Criminal Court at RightsCon: Upping its Cyber Game' (Huff Post, 11 March 2014) www.huffpost.com/entry/the-international-crimina_b_4936346.

[221] Office of the Prosecutor, 2023–2025 Strategic Plan [43].

[222] 'ICC Office of the Prosecutor partners with Microsoft in using AI to pursue justice' (YouTube, 22 September 2023) www.youtube.com/watch?v=7J-a6D9kqwA.

[223] Office of the Prosecutor (n 167) [65].

[224] L Kim, 'Tech Accountability in the Face of Genocide: Gambia v Facebook' (2022) 36 *Emory Law Review* 167, 169.

[225] ibid 168; *Application of the Convention on the Prevention and Punishment of the Crime of Genocide (The Gambia v Myanmar*; P Pillai, 'The Republic of The Gambia v. Facebook, Inc: Domestic Proceedings, International Implications' (Opinio Juris, 8 August 2020) opiniojuris.org/2020/08/08/the-republic-of-the-gambia-v-facebook-inc-domestic-proceedings-international-implications/.

assisting by sharing information that could be used as evidence.[226] As information needed for evidence of digital harm may likely be held by technology companies themselves, it could be argued that this provision obligates States Parties to ensure their domestic systems requires of companies operating within their jurisdictions to cooperate with ICCTs and to hand over the necessary information when requested to do so. This could consist of legislation either obligating companies to share information with State Party authorities, who could then pass on the information to the ICC, or obligating companies within the State's jurisdiction to share relevant information with the Court directly, both of which would be in accordance with the obligation under Article 88 to ensure national procedures for all forms of cooperation listed in Part 9 of the Rome Statute (and specifically the service of documents and the preservation of evidence as listed under Article 93(1)).[227]

In addition to States' or international organisations' obligations to ensure corporations within their jurisdictions comply with ICCTs, another way to create binding obligations for companies to cooperate with ICCTs would be through cooperation agreements entered into by the companies directly. In the case of the ICC, the Rome Statute allows for the Court to request cooperation from States Parties under Article 87, and private companies are not mentioned. First, this provision gives the ICC the ability to form cooperation agreements with States, which could provide for what was considered above in relation to States requiring companies within their jurisdictions to cooperate with the Court. This could be especially helpful in instances where a State is not party to the Rome Statute (and so is not obligated to comply with Article 88) but enters into an ad hoc agreement with the Court. In this scenario, if a cooperation agreement between a State and the Court included a provision that the State will take appropriate measures (such as enacting legislation) to ensure that companies operating within its territory cooperate and share information with the ICC, there would be a binding obligation for States to enforce these rules upon technology companies in their jurisdictions.

Second, given that there is also nothing in the Court's framework which would preclude the creation of cooperation agreements directly with private companies, it is conceivable that formal agreements between the Court and technology companies could be developed. The Negotiated Relationship Agreement between the International Criminal Court and the United Nations, adopted by UNGA Resolution 58/318, is a useful example of the ICC entering into an agreement with a non-State entity. This Agreement sets forth the ways in which the ICC and UN may cooperate.[228] Notably, the Agreement includes provisions for the exchange of

[226] Rome Statute arts 88 and 93; see also R Rastan and P Turlan, 'International Cooperation and Judicial Assistance' in A Babington-Ashaye, A Comrie, and A Adeniran (eds), *International Criminal Investigations: Law and Practice* (Eleven, 2018) 3.3.

[227] ibid. See also IBA International Criminal Court and International Criminal Law Programme, 'Strengthening the International Criminal Court and the Rome Statute System: A Guide for States Parties' (October 2021) www.ibanet.org/document?id=ICC-Report-Rome-Statute-October-2021.

[228] Negotiated Relationship Agreement between the International Criminal Court and the United Nations legal.un.org/ola/media/UN-ICC_Cooperation/UN-ICC%20Relationship%20Agreement.pdf.

information (Article 5), financial matters (Article 13), and testimony of UN officials (Article 16),[229] all of which could be relevant in a potential agreement between the Court and a private corporation. If such an agreement were to be negotiated with a major social media platform, provisions could outline how the company could best exchange information with the Court, in which matters company staff would be subject to providing expertise or testimony, who would bear the costs of such cooperation, and how users' data privacy would be respected.

The preserving and sharing of information with ICCTs is arguably the most pressing issue for investigations and prosecutions of digital harm given how social media platforms are actively deleting potential evidence of international crimes.[230] Guidance may be taken from TRIAL International's 2023 Comment ('the Comment') to the Meta Oversight Board on 'How Meta should approach preserving content depicting potential war crimes'.[231] The Comment highlights the importance of Meta developing a specific policy on 'preserving and archiving content depicting potential crimes under international law', which should be 'in accordance with, and informed by' relevant principles of international human rights law (IHRL), international humanitarian law (IHL), and international criminal law (ICL).[232] The Comment further notes that the policy should not be the 'object of a specific external request but be applied automatically in an independent and impartial manner', meaning that the policy should require the platform to preserve and share information without being requested by the relevant ICCT authorities.[233] This would be an important provision to include in a potential cooperation agreement with an ICCT such as the ICC as it would bind companies to share information with the Prosecutor without the need for a request, and therefore potential evidence that may be relevant to investigations that the OTP may not know about will not fall through the cracks.

However, there would be a need for the policy to outline how this would work in practice, which should be developed through discussions between companies and the Court, that would detail specific methods for information transfer and the roles of each party. In addition, the Comment suggests that Meta implement tools such as digital evidence lockers to archive content, and emphasises that as prosecutions of international crimes may take years to come to fruition, such tools should have the capacity to safely store the information for a long period of time.[234] This would also be imperative to include in a potential cooperation agreement with a platform and an ICCT, and additionally should stress that companies are transparent with how they are preserving content and establish a secure channel of

[229] ibid.
[230] Human Rights Watch, '"Video Unavailable": Social Media Platforms Remove Evidence of War Crimes' (10 September 2020) www.hrw.org/report/2020/09/10/video-unavailable/social-media-platforms-remove-evidence-war-crimes.
[231] TRIAL International, 'Public Comment submitted by Trial International to the Oversight Board' (March 2023) osbcontent.s3.eu-west-1.amazonaws.com/PC-11128.pdf.
[232] ibid.
[233] ibid.
[234] ibid.

communication to send over evidence from those digital lockers to the Prosecutor, both for admissibility purposes and in the interests of fair trial principles. Further, in the interests of protecting user privacy, in addition to establishing a secure line of communication with the ICCT, potential cooperation agreements should detail a process for how information that is deemed not relevant for investigations to be properly and promptly deleted.

ii. Non-binding Mechanisms

There are also some non-binding methods that may also foster cooperation between private companies and ICCTs. ICCTs may agree Memoranda of Understanding (MOUs) with relevant technology companies. MOUs are frequently used in various fields of international law and can be beneficial in securing cooperation when the parties are reluctant to sign an agreement that is legally binding.[235] However, while a MOU could help to outline modalities for cooperation and act as a precursor to a more concrete agreement, this solution could also be more problematic as it may give a large degree of deference to companies to pick and choose cases for which they wish to cooperate with, which goes against the overall function of ICCTs to conduct impartial trials and establish the truth. To date, the ICC has signed MOUs with a range of actors, including States,[236] international organisations,[237] and other international courts.[238] While there would not be recourse in the event of noncompliance, MOUs can still be beneficial in outlining how the parties will work together and the procedures for doing so. MOUs between an ICCT and a technology company could also highlight important elements considered previously, such as how digital information would be preserved and transferred to the court or tribunal, or serve as a prelude to a later binding agreement.

A more concrete framework for cooperation with private companies, such as through an agreement or MOU, would encourage (if not bind) companies to assist courts with investigations and prosecutions of international crimes by creating a

[235] M Kolb, 'The Memorandum of Understanding' in M Kolb, *The European Union and the Council of Europe* (Palgrave Macmillan London, 2013) 141–42.

[236] See, eg Memorandum of Understanding between the Bolivarian Republic of Venezuela and the Office of the Prosecutor of the International Criminal Court (3 November 2021) www.icc-cpi.int/sites/default/files/itemsDocuments/otp/acuerdo/acuerdo-eng.pdf. MOUs have also been adopted for groups of States, see Memorandum of Understanding between the International Criminal Court and the Commonwealth on Cooperation, ICC-PRES/10-04-11 (13 July 2011) www.legal-tools.org/doc/dc14ab/pdf.

[237] See, eg Memorandum of Understanding between the International Commission on Missing Persons and the Office of the Prosecutor of the International Criminal Court (7 July 2016) www.icc-cpi.int/sites/default/files/itemsDocuments/ICC_ICMP.pdf; Memorandum of Understanding between the International Criminal Court and the Asian-African Legal Consultative Organization, ICC-PRES/05-01-08 (5 February 2008) www.legal-tools.org/doc/121e2a/pdf.

[238] See, eg Memorandum of Understanding regarding Administrative Arrangements between the International Criminal Court and the Special Court for Sierra Leone, ICC-PRES/03-01-06 (13 April 2006) www.legal-tools.org/doc/9f10c8/pdf; Memorandum of Understanding between the International Criminal Court and the Inter-American Court of Human Rights, ICC-PRES/17-01-16 (15 February 2016) www.icc-cpi.int/sites/default/files/iccdocs/oj/MoU_CR_En.pdf.

formal channel of information-sharing. These mechanisms could also be helpful in the case of social media companies, which have been less (at least publicly) present in assisting the work of the Court than software developers such as Microsoft. While the tools being developed for the Court such as OTPLink are useful for sifting through vast quantities of digital data, the data first needs to be acquired, and in the case of open source photos and videos which would be relevant to investigations of digital harm, social media platforms are in possession of the information. As considered in chapter four, social media companies frequently delete potential evidence of international crimes quickly because of violations of policies against violent or graphic content,[239] or potentially for compliance with domestic laws regarding incitement or glorification of terrorism, and are not transparent about how and how long the content is preserved after it is removed.[240] An agreement or MOU could establish a specific secure channel for how evidence can be shared to avoid issues with transparency and potential evidence deletion later on.

In recent years, technology companies (and in particular, social media companies) have begun to employ the language of 'human rights' and adopt considerations based on IHRL into their business practices.[241] This has become especially apparent for Meta, who has explicitly affirmed its commitment to respecting IHRL frameworks including the Universal Declaration of Human Rights (UDHR), International Covenant on Civil and Political Rights (ICCPR), and the United Nations Guiding Principles on Business and Human Rights (UNGPs), which establish a basis for how private companies may incorporate human rights norms into their business practices.[242] Further, Meta's Oversight Board, an independent board that reviews decisions made by Facebook, Instagram, and Threads, has recognised the importance of the UNGPs in its case law and in its submission to the OHCHR.[243]

[239] See ch4, s IV.B of this book.

[240] Human Rights Watch (n 230). It is important to note that social media companies do not necessarily have the intention to delete potential evidence of international crimes, and in many cases, they are trying to fight terrorism online or protect other users. For example, YouTube introduced an algorithm to quickly delete terrorist content, but this resulted in hundreds of thousands of videos from the Syrian conflict disappearing from the website, as it was unable to distinguish between propaganda posted by ISIS and documentation posted by human rights activists; RJ Hamilton, 'Social Media Platforms in International Criminal Investigations' (2020) *52 Case Western Reserve Journal of International Law* 213.

[241] S Di Stefano, 'International Human Rights Law in Content Moderation and the Risks of "Misdiagnosing" its Limits' (2025) 16 *Transnational Legal Theory* 519; S Di Stefano, 'Regulating Freedom of Expression in the Age of Social Media: New Actors as Drivers of Change in International Law', PhD Thesis, Graduate Institute of International and Development Studies, Geneva, 2025 (on file with the author).

[242] Meta, 'Human Rights Report: Insights and Actions 2020-2021' (July 2022) about.fb.com/wp-content/uploads/2022/07/Meta_Human-Rights-Report-July-2022.pdf, 22. See also Meta, 'Human Rights Report: Insights and Actions 2023' (September 2024) humanrights.fb.com/wp-content/uploads/2024/09/2023-Meta-Human-Rights-Report.pdf.

[243] Meta Oversight Board, 'Operationalizing the UN Guiding Principles on Business and Human Rights: Submission to the Office of the High Commissioner for Human Rights, United Nations on the practical application of the UNGPs to the activities of technology companies' (February 2022) www.ohchr.org/sites/default/files/2022-03/Oversight-Board.pdf.

Even though IHRL treaties do not legally bind companies, it is possible that this increased focus on human rights within the social media sphere has created normative change in the interpretation of international law.[244] It has been argued that IHRL is inadequate to address challenges posed by new technologies and actors, mainly due to the fact that IHRL is designed to constrain government and not corporate entities, and has no real binding effect on companies.[245] In response to social media companies using the language of IHRL, some have even offered a more cynical view that platforms have embraced this terminology 'because they know that in reality in will not act as much of a constraint at all'.[246] Yet, as argued by Di Stefano, who draws upon the theories put forth by Krisch,[247] the way in which IHRL is interpreted does not necessarily have to be universal, but can be highly authoritative in specific areas while being less authoritative in others.[248] Di Stefano notes that the emergence of IHRL as a '*lingua franca*' in discourse around social media policies (specifically content moderation) demonstrates that at least in the limited sphere of social media platform governance, IHRL can be seen as an authoritative body of law.[249]

While social media companies may not always adhere to their commitments to human rights in practice, this problem is not unique to the corporate sector, as States who are bound to IHRL treaties may still not fulfil their obligations. As argued by Di Stefano, 'misdiagnosing' the limits of IHRL in the context of social media companies can result in the 'pigeonholing' of new phenomena into predetermined and potentially outdated international law categories, and place too much focus on the overall inadequacy of IHRL as opposed to how to facilitate change.[250] Taking this into account, it is still therefore valuable to consider how IHRL can be used to foster cooperation between technology companies and ICCTs.

For instance, as stated above, Meta has confirmed its commitment to upholding the rights enshrined in the ICCPR, amongst other human rights treaties. Article 2 of the ICCPR provides for the right to remedy when an individual's rights or freedoms are violated, including through 'judicial' authorities.[251] It follows that if Meta genuinely intends to respect this right to remedy, it will need to ensure that victims who experience harm from its platforms have appropriate redress mechanisms. In

[244] ibid.

[245] See B Dvoskin, 'Expert Governance of Online Speech' (2023) 64 Harvard International Law Journal 85; E Douek, 'The Meta Oversight Board and the Empty Promise of Legitimacy' (2023) *37 Harvard Journal of Law & Technology* ssrn.com/abstract=4565180; E Douek, 'The Limits of International Law in Content Moderation' (2021) 6 *UC Irvine Journal of International, Transnational, and Comparative Law* 37.

[246] Douek (n 245).

[247] Krisch argues that international law is not static, but a dynamic field that is changing frequently in many different areas. See N Krisch, 'The Dynamics of International Law Redux' (2021) 74 *Current Legal Problems* 269–97, 271: 'In many instances, international law is changing much more flexibly than the traditional picture leads us to believe – states are not always at the centre, legality is not necessarily treated as binary, and the ways in which international law changes also vary significantly across issue areas and institutional contexts'.

[248] ibid.

[249] ibid.

[250] Di Stefano (n 241).

[251] ICCPR art 2(3)(b).

cases where digital harms are grave enough to be considered international crimes, and State authorities are unwilling or unable to prosecute those crimes, the most appropriate remedy for victims to achieve justice may be through ICCTs. In order to facilitate those international criminal trials, it would be imperative for companies to cooperate with prosecutors by sharing information that may be used as evidence during their investigations. Additionally, Principle 22 of the UNGPs states that companies must 'provide for or cooperate in their remediation through legitimate processes'.[252] In the commentary provided for Principle 22, it is stated that '[s]ome situations, in particular where crimes are alleged, typically will require cooperation with judicial mechanisms'.[253] This further reinforces the responsibility of companies to cooperate with judicial mechanisms, including ICCTs, in order to be compliant with the rights enshrined in IHRL, and this framing could be utilised in discourse surrounding cooperation to further encourage cooperation.

C. Cooperation With Non-State Investigators and CSOs

Cooperation with CSOs is beneficial for ICCTs as they can provide a lived experience and policy expertise to the development of court practice, and bring the work of courts closer to affected communities.[254] Further, as noted by McGonigle Leyh, CSOs also play a critical role in collecting and documenting information relevant to international crimes.[255] To be most effective when dealing with evidence of digital harm, it is important that ICCTs work with open source investigators and other CSOs with expertise in the collection, documentation, authentication, and preservation of digital evidence. Of course, prosecution teams should ensure they can carry out such work themselves as outlined in section 6.3,[256] but collaborating with technology experts where possible will increase investigative capacity and quality. Organisations such as Bellingcat,[257] who specialise in open source investigations, Mnemonic and Syrian Archive,[258] who specialise in documenting and preserving evidence for accountability purposes, and other third party fact-finding mechanisms such as the IIIM therefore need to be able to communicate with international courts effectively and efficiently.[259] These organisations are also especially

[252] OHCHR, 'Guiding Principles on Business and Human Rights' (2011) HR/PUB/11/04, principle 22.

[253] ibid.

[254] E Evenson, 'The International Criminal Court at 20: the Role of Civil Society' in C Stahn and R Braga de Silva (eds), *The International Criminal Court in Its Third Decade* (Brill, 2023) 71.

[255] B McGonigle Leyh, 'Changing Landscapes in Documentation Efforts: Civil Society Documentation of Serious Human Rights Violations' (2017) 33 *Utrecht Journal of International and European Law* 44–58, 45.

[256] See s III of this chapter.

[257] See 'Bellingcat' (Bellingcat) www.bellingcat.com.

[258] See 'Mnemonic' (Mnemonic) www.mnemonic.org; 'Syrian Archive' (Syrian Archive) www.syrianarchive.org.

[259] See 'International, Impartial and Independent Mechanism to Assist in the Investigation and Prosecution of Persons Responsible for the Most Serious Crimes under International Law Committed in the Syrian Arab Republic since March 2011' (IIIM) iiim.un.org/; Burgis-Kasthala (n 154).

helpful in the absence of cooperation from social media platforms, as they are able to retrieve and store open source information before it is potentially deleted by the platform. In addition, organisations like WITNESS have been working to educate human rights defenders about the prevalence of synthetic media and deepfakes,[260] which have been increasingly found in the media and online,[261] which could provide valuable assistance to ICCTs in authenticating digital evidence. However, as argued by McGonigle Leyh, it is important that as new actors focusing on digital documentation enter the international accountability arena, they adhere to the general principles of human rights documentation, including the 'do no harm' principle and obtaining informed consent where possible.[262]

At present, organisations can submit information to the ICC through Article 15 communications,[263] or raise with the Court at bi-annual roundtables between ICC representatives and NGOs.[264] Yet, as considered by Braga da Silva, a main challenge that arises is the lack of consistency and comparability between different investigative standards, as each organisation will have its own protocols, which will likely also differ from that of the Court.[265] If the information submitted to the Court is not in line with the evidentiary standards used during trial, this can hinder the ability of the OTP to build a strong case.[266] Further, if investigators use diverse approaches to analyse the evidence and come up with different conclusions, this can create uncertainty and undermine the legitimacy of the investigation.[267] Finally, the differences in standards between third parties and courts can lead to 'ethical dilemmas' if there are disagreements about professionalism – for example, third-party investigators do not have the same obligation to investigate both inculpatory and exculpatory evidence as the OTP of the ICC, which could lead to one-sided evidence and pose a detriment to fair trial rights.[268] A solution to the aforementioned issues could be the issuance of a clear internal

[260] 'Deepfakes, Synthetic Media and Generative AI' (WITNESS) www.gen-ai.witness.org/?pk_vid =ab24adb66c8948da170540873970fe96.

[261] Deepfakes and synthetic media have been increasingly used to depict international leaders saying or doing things that did not happen or to portray false events, which can throw off investigations if not properly identified and spread misinformation. See Europol, 'Facing reality: Law enforcement and the challenge of deepfakes' (2022) www.europol.europa.eu/cms/sites/default/files/documents/Europol _Innovation_Lab_Facing_Reality_Law_Enforcement_And_The_Challenge_Of_Deepfakes.pdf; A Koenig, '"Half the Truth is Often a Great Lie": Deepfakes, Open Source Information, and International Criminal Law' (2019) 113 *AJIL Unbound* 250.

[262] McGonigle Leyh (n 255) 51–55.

[263] Under Article 15 of the Rome Statute, any individual, group, or organisation can submit information to the OTP about alleged crimes. Communications can be sent by post or through OTPLink. Rome Statute Art 15, see also 'How to file a communication to the ICC-Prosecutor' (Coalition for the International Criminal Court) coalitionfortheicc.org/how-file-communication-icc-prosecutor; 'FAQs' (ICC OTPLink) otplink.icc-cpi.int/faqs.

[264] 'Civil Society and the ICC' (ICC) www.icc-cpi.int/get-involved/ngos.

[265] Rafael Braga da Silva, 'Collaboration between the Office of the Prosecutor and Third-Party Investigators' in C Stahn and R Braga da Silva (eds), *The International Criminal Court in Its Third Decade* (Brill, 2023) 133.

[266] ibid.

[267] ibid.

[268] ibid.

policy (such as an OTP Policy Paper) for cooperation with investigators and other technology-specific CSOs to encourage more consistency amongst approaches, which would be beneficial for the efficiency, credibility, and fairness of international criminal investigations.

To standardise the collection of evidence and minimise the risk of overdocumentation, in 2022, Eurojust and the ICC OTP released guidelines for CSOs on documenting international crimes and human rights violations for accountability purposes.[269] The guidelines include a section on documenting digital information and conducting online investigations, outlining best practices for organisations to ensure the evidence they collect can be used at by the Court.[270] As was raised in relation to cooperation with companies, formal agreements like the agreement between the UN and the ICC or MOUs can also be helpful in establishing a framework for how courts will cooperate with CSOs. In the context of digital harm, it would be beneficial for the Court to have a solidified agreement with organisations that specialise in the collection and preservation of digital evidence to streamline their processes and ensure that the evidence already meets criteria for admissibility and weight at trial.

V. Conclusion

In this chapter, I considered the obstacles that ICCTs will likely face to successfully adjudicate digital harm once it is criminalised, including jurisdictional, internal, and external challenges. Regarding jurisdictional challenges, the chapter assessed how ICL prosecutors could establish jurisdiction for digital harms perpetrated through cyberspace based on personal, territorial, and universal jurisdiction. I conclude that personal jurisdiction through active personality (as provided in the Rome Statute) may be a more straightforward way to establish jurisdiction than assessing the meaning of territorial jurisdiction in cyberspace, but that personal jurisdiction's utility may be limited given ICL prosecutors' apparent policy not to pursue jurisdiction on that basis. Regarding territorial jurisdiction, I suggest that the clearest avenue for jurisdiction would be to link the digital harm to a physical element, which can most directly be done through interpreting the 'conduct' element of crimes as occurring on the territory where the perpetrator is or where the harm manifests. Finally, concerning universal jurisdiction, I conclude that the ICC will be able to enforce universal jurisdiction in very limited circumstances (ie,

[269] Eurojust and ICC (n 212). In addition, Public International Law and Policy Group (PILPG) released its report 'Human Rights Documentation by Civil Society – Technological Needs, Challenges, and Workflows' in 2020, which contains sections on how to preserve digital information and verify its accuracy for use as evidence; PILPG in collaboration with The Engine Room and HURIDOCS, 'Human Rights Documentation by Civil Society – Technological Needs, Challenges, and Workflows' (November 2020) static1.squarespace.com/static/5900b58e1b631bffa367167e/t/5fb58bcb67862d7d964cf27a/1605733350976/PILPG+-+HR+Doc+Solutions+-+Assessment+Report.pdf.

[270] ibid 30–32.

a UNSC referral or through agreements with non-States Parties), and that a future tribunal created based on universal jurisdiction may be a viable way to account for digital harms.

Concerning internal challenges, issues relating to the anonymity of perpetrators, challenges raised by digital evidence, security, and technological expertise were discussed. While international courts like the ICC have demonstrated progress in overcoming these issues, there is still room for improvement to ensure that evidence is stored securely, that new technologies used by the Court are not biased, and that all staff are equally trained. Regarding external challenges, although issues with State cooperation may have posed problems for ICCTs in the past, it is possible that the nature of digital harms would render State cooperation less essential for carrying out international criminal investigations and trials. This is because new technologies and digital investigative methods allow for courts and other organisations to carry out searches and find evidence themselves. Non-State actors such as corporations will have bigger roles to play in the context of digital harm, as social media companies and internet service providers are likely to have greater and/or earlier access to digital evidence than national authorities. In the event of non-cooperation from such corporations, increasing the capacity of courts to conduct their own digital investigations, combined with the potential collaboration with CSOs, will be critical in ensuring that courts can effectively prosecute digital harm.

7

Case Studies of Digital Harm

I. Introduction

The first six chapters of this book theorised how digital harms could be criminalised under international criminal law (ICL) and the potential challenges international criminal courts and tribunals (ICCTs) could face should digital harm be adjudicated. To form a more concrete picture of how criminalisation of digital harm could work in practice at an ICCT, this chapter will apply that analysis to two real-world case examples of digital harm – the beheading of American journalist James Foley by the Islamic State (ISIS), which was filmed and circulated online, and the use of digital surveillance technologies to suppress the Uyghur population in Xinjiang, China. Although other additional international crimes are relevant to both case examples (ie the killing of a journalist and the detention and torture of Uyghurs in internment camps), only those crimes pertaining to the new forms of digital harm set out in the preceding chapters will be considered.

The case studies are structured similarly. For the first case study, which concerns potential jurisdiction in cyberspace, jurisdiction is considered first – as the analysis of jurisdiction is not different from 'traditional' cases because of the nature of the digital harms in the second case study, which will be explained in that section, jurisdiction will not be considered in detail for the second case study. Then, for both case studies, the potential crimes that could be charged will be analysed. For the first case study, this will consist of the war crimes of outrages upon personal dignity and torture and cruel treatment, and the crimes against humanity of torture and other inhumane acts. For the second case study, the crimes considered will be the crimes against humanity of persecution and apartheid. As the main ICCT available for such acts is the ICC, the legal analysis is centred around Rome Statute crimes and their elements, however this analysis is intended to be applicable to any future ICCT that may be established. Next, the relevant challenges that might arise as a result of the specific digital harm in question will be explored, in particular, issues with digital investigations for the first case study, and gravity for both case studies. At the end of the chapter, the two case studies are compared and contrasted as part of a broader analysis of how digital harms may be criminalised and prosecuted at ICCTs in practice.

II. Case Study 1: Sharing Degrading Content

This case study concerns the beheading of United States journalist James Foley by ISIS in 2014, which was filmed and circulated online and in mainstream news media.[1] Foley was a conflict journalist and videographer with an esteemed career, reporting in Iraq, Afghanistan, Libya, and Syria.[2] In November 2012, Foley was kidnapped by ISIS and was murdered by decapitation on 19 August 2014 in the Raqqa region of Syria.[3] Later the same day, a video of the beheading titled 'A Message to America' appeared on Al-Hayat Media Center's (ISIS' leading distributor of western-aimed propaganda) account on the social networking platform Diaspora,[4] and on YouTube.[5] The video, which is four minutes and 40 seconds long, shows Foley kneeling in an orange jumpsuit in what appears to be a desert next to a masked militant standing in all black.[6] Foley's face is clearly visible as he states (under duress), 'I call on my friends, family and loved ones to rise up against my real killers, the US government, for what will happen to me is only a result of their complacency and criminality'.[7] The masked militant then delivers a warning to the United States government before taking out a knife and beginning to cut at Foley's neck, and the video fades to black.[8] A decapitated body is then shown lying on the ground posed with a head placed on the back, presumably Foley's.[9] The video concludes with the masked militant returning holding another kneeling hostage (later identified as American journalist Steven Sotloff) and

[1] Although there have been more recent instances of acts of this nature, especially in the contexts of Ukraine and Palestine, this case example was chosen due to both the amount of information publicly available about it and the fact that the family of James Foley openly discuss his case, indicating their consent for publicising their harms and a desire to raise awareness (see also the subsequent footnote). While this specific case involves more 'dated' social media (as opposed to current fora such as Instagram and TikTok), the analysis is still equally applicable in the present day. I have written briefly about more recent examples post-2020: S Zarmsky, 'Contemporary International Criminal Law After Critique Symposium: ICL's Potential to Address Online Harms in Ukraine, Palestine, and Beyond' (Opinio Juris, 10 September 2024) opiniojuris.org/2024/09/10/contemporary-international-criminal-law-after-critique-symposium-icls-potential-to-address-online-harms-in-ukraine-palestine-and-beyond/.

[2] 'About Jim' (James W. Foley Legacy Foundation) jamesfoleyfoundation.org/james-w-foley. The James W. Foley Legacy Foundation was founded by James' mother, Diane Foley, and advocates for the freedom of all Americans held hostage abroad.

[3] ibid.

[4] Diaspora is a free, decentralised and community-run network. It has been reported that as of 2014, all of ISIS's accounts on the platform had been deleted; SM Friis, '"Beyond Anything We Have Ever Seen": Beheading Videos and the Visibility of Violence in the War against ISIS' (2015) 91 *International Affairs* 725.

[5] CJ Carter, Video shows ISIS beheading US journalist James Foley' (CNN, 20 August 2014) edition.cnn.com/2014/08/19/world/meast/isis-james-foley/index.html.

[6] ibid; 'American journalist beheaded by ISIS' (CNN, 19 August 2014) edition.cnn.com/videos/world/2014/08/19/sot-journalist-james-foley-isis-beheading.cnn.

[7] 'James Foley: Islamic State militants 'behead reporter'' (BBC News, 20 August 2014) www.bbc.co.uk/news/world-middle-east-28862268.

[8] ibid.

[9] ibid; Friis (n 4).

warning President Obama that 'the life of this American citizen depends on your next decision'.[10]

The members of ISIS who carried out Foley's murder were later identified by United States authorities as belonging to the group of four British militants known as the 'ISIS Beatles'.[11] The 'Beatles' carried out three similar beheadings in 2014, one of another American journalist and two of British aid workers.[12] Two of the members, Alexanda Amon Kotey and El Shafee Elsheikh, were captured and brought to the United States to face domestic criminal prosecutions,[13] while Aine Davis was prosecuted and convicted in Turkey and deported back to the United Kingdom, where he was charged with terrorist offences.[14] The fourth member, Mohamed Emwazi, who physically conducted the videotaped beheadings, was killed by an airstrike in Syria in November 2015.[15]

The video was deleted by YouTube within an hour of its original publication, but had already begun to circulate both on other social media websites and in mainstream news.[16] Dozens of accounts were suspended on Twitter (now X) for sharing the video in violation of community standards, and decentralised networks like Diaspora and LiveLeak initiated censorship for the first time to stop its dissemination by removing the video and banning any future Islamic State beheading videos.[17] LiveLeak's co-founder, Hayden Hewitt, stated that this decision was guided 'by our own concerns regarding this slickly presented style of recruitment video and what we believed was best for the site overall', and that the co-founders feared this viral video would set off a wave of similar videos.[18] However, even in 2024, still images and excerpts of the video can be easily found online through a simple search, demonstrating the impossibility of completely removing content from the internet once it is uploaded.

This case study focuses on the potential criminalisation of the harm resulting from filming and sharing the execution video online. At its root, and as explained in chapters three and four,[19] the harm that arises from sharing such degrading content is an assault on the human dignity of the victim. This case study will

[10] ibid.

[11] 'ISIS Militant Pleads Guilty to Role in Deaths of Four Americans in Syria' (US Department of Justice Office of Public Affairs, 2 September 2021) www.justice.gov/opa/pr/isis-militant-pleads-guilty-role-deaths-four-americans-syria.

[12] 'Elshafee El Sheikh: Ex-Briton "Isis Beatle" sentenced to life in prison' (BBC News, 19 August 2022) www.bbc.co.uk/news/world-us-canada-62609217.

[13] ibid.

[14] D Gardham and Associated Press, 'Alleged member of ISIS "Beatles" charged in UK with terrorism' (NBC News, 11 August 2022) www.nbcnews.com/news/world/alleged-member-isis-beatles-charged-uk-terrorism-rcna42591.

[15] US Department of Justice (n 11).

[16] Friis (n 4) 740.

[17] ibid.

[18] S Nelson, 'LiveLeak Bans Future Islamic State Beheading Videos' (US News, 22 August 2014) www.usnews.com/news/articles/2014/08/22/liveleak-bans-islamic-state-beheading-videos-after-james-foley-murder.

[19] See chs 3 and 4 of this book.

demonstrate that this harm can potentially constitute war crimes and crimes against humanity. It will also consider the specific challenges that could arise in relation to the use of digital open source information.

A. Jurisdiction

In this case, jurisdiction is a relevant challenge to consider, as adjudicating the conduct associated with sharing execution videos online would involve establishing jurisdiction over acts committed in cyberspace. This is because the harm arising from sharing the video was likely inflicted from a different jurisdiction than where the harm was experienced, and as noted in chapter six,[20] the jurisdiction of an ICCT over this harm could therefore be interpreted in multiple ways. As also explained in chapter six,[21] jurisdiction can have various bases, including territorial, nationality-based, and universal jurisdiction. At the ICC, the Court may exercise jurisdiction if (a) the situation is referred to the Prosecutor by a State Party, (b) the situation is referred to the Prosecutor by the United Nations Security Council (UNSC) under Chapter VII of the UN Charter, or (c) the Prosecutor initiates an investigation on the basis of information on crimes within the jurisdiction of the Court.[22] For (a) and (c), the alleged crime must have been committed on the territory of a State Party or by a national of a State Party.[23] In this case, the relevant States to consider based on where the acts took place and the nationalities of the perpetrators and victims are Syria, Iraq, the United States, and the United Kingdom, the only State Party to the Rome Statute being the United Kingdom.

In line with Article 13, this case could be referred to the Court via a State Party, the UNSC, or initiated by the Prosecutor. At present, the crimes committed by ISIS in Syria and Iraq have not been referred to the Court by a State Party and the UNSC has also not referred the situation to the International Criminal Court (ICC), although these avenues remain open as future possibilities. As mentioned in chapter six,[24] former ICC Prosecutor Bensouda announced in 2015 that her office had inquired into alleged crimes committed by ISIS but ultimately decided that there was 'too narrow' a jurisdictional basis to open a preliminary examination because it would only allow for prosecutions of 'lower level' foreign fighters and not ISIS leaders, which would (in her view) not arise to a sufficient level of gravity.[25] However, it can be argued that this decision was flawed, and that the ICC Office of the Prosecutor (OTP) should reconsider opening a preliminary examination

[20] See ch 6, s II.B of this book.
[21] ibid.
[22] Rome Statute art 13.
[23] ibid art 12.
[24] See ch 6, s II.B.i of this book.
[25] 'Statement of the Prosecutor of the International Criminal Court, Fatou Bensouda, on the alleged crimes committed by ISIS' (ICC, 8 April 2015) www.icc-cpi.int/news/statement-prosecutor-international-criminal-court-fatou-bensouda-alleged-crimes-committed-isis.

into ISIS crimes.[26] Concerning the case example, the acts in question were allegedly perpetrated by the ISIS Beatles, a group of militants who were known to be particularly brutal and harsher than other ISIS guards, allegedly torturing hostages with electroshock weapons and subjecting them to mock executions, crucifixions, and waterboarding (amongst other heinous acts).[27] According to US authorities, the group also beheaded 27 hostages including Foley, and it was common practice for videos of the murders to be shared online like in the present case.[28] Members of the group who were later prosecuted in the United States, Alexanda Kotey and El Shafee Elsheikh, were known to hold leadership positions within ISIS.[29] Thus, while the Prosecutor did not refer to the ISIS Beatles specifically in her statement, given their notoriety and cruelty, it is unclear why they would not be considered as some of those 'most responsible' for ISIS crimes.[30]

In the event that this situation was referred to the ICC by a State Party or a preliminary examination was opened by the Prosecutor, there would need to be either territorial or personal jurisdiction as required by Article 12. Concerning territorial jurisdiction, in this case example, the execution was alleged to have taken place in Raqqa, Syria.[31] The footage of the execution was posted to an official ISIS account, presumably by those who filmed it, although this cannot be confirmed without details about the IP address of the uploading device (which as explained in chapter six, can be faked or hidden) or through other methods such as witness testimony or a confession.[32] It is therefore unknown where exactly the video was uploaded, and whether this occurred on State Party territory. If, however, it is assumed that the footage was shared online by alleged perpetrators in Syria, and the 'conduct' element is understood as taking place at the location of the perpetrator,[33] the ICC would not have jurisdiction on the basis of territory because Syria is not a party to the Rome Statute.

The digital harms associated with this scenario consist of those experienced by the direct victim, his family and friends, and potentially anyone who comes across

[26] For an explanation of critiques of the Prosecutor's decision, see ch 6, s II.B.i.

[27] A Mitchell, 'ISIS "Waterboarded" James Foley: Sources' (NBC News, 29 August 2014) www.nbcnews.com/storyline/james-foley/isis-waterboarded-james-foley-sources-n191876; 'Who were the jihadists nicknamed the Islamic State 'Beatles'?' (BBC News, 11 August 2022) www.bbc.co.uk/news/world-middle-east-42993715.

[28] ibid.

[29] The Associated Press, 'A Man Pleads Guilty in Islamic State Beheadings of US Hostages' (NPR, 2 September 2021) www.npr.org/2021/09/02/1033841860/islamic-state-james-foley-beheadings-guilty-plea-alexanda-kotey; 'US v Kotey, et al.' (The Investigative Project on Terrorism) www.investigativeproject.org/case/1125/us-v-kotey-et-al.

[30] The seriousness of the harm inflicted by the perpetrators in the present case study will be considered in detail in s II.C. Further, although Prosecutor Bensouda stated that it was the 'scope of the OTP's policy' to 'focus on those most responsible for mass crimes', this is notably not a formal test under the Rome Statute.

[31] Although the video has since been verified by domestic authorities, if this case were to appear as new before an ICCT, the footage and perpetrators would not have been confirmed yet. The language of this case study is intended to reflect the degree of certainty the Court would have at the relevant stages.

[32] See ch 6, s III.A of this book.

[33] See discussion of the 'conduct' element regarding territorial jurisdiction in ch 6, s II.B of this book.

such violent content online (as has been described in previous chapters in relation to sharing footage of crimes).[34] This has implications for the assessment of jurisdiction because the place the harm manifested may differ depending on who are considered the victims. If territorial jurisdiction is assessed not through the location of the alleged perpetrators where the content was filmed and uploaded but in line with the principle of ubiquity (ie the location of its effects), multiple locations could be considered. First, the harm to Foley himself (which will be elaborated upon in a later section but can be summarised as the degrading treatment and assault on dignity of knowing his murder was filmed and would be shared) took place in Syria where the physical crime occurred. In this respect, territorial jurisdiction at the ICC could not be established as the conduct occurred on non-State Party territory. However, applying this principle to the harm experienced by Foley's loved ones, the 'conduct' may be considered as having occurred where the video was viewed. As Foley's family is based in the United States, which is also not a State Party to the Rome Statute, the ICC would still not have jurisdiction on the basis of territory unless the content was viewed on State Party territory.

A third category of potential victims in this example are those who may have accidentally come across the video online, which is extremely graphic and could lead to secondary trauma.[35] This was reported on by BBC News in 2014 shortly after the video went viral, where experts who were interviewed warned that those who 'find [the video] popping up unexpectedly in their Twitter or Facebook feeds' would be at 'more risk of harm'.[36] This is because although psychological effects of viewing graphic content are well-documented in professionals such as security forces and journalists,[37] individuals who are not prepared to see such content and have no experience dealing with it can make them even more vulnerable.[38] It is therefore possible that those who stumbled across the video online were harmed, potentially large numbers and in a way that would give rise to the required harm elements of the crimes to be discussed in section II.B (such as other inhumane acts).[39] If this harm occurred on State Party territory (for example, a person browsing the internet in the United Kingdom), there could theoretically be territorial jurisdiction for the ICC.[40]

Under the ICC framework, the alternative under Article 12 (in addition to a UNSC referral or an ad-hoc acceptance of jurisdiction by a non-State Party) would be to establish jurisdiction using the nationality of the perpetrator(s). In this case, the ISIS Beatles were known to be of British nationality, and the United Kingdom is a State Party to the Rome Statute. As mentioned above, this approach would be

[34] See ch 4 of this book.

[35] See ch 4, ss III and IV of this book.

[36] S Mundasad, 'Experts warn of trauma after watching Foley death video' (BBC News, 21 August 2014) www.bbc.co.uk/news/health-28878602.

[37] ibid.

[38] ibid. These points will also be discussed further in the following section in reference to gravity.

[39] See s II.B of this chapter.

[40] Of course, this scenario would also need to meet additional admissibility criteria, including being considered of sufficient gravity, to be considered a crime that may be prosecuted before the ICC.

inconsistent with the former Prosecutor's approach to ISIS cases in 2015, as she determined there would be too narrow a basis for jurisdiction because the Court would only have jurisdiction over foreign fighters with State Party nationalities.[41] However, as noted in chapter six, this argument does not mean that the Court does not have jurisdiction, and gravity or the ability to punish those 'most responsible' arguably should have been assessed at a later point of the case.[42] Should this approach be overturned by the current or a future ICC Prosecutor in favour of the contrary argument that the Court does not only need to have jurisdiction over those highest in command to proceed with a case, the ICC would have jurisdiction over the alleged crimes (provided the other elements of jurisdiction and admissibility are met).

B. Applicable Crimes

This section will consider the applicable crimes to the case example, including war crimes and crimes against humanity. At the ICC, perpetrators may be held criminally responsible for crimes within the Court's jurisdiction for acts committed as individuals or jointly with or through another person.[43] In addition, those acting as military commanders may be responsible for crimes committed by their subordinates where they (a) knew or should have known that the forces were committing such crimes and (b) failed to take all necessary actions within their power to prevent the commission of those crimes.[44] As this case study focuses on the digital harm of filming and posting footage of the execution online, the potential perpetrators could therefore include the militant depicted in the footage, the person(s) filming, those who uploaded the content to the internet, and any individual who may have ordered the acts to take place.

i. War Crimes

The perpetrators who filmed and shared footage of Foley's beheading online could be liable for the war crimes of outrages upon personal dignity and torture or inhuman treatment. The elements of each of these crimes will be considered in detail, but it is first necessary to establish the connection to an armed conflict. As at the time of the video and its sharing, ISIS (a non-State group) was engaged in long-standing conflicts with Iraq and Syria, this conflict may be classified as a non-international armed conflict (NIAC).[45] NIACs require a certain level of

[41] ICC (n 25).
[42] See ch 6, s II.B of this book.
[43] Rome Statute art 25(3).
[44] ibid art 28(1)(a).
[45] Multiple UNSC Resolutions on the conflicts between ISIS and Syria and ISIS and Iraq have condemned the group for alleged violations of IHL and war crimes. Although none of the resolutions explicitly state that these are NIACs, the assertion that the non-State armed group has committed

intensity and a degree of organisation of the parties to be classified as armed conflicts as opposed to internal disturbances.[46] The serious and protracted hostilities between ISIS and the States of Iraq and Syria, and the clear command structure within ISIS, contribute to why the conflicts are widely accepted as being classified as NIACs.[47] It can therefore be said that the necessary link to an armed conflict for individuals to be liable for war crimes under Article 8 exists.

a. Outrages Upon Personal Dignity

As described in chapter four, the harm of sharing footage of crimes online can be considered an outrage upon personal dignity, and has been prosecuted as such in domestic war crimes trials.[48] Under the Rome Statute, in relation to NIACs, 'committing outrages upon personal dignity, in particular humiliating and degrading treatment' is prohibited by Article 8(2)(c)(ii).[49] As provided in the Elements of Crimes, to constitute the actus reus of the offence, in addition to the conduct taking place in the context of a NIAC, the perpetrator must 'humiliate, degrade, or otherwise violate the dignity of one or more persons' and the 'severity of the humiliation, degradation or other violation' must be of 'such a degree as to be generally recognized as an outrage upon personal dignity'.[50] Additionally, the person(s) must be either hors de combat or a civilian taking no active part in the hostilities.[51] Further, it is provided that 'persons' can also include dead persons, and that the victim 'need not be personally aware of the existence of the humiliation or degradation or other violation'.[52] As for the mens rea, in addition to the requirements of the material elements being committed with intent and knowledge in accordance with Article 30, the perpetrator must be aware of the factual circumstances that established (1) the victim's status as hors de combat or a civilian and (2) the existence of an armed conflict.[53]

In this example, as will also be elaborated upon in relation to gravity in section II.C,[54] it is likely that filming and publishing a video online of a man in which he

violations of IHL implies an existence of a conflict that would be governed by IHL, and that the group had capacity to comply with the law. See for example UNSC Res 2170 (15 August 2014) UN Doc S /RES/2170; UNSC Res 2249 (20 November 2015) UN Doc S/RES/2249; UNSC Res 2331 (20 December 2016) UN Doc S/RES/2331. The distinction between an IAC and a NIAC stems from Common Articles 2 and 3 of the Geneva Conventions; A Haque, 'Whose Armed Conflict? Which Law of Armed Conflict?' (2017) 45 *Georgia Journal of International and Comparative Law* 475–93.

[46] ibid; Eurojust, 'Cumulative Prosecution of Foreign Terrorist Fighters for Core International Crimes and Terrorism-Related Offences' (May 2020) www.eurojust.europa.eu/sites/default/files/Partners /Genocide/2020-05_Report-on-cumulative-prosecution-of-FTFs_EN.PDF, 8.

[47] Eurojust, ibid 8–10. See also N Zamir, 'The Armed Conflict(s) Against the Islamic State' (2015) 18 *Yearbook of International Humanitarian Law* 91–121, 105.

[48] See ch 4, ss III.C and IV.C of this book.

[49] Rome Statute art 8(2)(c)(ii).

[50] Rome Statute Elements of Crimes arts 8(2)(c)(ii)(1), (2) and (5).

[51] ibid art 8(2)(c)(ii)(3).

[52] ibid art 8(2)(c)(ii)(1) fn 57.

[53] Rome Statute art 30(1); Elements of Crimes arts 8(2)(c)(ii)(4) and (6).

[54] See section II.C of this chapter.

knows he is being recorded, forcing him to address his family while kneeling on the ground, and then decapitating him and positioning the body in a humiliating position with the bloodied head on the corpse is humiliating and degrading enough to be generally recognised as an outrage upon his personal dignity.[55] This same logic was applied by domestic courts such as in The Netherlands, Finland, and Germany, as mentioned in chapter four.[56] Further, Foley was a well-known American journalist (ie a civilian) covering hostilities in the region, which is why he was captured by ISIS in the first place. It is therefore also clear that those who filmed, committed, and shared his execution were aware of the broader context and of Foley's status as a non-combatant.

In terms of the intent and knowledge to commit the outrage upon personal dignity, the fact that the video was posted to official ISIS channels demonstrates the perpetrators' desire to share the footage to a wide audience, knowing it would also be picked up by international media. Additionally, the fact that such a grotesque method of execution was chosen and that afterwards the body was deliberately manipulated with the head on the back suggests that the perpetrators wanted to degrade the victim and demonstrate their power over him. Although the victim was aware of the existence of the camera and therefore likely the humiliation and degradation, it is also not necessary for him to have known about the manipulation of his body after his death to suffer a violation of his dignity.[57]

Given that this example of digital harm is mainly characterised by its dehumanising nature, and that case law already exists where domestic courts have successfully prosecuted individuals for the same offence,[58] the crime of outrages upon personal dignity is likely the best to accommodate the digital element of the situation. Also, in line with the principle of fair labelling and the expressivist theory of criminalisation explained in chapter five, it is important that the name of the offence reflect the nature of the harm associated with the crime.[59] There is therefore a strong case for prosecuting the offence of outrages upon personal dignity in this case scenario and situations like it where footage of crimes with a nexus to armed conflict are deliberately shared on social media.

[55] As noted in ch 4, the humiliation and degradation that comes from crimes being made public or being shared online has been recognised in both international and domestic case law.

[56] For example, in The Netherlands, a Hague Court found that an accused committed an outrage upon personal dignity when he shared a photo of himself posing with a body to Facebook. In its assessment of whether this act constituted what would generally be considered an outrage upon personal dignity, the Court stated that by posting the photo to social media, 'the suspect ensured that a large number of people were given the opportunity to take note of the photo', and that 'the fact that he posed for the photo himself and had it taken … further continued the assault on the personal dignity of the deceased person'. ECLI:NL:GHDHA:2021:103, translated from Dutch.

[57] Rome Statute Elements of Crimes art 8(2)(c)(ii)(1) fn 57: the victim 'need not be personally aware of the existence of the humiliation or degradation or other violation'.

[58] Eurojust, 'Prosecuting war crimes of outrage upon personal dignity based on evidence from open sources - Legal framework and recent developments in the Member States of the European Union' (2018) www.eurojust.europa.eu/sites/default/files/Partners/Genocide/2018-02_Prosecuting-war-crimes-based-on-evidence-from-open-sources_EN.pdf.

[59] See ch 5, ss II.C and III.A of this book.

b. Torture and Cruel Treatment

The digital component of this case example could also constitute the war crimes of torture and cruel treatment prohibited by Article 8(2)(c)(i) in relation to a NIAC, potentially both to the victim and his family. First, in addition to the required nexus to armed conflict and the fact that the victims are not taking part in hostilities, the actus reus of torture is that the perpetrator must inflict 'severe physical or mental pain or suffering' for 'such purposes as: obtaining information or a confession, punishment, intimidation or coercion or for any reason based on discrimination of any kind'.[60] For the mens rea, in addition to intent and knowledge, the perpetrator must be aware of the factual circumstances establishing the armed conflict and the victim's status as a civilian or hors de combat.[61] The crime of cruel treatment requires the same elements except for the need for a specific purpose.[62]

Concerning the victim himself, filming and sharing a video of his beheading would constitute cruel treatment, because as described previously, recording the execution is a particularly cruel act. Knowing that one is being filmed in an extremely vulnerable state and that the video will likely be shared to their family and friends is arguably a form of 'severe mental suffering' as required for both cruel treatment and torture. This is in line with case law discussed in chapter three,[63] for example *Furundžija*, where the International Criminal Tribunal for the former Yugoslavia (ICTY) Trial Chamber found that 'among the possible purposes of torture one must also include that of humiliating the victim'.[64] The humiliation that accompanies one's gruesome last moments being filmed and having to address one's family and friends under duress can be considered as a serious form of psychological suffering, as severe public humiliation has been found to cause grave mental health effects (including those which result in suicide or homicide).[65] The degradation in this case can also be considered even more de-humanising due to the fact that Foley is seemingly used as a means to an end by ISIS to send a message to President Obama. The use of a human being as a 'tool' implies that they are not worthy of dignity and respect, which can also arguably amount to serious mental suffering to constitute torture or cruel treatment. This was alluded to by the ICTY Trial Chamber in *Aleksovski*, which noted that the use of detainees as human shields or trench-diggers constituted 'particularly degrading or humiliating treatment' as they were used as means to an end and helplessly placed in a 'situation of

[60] Rome Statute Elements of Crimes arts 8(2)(c)(i)-4(1), (2), (3), and (5).

[61] ibid arts 8(2)(c)(i)-4(4) and (6).

[62] ibid art 8(2)(c)(i)-3.

[63] See ch 3, s II.B.i of this book.

[64] *Prosecutor v Furundžija* (Judgment) IT-95-17/1-T, Trial Chamber (10 December 1998) ('*Furundžija* Trial Judgment') [162].

[65] WJ Torres and RM Bergner, 'Severe Public Humiliation: Its Nature, Consequences, and Clinical Treatment' (2012) 49 *Psychotherapy* 492–501. See also D Shultziner and I Rabinovici, 'Human Dignity, Self-Worth, and Humiliation: A Comparative Legal–Psychological Approach' (2012) 18 *Psychology, Public Policy, and Law* 105–43.

inferiority'.[66] The scenario in the present case example is similar, as the victim is reduced to a tool to spread the perpetrators' political message, having no choice but to read from the script and knowing his violent death will be publicly shared.

Also, as established above, it is evident that the perpetrators must have known Foley's status as a civilian journalist and were aware of the armed conflict between ISIS and Syria and Iraq. The requirements for the act to constitute the crime of cruel treatment would therefore be met. Regarding the purpose requirement for torture as a war crime under Article 8, it could be inferred from the dialogue of the video that the recording and distribution of the video was intended to both punish Foley for the actions of the US government (Foley states, 'I call on my friends, family and loved ones to rise up against my real killers, the US government, for what will happen to me is only a result of their complacency and criminality') and to coerce the government to meet ISIS' demands (the militant addresses President Obama, stating that the life of the next American depicted in the video 'depends on your next decision').[67] The requirements for torture are thus likely be met concerning Foley as a victim.

In addition, the perpetrators could potentially be liable for cruel treatment and torture in reference to Foley's family. This is because, as described above and in chapter three, being forced to watch crimes being committed against a loved one has been found to constitute the 'severe mental suffering' requirement in ICL jurisprudence.[68] The elements analysed in the preceding paragraphs apply similarly to Foley's family as victims, although two elements may differ. First, it could be argued that the victim's family were not forced to view the footage, as they viewed it on their own devices at home. However, given that the video went 'viral' and was widely shared on social media platforms and covered by the mainstream media, it could be argued that the family seeing the video would be reasonably foreseeable, and that the perpetrators would have to have either intended for this or were indifferent, negligent, or reckless as to the consequences. The perpetrators uploaded the video online with the knowledge that doing so would allow it to be viewed by a virtually infinite audience, that people would be forced to hear about it, and did so with the intent to spread their message and instil fear in Americans, including

[66] *Prosecutor v Aleksovski* (Judgment) IT-95-14/1, Trial Chamber (25 June 1999) ('*Aleksovski* Trial Judgment) [227]–[229].

[67] BBC News (n 7). It has been recognised in jurisprudence from ICCTs that intent for crimes can be inferred. For example, in *Kayishema and Ruzindana*, the ICTR Appeals Chamber, affirming the findings of the Trial Chamber, noted that 'explicit manifestations of criminal intent are, for obvious reasons, often rare in the context of criminal trials. In order to prevent perpetrators from escaping convictions simply because such manifestations are absent, the requisite intent may normally be inferred from relevant facts and circumstances'; *Prosecutor v Kayishema and Ruzindana* (Judgment) ICTR-95-1-A, Appeals Chamber (1 June 2001) [159].

[68] *Furundžija* Trial Judgment (n 64) [162]; *Prosecutor v Fofana and Kondewa* (Judgment) SCSL-04-14-T, Trial Chamber I (2 August 2007) ('*Fofana and Kondewa* Trial Judgment') [153]; see also ch 3, s II of this book.

Foley's family. Therefore, the perpetrators could also be liable for the war crimes of cruel treatment and torture in relation to the victim's family.

ii. Crimes Against Humanity

The perpetrators could also be liable for the crimes against humanity of torture and other inhumane acts for the digital harms of this case as prohibited by Article 7 of the Rome Statute. First, the contextual elements must again be established. Crimes against humanity must be committed as part of a widespread or systematic attack against a civilian population.[69] 'Widespread' refers to the 'large-scale nature of the attack and the number of victims', whereas 'systematic' refers to 'the organised nature of the acts of violence and the improbability of their random occurrence'.[70] Further, an 'attack against the civilian population' refers to 'a course of conduct involving the multiple commission of acts referred to in article 7, paragraph 1, of the Statute against any civilian population, pursuant to or in furtherance of a State or organizational policy to commit such attack'.[71] It is also provided in the Elements of Crimes, Article 7(3) that the act 'need not constitute a military attack', and that a 'policy to commit such attack' requires that 'the State or organization actively promote or encourage such an attack against the civilian population'.[72]

The crimes committed in this case study were perpetrated in the context of arguably both a widespread and a systematic attack against the civilian population. This is because the attacks perpetrated by ISIS (which this particular crime against Foley was a part of) have a large scale in terms of geographical reach, as the group was involved with multiple conflicts across different States, and the number of victims is high – the group has claimed responsibility for deadly attacks in nearly 20 countries, as reported by Human Rights Watch,[73] and allegedly killed over 25,000 Iraqi civilians alone from 2014–2016.[74] The attacks were also systematic given their patterned nature, as the group regularly employs certain methods (including beheading videos) to gain power and spread their message.[75] In addition, there could be said to be an 'attack against the civilian population', as ISIS routinely committed crimes against civilians in Syria and Iraq in furtherance of spreading their ideology. Therefore, the contextual elements for crimes against humanity are likely met.

[69] Rome Statute art 7.

[70] *Prosecutor v Nahimana, Barayagwiza and Ngeze* (Judgment) ICTR-99-52-A, Appeals Chamber (28 November 2007) ('*Nahimana et al* Appeal Judgment') [920]; *Prosecutor v Kordić and Čerkez* (Judgment) IT-95-14/2-A, Appeals Chamber (17 December 2004) [94]; *Prosecutor v Blaškic* (Judgment) IT-95-14-A, Appeals Chamber (29 July 2004) ('*Blaškic* Appeal Judgment') [101]; *Prosecutor v Kunarac et al* (Judgment) IT-96-23-7 & IT-96-23/1-A, Appeals Chamber (12 June 2002) [94].

[71] Rome Statute Elements of Crimes art 7(3).

[72] ibid.

[73] 'ISIS' (Human Rights Watch) www.hrw.org/tag/isis.

[74] 'Database' (Iraq Body Count) www.iraqbodycount.org/database/.

[75] See for example Friis (n 4); A Koch, 'Jihadi Beheading Videos and their Non-Jihadi Echoes' (2018) 12 *Perspectives on Terrorism* 24–34.

a. Torture

The alleged perpetrators could be liable for the crime against humanity of torture for filming and sharing the beheading video online. The analysis is similar to that of the war crime of torture and cruel treatment considered above because some of the elements are the same,[76] and therefore will not be repeated in full in this section. However, for torture as a crime against humanity, in addition to the contextual elements, there are two different requirements: (1) that the severe physical or mental pain or suffering was inflicted upon persons 'in the custody or under the control of the perpetrator' and (2) that the 'pain or suffering did not arise only from, and was not inherent in or incidental to, lawful sanctions'.[77]

Concerning the second requirement, there is no evidence to suggest that this case example involved lawful sanctions, as a civilian journalist was detained and killed by non-State armed militants. Yet, the first requirement in relation to custody is relevant to consider because the crime against humanity of torture may not be applicable to Foley's family, in contrast to the war crime of torture analysed above. The Rome Statute and the Elements of Crimes do not provide that perpetrators of torture need to be public or State officials acting in their official capacity, unlike what was determined in some earlier rulings at the *ad-hoc* tribunals,[78] however the victims do need to be in the custody of or under the control of the perpetrator. From the video itself where Foley is kneeling next to an armed militant who is holding onto him, and the context that Foley had been imprisoned by ISIS for years prior to his murder, Foley was under the control of the direct perpetrators because he was obviously not free to leave.[79] However, since his family viewed the footage from their home in the United States and were not under the control of ISIS, it would not be possible to consider them victims of the crime against humanity of torture in this case. In this sense, the war crime of torture would have a broader applicability in terms of who could legally be considered victims. This also signifies that the custodial provision for torture was arguably not developed

[76] As with the war crime of torture, the perpetrator must inflict 'severe physical or mental pain or suffering upon one or more persons', and must do so with knowledge and intent; Rome Statute art 30; Elements of Crimes art 7(1)(f)(1). Unlike the war crime of torture, no specific purpose requirement exists for the crime against humanity of torture; Rome Statute Elements of Crimes art 7(1)(f) fn 14.

[77] Rome Statute Elements of Crimes art 7(1)(f)(2).

[78] For example, in early decisions of the ICTY, it was held that at least one of the perpetrators of torture needed to be a public official or someone acting not in a private capacity, based on the inclusion of such a criterion in the Torture Convention; see *Prosecutor v Delalić et al* (Judgment) IT-96-21-T, Trial Chamber (16 November 1998) ('Delalić et al Trial Judgment') [494]–[496], *Furundžija* Trial Judgment (n 64) [162]; *Prosecutor v Furundžija* (Judgment) IT-95-17/1-A, Appeals Chamber (21 July 2000) [111]; *Prosecutor v Akayesu* (Judgment) ICTR-96-4-T, Trial Chamber I (2 September 1998) ('Akayesu Trial Judgment') [593]–[595], [681]. However, in *Kvočka*, the Trial Chamber found that 'the state actor requirement imposed by international human rights law is inconsistent with the application of individual criminal responsibility for international crimes found in international humanitarian law and international criminal law'; *Prosecutor v Kvočka et al* (Judgment) IT-98-30/1-T, Trial Chamber (2 November 2001) ('*Kvočka et al* Trial Judgment') [139]; W Schabas, *The International Criminal Court: A Commentary on the Rome Statute* (2nd edn, OUP, 2016) 183.

[79] BBC News (n 7).

with digital harms in mind, as although Foley's family viewing the content seems to meet other elements required for the offence, this type of digital harm will fail to meet the criteria for the crime against humanity of torture unless the provision is removed or deemed inapplicable to digital harms. In this instance where war crimes may be considered due to the existence of an NIAC, this may not be so much of an issue, but the present framework leaves a gap of this type of digital harm that will not be able to be charged as torture as a crime against humanity if there is no nexus to a conflict.

In addition to the actus reus of the crime against humanity of torture described above, the perpetrators must have the mental element required by Article 30 (which was considered in the previous section and thus will not be analysed again in this section) and the knowledge that the conduct was part of or intended to be part of the widespread or systematic attack directed against a civilian population.[80] Given that the members of ISIS identified in relation to Foley's killing were members of the notorious 'Beatles', who regularly captured, tortured, and murdered civilians, journalists, and aid workers,[81] it could be argued that they were aware of their conduct being a part of both a widespread and systematic attack against the civilian population, as was established in the first part of this section.

b. Other Inhumane Acts

Another crime against humanity the alleged perpetrators could be liable for is other inhumane acts, which is prohibited by Article 7(1)(k).[82] To commit the crime of other inhumane acts, the alleged perpetrator must inflict 'great suffering, or serious injury to body or mental or physical health, by means of an inhumane act' and such act must be of 'a character similar to any other act referred to in article 7, paragraph 1, of the Statute'.[83] The mental element is nearly the same as for the crime against humanity of torture, as in addition to the intent to cause other inhumane acts, the perpetrator must be aware of the factual circumstances that established the character of the act and have known that the act would be part of a widespread or systematic attack against the civilian population.[84]

As described in the previous section and for the war crimes of torture and cruel treatment, filming and sharing the execution video can cause great suffering or serious injury to mental health (both to the victim and his family) and is undoubtedly an inhumane act. Further, given that the act could potentially constitute torture (but for the lack of a custodial situation), it is similar in nature to another crime against humanity. For the reasons mentioned above as well, it is also clear that the perpetrators were aware of the circumstances of their acts and that sharing the footage would be part of their widespread and systematic attack on the civilian

[80] Rome Statute Elements of Crimes art 7(1)(f)(5).
[81] BBC News (n 27).
[82] Rome Statute art 7(1)(k).
[83] Rome Statute Elements of Crimes arts 7(1)(k)(1) and (2).
[84] ibid arts 7(1)(k)(3), (4), and (5).

population. Unlike with the crime against humanity of torture, the crime of other inhumane acts does not require that the victims be in the custody or under the control of the perpetrator, meaning that it could also be applicable in this situation to the victim's family – the analysis of which would be virtually the same for the 'severe mental suffering' considered in relation to torture in section II.B.i.[85]

C. Gravity

This section will consider the gravity of the digital harms pertaining to the case example, namely filming the execution and sharing the footage online. As explained in chapter six, the gravity of an offence may be assessed in terms of various elements, including its scale, nature, manner of commission, and impact.[86] The seriousness of the harm inflicted through filming and sharing the degrading beheading video online in this case is similar to what was discussed in chapters two, three, and four, in relation to posting footage of crimes online – its gravity is most serious in terms of the nature and impact of the acts, as the core harms are the severe humiliation of the victim and the traumatic effects experienced by his family. Concerning the harm to the direct victim (Foley), before the execution takes place, he is aware that he is being filmed and that the video will be shared, as he is forced to speak to the camera to his 'friends, family, and loved ones'.[87] The knowledge that a victim is being filmed can exacerbate the harm of criminal offences because it brings about a sense of helplessness and loss of control, as the individual knows the footage will likely be shared and that they cannot stop its dissemination.[88] In the video, the camera zooms in clearly showing his face, he is wearing an orange jumpsuit like one typically worn by prisoners, and is kneeling on the ground while being held by the militant beside him, all which contribute to a further sense of humiliation. The mental suffering that Foley likely endured knowing that he would be seen in this state by his parents, siblings, friends, and colleagues is unconscionable.[89] In addition to the knowledge that his murder would be shown to his loved ones and cause them pain, Foley was further degraded by being forced to participate in the performance and read a from a script.[90] This level of psychological harm would likely be grave enough to satisfy the harm requirement for the relevant international crimes, including torture ('severe mental suffering'), outrages upon personal

[85] See section II.B.i of this chapter.

[86] See ch 6, s II.A of this book; Office of the Prosecutor, Policy Paper on Case Selection and Prioritization (September 2016).

[87] BBC News (n 7).

[88] S Sandberg and T Ugelvik, 'Why Do Offenders Tape Their Crimes? Crime and Punishment in the Age of the Selfie' (2017) 57 *British Journal of Criminology* 1023–40. 1030; see also A Dodge, 'Digitizing Rape Culture: Online Sexual Violence and the Power of the Digital Photograph' (2016) 12 *Crime, Media, Culture* 65–82.

[89] Friis (n 4) 729.

[90] SM Friis, '"Behead, Burn, Crucify, Crush": Theorizing the Islamic State's Public Displays of Violence' (2017) 24 *European Journal of International Relations* 243–67.

dignity ('humiliation, degradation or otherwise violated the dignity'), and other inhumane acts ('great suffering to mental or physical health').[91]

Following his execution, Foley's body is positioned on the ground with the head on top of the back, showing that his killers deliberately manipulated the corpse in a degrading manner. This further violates the dignity of the victim and demonstrates an additional layer of heinousness, as the killers treated the body as a prop in their propaganda video, not to be remembered as a human being but as part of a violent spectacle. The digital component in this instance greatly exacerbates the harm because unlike, for example, a printed photo on a flyer in a public square available in a finite quantity that could be taken down and discarded, the images of the victim's desecrated corpse can never be completely erased from the internet. The harm incurred after Foley's death therefore also contributes to the gravity of the offence, and can constitute a 'violation of dignity' as provided in the elements of outrages upon personal dignity, which also apply to deceased persons.[92]

The gravity of this case is also reflected by the impact on Foley's family and friends, particularly his parents, who have been outspoken about the immeasurable mental harm their son's murder and the video of it has caused them.[93] For instance, Foley's mother, Diane Foley, has described how she heard about her son's beheading after the video started to go viral online, and that a journalist called her during her afternoon coffee mentioning what they had seen on Twitter (now X). Confused, Ms Foley opened her laptop and began to look on Twitter, and shortly after, without warning, saw her son with his 'bloodied head upon his back'.[94] In an article in *The Telegraph*, Ms. Foley wrote, 'The ache inside cannot be described except by its own pain. I was sundered, torn apart', and later,

> I heard his name everywhere. I never watched the video of the beheading and I never will. The static image was more than enough. It had burned itself into my brain. There are so many times I wish I hadn't seen it.[95]

The gravity of this harm can be analogised to what has previously constituted torture in ICL jurisprudence, as considered in chapter three.[96] As previously mentioned, the *Furundžija* case at the ICTY and the *Fofana and Kondewa* case at the Special Court for Sierra Leone (SCSL) found that witnessing crimes committed against

[91] Rome Statute Elements of Crimes art 7(1)(f) torture, 8(2)(c)(i) torture and cruel treatment, 8(2)(c)(ii) outrages upon personal dignity, and 7(1)(k) other inhumane acts.

[92] ibid art 8(2)(c)(ii) fn 57.

[93] E Brockes, '"We all lost. That's where hatred leads": 10 years after her son was beheaded, Diane Foley on why she met one of his killers' (*The Guardian*, 10 February 2024) www.theguardian.com/global/2024/feb/10/diane-foley-mother-james-foley-beheaded-islamic-state-interview; C McCann and D Foley, *American Mother* (Etruscan Press, 2024).

[94] D Foley, 'I turned on social media and there was my son with his bloodied head upon his back' (*The Telegraph*, 1 February 2024) www.telegraph.co.uk/family/life/diane-foley-james-isis-jihadists-hostage-obama-government/.

[95] ibid.

[96] See ch 3, s II.B.i of this book.

others (even with less of a personal connection than being family members) could constitute the level of severe mental suffering required for torture.[97] In this case, the fact that the execution was viewed through a screen does not reduce the gravity of the situation, especially given the grotesque method of the murder and the viewers' personal connections to the victim depicted, as was considered in chapter four.[98]

Aside from the trauma incurred through watching the footage, Foley's loved ones have also been harmed by the fact that the nature of his execution has taken over his memory in the public eye. Given that Foley's murder was carried out in such a grotesque way that was filmed and shared online, and reported on in mainstream news, this tends to 'overshadow everything else about him'.[99] In this sense, sharing footage of an execution further dehumanises the victim, as they will be remembered not for the life they led (in Foley's case, the life of an esteemed journalist and human rights advocate) but the horrible way in which they died, and the images of that death will never be fully scrubbed from the internet.

Finally, the impact of the video on the broader population (outside of those who knew Foley personally) also adds to the gravity of the offence in terms of scale. Although the original video was deleted on YouTube within an hour of being uploaded and other platforms attempted to remove it from circulating further on their sites,[100] the video still was viewed by a large number of people, some of which likely stumbled across it by accident, or could have been minors. As considered in chapter four, viewing violent content online can result in vicarious trauma that manifests in many different mental health ailments.[101] Moreover, as noted by Friis, the public display of violence through beheading videos can also serve to provoke more violence and influence the beliefs of a group's enemies in a way that aids their own cause.[102] In this respect, such videos have been described as 'psychological weapons' or 'strategic tools' for terrorist groups,[103] and can inflict the additional harms of inciting violence and/or hatred against certain individuals or groups.

These considerations demonstrate that separate to Foley's actual execution, the harm of filming and sharing the video of the murder matches the harm elements of multiple war crimes and crimes against humanity. Further, this harm is grave enough to be admissible before the ICC, especially in terms of the nature and impact of the digital harm.

[97] *Furundžija* Trial Judgment (n 64) [162]; *Fofana and Kondewa* Trial Judgment (n 68) [153]; see also ch 3, s II.B.i of this book.

[98] See ch 4, ss III and IV of this book; see also A Koenig and A Lampros, *Graphic: Trauma and Meaning in Our Online Lives* (CUP, 2023).

[99] Brockes (n 93).

[100] BBC News (n 7).

[101] See ch 4, s III.C of this book.

[102] Friis (n 4) 729.

[103] ibid 730.

D. Investigating Open Source Content

Another relevant challenge to consider for this case study is the potential obstacles involved with investigating open source content. Although the OTP will of course investigate further than the video and related online content, such as through collecting physical evidence and witness testimony, at least part of the investigation is likely to be focused on digital open source information. As considered in chapter six, a main challenge associated with using digital evidence, particularly that which is open source, is that it can be difficult to authenticate given how easily content can now be difficult to authenticate, manipulated online or faked using generative AI.[104] It would therefore be necessary for investigators to verify that the video in question is real before proceeding further with the investigation and relying upon it as evidence.

The fact that the video was posted to official ISIS channels can help to prove that the video is authentic, but this alone does not mean that the video is what it is purported to be – for instance, those who posted the video could have staged or faked the murder and could have shared it just to spread propaganda or misinformation. Additionally, although this is not a very relevant concern for this case given that the video was created in 2014 when generative AI was not readily available, it is possible in future similar cases that the face and voice of the victim could be 'deepfaked' completely or juxtaposed onto another body. These concerns raise the need to verify the video using techniques commonly used by open source analysts, such as through using contextual clues in the image, geolocation, and chronolocation.[105]

For this particular video, which was filmed in what appears to be a desert with very limited visible landmarks, determining the location and time in which it was filmed (which is important to establish the authenticity of the evidence as explained in chapter six) would be challenging and would require expert analysis.[106] The militant in the video standing next to Foley is also wearing no identifiable uniform with insignia, only a plain all-black ensemble, with only his eyes visible. Moreover, because the video was uploaded to YouTube, any metadata (such as time and location data) that would have accompanied the original video would have been stripped when it was uploaded.[107] It would therefore be

[104] See ch 6, s III.B of this book.

[105] For a detailed explanation of these terms and guidance as to how such investigations can be conducted, see OHCHR and Human Rights Center at the University of California, Berkeley, School of Law, 'Berkeley Protocol on Digital Open Source Investigations: A Practical Guide on the Effective Use of Digital Open Source Information in Investigating Violations of International Criminal, Human Rights and Humanitarian Law' (3 January 2022).

[106] For example, the arrest warrants in the case against Al-Werfalli at the ICC were based on social media videos. These videos were verified by Bellingcat, who were able to determine the time and location they were taken.; Christiaan Triebert, 'Geolocating Libya's Social Media Executioner' (Bellingcat, 4 September 2017) www.bellingcat.com/news/mena/2017/09/04/geolocating-libyas-social-media-exe-.cutioner/. See also ch 6, s III.B of this book.

[107] When photos and videos are uploaded to social media platforms like YouTube, the files are 'ingested' into the ecosystem of the platform and a new file is created, without the original metadata. This is commonly

difficult if not impossible to determine where and when the video was taken based on clues within the video alone. No information is available to the public about how United States authorities verified the footage and found those responsible, but aside from State intelligence sources and surveillance, this likely would require some level of cooperation from the social media platforms that hosted the video, as they would be in possession of the video after it was removed, potentially with its original metadata, and could also assist in determining the identity and location of the uploader. Additionally, ISPs could assist with determining the IP address of the device the content was uploaded from. However, a critical difference between investigations carried out by domestic authorities versus by those at ICCTs is that courts have the power to subpoena companies for the required information. As explained in chapter six, if this case were to be investigated and prosecuted by an ICCT like the ICC, at present, the Court would need to rely on voluntary cooperation either from States to request the necessary information from technology companies or from the companies themselves.

On another note, as the Prosecutor is required to investigate incriminating and exonerating circumstances equally,[108] the OTP should ensure further inquiries based on open source information are conducted in a neutral manner that avoids imposing pre-conceived notions of guilt and potentially 'cherry-picking' other evidence (also known as 'confirmation bias').[109] This risk can arguably be heightened in a case like Foley's, where compelling graphic footage may be uploaded by the group itself, as there can be an inclination (even subconsciously) to jump to conclusions, immediately assuming that the video is authentic and that members of ISIS would be responsible for the crime. In this sense, while having actual footage of an international crime can be very valuable as evidence at an ICCT, it also warrants more attention to ensure that the rights of the accused are fully safeguarded.

More generally, cases based upon digital open source evidence can be particularly difficult for Defence teams, who have significantly less resources than ICCT prosecutors.[110] At the ICC, where Defence teams are externally contracted and do not have the same technologies to sift through mass volumes of digital data, or the same budget to hire experts or train their staff on verifying open source imagery, it is arguably even more critical in a digital age that the OTP fulfil its mandate of

referred to as 'scrubbed' metadata; 'Social Media Stripped My Metadata: A Cleaner Understanding of "Scrubbed" Metadata' (Medex Forensics, 2 January 2024) medexforensics.com/2024/01/02/social-media-stripped-my-metadata-a-cleaner-understanding-of-scrubbed-metadata/.

[108] Rome Statute art 54(1)(a).

[109] This form of cognitive bias can be present in open-source investigations, along with other forms of technical and cognitive biases. See Y McDermott, A Koenig, and D Murray, 'Open Source Information's Blind Spot: Human and Machine Bias in International Criminal Investigations' (2021) 19 *Journal of International Criminal Justice* 85.

[110] For example, as reported in 2016, the legal aid budget for the Defence at the ICC was only 3.25 per cent of the total Court budget; RJ Rogers, 'Assessment of the ICC's Legal Aid System' (5 January 2017) www.icc-cpi.int/sites/default/files/itemsDocuments/legalAidConsultations-LAS-REP-ENG.pdf,[12].

investigating exonerating circumstances equally and sharing this information with the Defence.[111]

In conclusion, this case study demonstrated that sharing footage of international crimes online can meet the definitions of existing offences, and further that victims like James Foley and his family deserve recognition for the additional harm inflicted when such degrading acts are filmed and shared for the world to see. Given that this example of a digital harm is so similar in nature to the harms of certain crimes against humanity and war crimes, ICCT prosecutors can and should follow the lead of domestic courts that have already prosecuted similar conduct and recognise when crimes are maliciously shared online in addition to the offline offence. How this can be done in practice will be considered further in section IV.[112]

III. Case Study 2: Digital Surveillance

The second case study focuses on the digital surveillance methods used by the Chinese government in Xinjiang to suppress the rights of the Uyghur population. While this situation has a broad scope that also includes non-digital harms (such as the alleged arbitrary detention of Uyghurs in internment camps),[113] this case study will only focus on the digital element (the use of digital technologies to heavily monitor the group and what that monitoring facilitates).

In this region, a variety of digital technologies, such as facial recognition software designed to distinguish Uyghur faces and to facilitate tracking of individuals across time and space, QR codes attached to the exterior of homes with information about the residents, wi-fi 'sniffers' used to extract data from electronic devices, and GPS trackers attached to vehicles, are all allegedly used to heavily monitor and suppress the Uyghur population.[114] Individuals have been forced to provide the government with their phone numbers, access to the content of their phones, and their social media accounts for monitoring purposes.[115] Further, having unsanctioned software on one's personal devices, such as VPNs or encrypted messaging platforms like WhatsApp, has been reported as grounds for being detained and

[111] S Zarmsky and J Mionki, 'Defence Perspectives on Digital Evidence: Insights from the ICC' in S Dubberley, A Koenig, D Murray, and Y McDermott (eds), *Digital Witness: Using Open Source Information for Human Rights Investigation, Documentation, and Accountability* (2nd edn, OUP, 2026).

[112] See s IV of this chapter.

[113] A Ramzy and C Buckley, '"Absolutely No Mercy": Leaked Files Expose How China Organized Mass Detentions of Muslims' (The New York Times, 16 November 2019) www.nytimes.com/interactive/2019/11/16/world/asia/china-xinjiang-documents.html; A Killing, M Rajagopalan, and C Buschek, 'Blanked-Out Spots on China's Maps Helped Us Uncover Xinjiang's Camps' (Buzzfeed News, 27 August 2020) www.buzzfeednews.com/article/alison_killing/satellite-images-investigation-xinjiang-detention-camps.

[114] R Khatchadourian, 'Surviving the Crackdown in Xinjiang' (The New Yorker, 12 April 2021) www.newyorker.com/magazine/2021/04/12/surviving-the-crackdown-in-xinjiang.

[115] Amnesty International, '"Like We Were Enemies In A War": China's Mass Internment, Torture and Persecution of Muslims in Xinjiang' (2021) xinjiang.amnesty.org/, 40.

sent to an internment camp.[116] Uyghur individuals have also been allegedly told by government officials not to visit websites related to Islam or other aspects of their Muslim culture, otherwise they risk being sent to the detention camps.[117] It is for these reasons that Amnesty International has described the Muslim population in Xinjiang as 'the most closely surveilled population in the world'.[118]

Further, as evidenced by hundreds of leaked internal Chinese government documents and through investigations by journalists of blanked-out spots found using open-source satellite imagery analysis,[119] the government has engaged in the practice of sending Uyghurs to 're-education' internment camps.[120] Interviews conducted by Amnesty International with those who were detained and subsequently released from these camps revealed that the Uyghurs were subject to inhumane conditions, including inadequate hygiene measures and being unable to contact family, and torture through being sent to 'punishment rooms' where they may be subjected to physical torture and forced to write coerced confessions about exercising their religious practices.[121] The Uyghur population therefore not only faces the constant infringement upon privacy of mass surveillance, but the fear of their surveilled actions resulting in them being identified and taken to an internment camp and tortured, which can reasonably lead to a significant chilling effect on exercising their cultural identities.

Though the broader context is relevant to consider because the fear of physical violence or detention exacerbates the situation, this case study is only concerned with the digital elements, namely the use of technology to surveil the Uyghurs both inside and outside the home, which I argue on its own can constitute international crimes. The nature of the digital harm is twofold – on one hand, there are individual harms associated with the invasive use of technology, as the constant monitoring through remote data collection (such as 'wi-fi sniffers' or cell phone monitoring) and video surveillance (even in intimate areas of targeted homes) is extremely invasive and eradicates one's sense of privacy, which can lead to chilling effects on freedom of expression.[122] On the other hand, the chilling effects this invasive surveillance has upon individuals to exercise their culture results in the collective harm of the loss of the Uyghur culture, which, in line with the view of scholars previously discussed in chapter three such as Arendt and Lederman,[123] is a loss that can also be felt by global society.

[116] ibid.
[117] ibid.
[118] ibid 12.
[119] Ramzy and Buckley (n 113); Killing, Rajagopalan, and Buschek (n 113).
[120] ibid.
[121] Amnesty International (n 115).
[122] For more examples of the technology used against the Uyghur population, see R Asat and Y Diamond, 'The World's Most Technologically Sophisticated Genocide is Happening in Xinjiang' (Foreign Policy, 15 July 2020) foreignpolicy.com/2020/07/15/uighur-genocide-xinjiang-china-surveillance-sterilization/.
[123] H Arendt, *The Promise of Politics* (Schocken Books, 2005); S Lederman, 'A Nation Destroyed: An Existential Approach to the Distinctive Harm of Genocide' (2017) 19 *Journal of Genocide Research* 112–32.

In contrast with the previous case example, this case study will not consider issues with jurisdiction because the digital infrastructure that facilitates the surveillance is physically located in China and carried out by Chinese officials. Consequently, the analysis would not differ from a 'traditional' assessment of jurisdiction (which would not be established for the ICC under Article 12). This case study will therefore begin with an analysis of the applicable crimes. Following this, it will consider how the digital harm in this case may meet the gravity threshold, including whether (a) gravity may be assessed based on individual versus cumulative acts of surveillance, and (b) the digital surveillance on its own can be considered grave enough to be prosecuted as an international crime.

A. Applicable Crimes

This section will consider the crimes that could potentially be applied to the case example, including the crimes against humanity of persecution and apartheid. It is important to note that some scholars and even foreign governments have suggested that the acts against the Uyghurs in Xinjiang amount to genocide, however because these allegations are concerned mainly with non-digital harms (ie forced sterilisation, arbitrary detention, forced assimilation, and physical killings or disappearances), genocide will not be assessed as part of this case study.[124]

i. Persecution

The most relevant crime under the framework of the Rome Statute for this case example is the crime against humanity of persecution under Article 7(1)(h).[125] First, as described in the previous case study, the chapeau elements for crimes against humanity (a widespread or systematic attack against a civilian population) must be met. The persecution in Xinjiang is both widespread, given the use of surveillance

[124] See for example L Maizland, 'China's Repression of Uyghurs in Xinjiang' (Council on Foreign Relations, 22 September 2022) www.cfr.org/backgrounder/china-xinjiang-uyghurs-muslims-repression-genocide-human-rights#chapter-title-0-8; lawmakers in several States including Canada, the United States, and the United Kingdom have declared that China was committing genocide against the Uyghurs: Canada House of Commons, Report of the Standing Committee on Foreign Affairs and International Development, Subcommittee on International Human Rights, 'The Human Rights Situation of Uyghurs in Xinjiang, China' (March 2021); M Pompeo, 'Press Statement: Determination of the Secretary of State on Atrocities in Xinjiang' (US Secretary of State, 19 January 2021) 2017-2021.state.gov/determination-of-the-secretary-of-state-on-atrocities-in-xinjiang/; P Wintour, 'UK MPs declare China is committing genocide against Uyghurs in Xinjiang' (The Guardian, 22 April 2021) www.theguardian.com/world/2021/apr/22/uk-mps-declare-china-is-committing-genocide-against-uyghurs-in-xinjiang. See also M Munsterhjelm, 'Scientists Are Aiding Apartheid in China' (Just Security, 18 June 2019) www.justsecurity.org/64605/scientists-are-aiding-apartheid-in-china/; JS Finley, 'Why Scholars and Activists Increasingly Fear a Uyghur Genocide in Xinjiang' (2021) 23 *Journal of Genocide Research* 348–70.

[125] Rome Statute art 7(1)(h).

across the entire region inhabited by approximately 10 million Uyghurs,[126] and systematic, as the facts mentioned above suggest a clear government policy to employ digital surveillance methods against the Uyghur population.

As provided by the Elements of Crimes, persecution refers to when the perpetrator 'severely deprived, contrary to international law, one or more persons of fundamental rights' and that the perpetrator 'targeted such person or persons by reason of the identity of a group or collectivity or targeted the group or collectivity as such'.[127] Further, the targeting was 'based on political, racial, national, ethnic, cultural, religious, gender, . . . or other grounds that are universally recognized as impermissible under international law'.[128] In the situation of Xinjiang, where Uyghurs are targeted by the Chinese government on the basis of their cultural and religious practices and suppressed into abandoning their identities, these elements of persecution are arguably met. This is because first, as established by the facts in previous sections, the discriminatory acts of surveillance may be considered acts of persecution in line with ICL jurisprudence. As found by the ICTY Trial Chamber in *Kvočka et al.*, a large spectrum of acts may be considered acts of persecution when committed with discriminatory intent, including 'infringement upon individual freedom'.[129] In *Kupreškić et al.*, the Trial Chamber also found that 'restrictions placed on a particular group to curtail their rights to participate in particular aspects of social life (such as visits to public parks, theatres or libraries)' could also amount to acts of persecution if 'weighed for their cumulative effect'.[130] Further, in the recent *Al Hassan* judgment at the ICC, the Trial Chamber found that the discriminatory policies implemented against religions other than the Muslim faith, including the regulation or banning of certain religious practices like celebrating saints or wearing protective amulets, not allowing any sign of another faith to be shown in public, and 'indirectly asking' Christians to 'hide in their homes' contributed to the persecution committed by the accused.[131]

The acts which were classified as acts of persecution in the above cases are similar in nature to those present in the situation in Xinjiang. As argued in an earlier section, the use of surveillance technologies both inside and outside the home, on virtually all personal devices and which affect all areas of life, amount to a gross invasion of privacy and chilling effects on freedom of expression and religion that may be characterised as 'infringements upon individual freedom'. These acts are also discriminatory towards the Uyghur population, as evidenced by leaked policy documents and the stories of those who have witnessed the use of technologies

[126] S Feldstein, 'How Artificial Intelligence and Big Data are Transforming Repression' in S Feldstein, *The Rise of Digital Repression: How Technology is Reshaping Power, Politics, and Resistance* (OUP, 2021) 222.

[127] Rome Statute Elements of Crimes arts 7(1)(h)(1) and (2).

[128] ibid art 7(1)(h)(3).

[129] *Kvočka et al* Trial Judgment (n 78) [186].

[130] *Prosecutor v Kupreškić et al* (Judgement) IT-95-16-T, Trial Chamber (14 January 2000) ('*Kupreškić et al* Trial Judgment') [615].

[131] *Prosecutor v Al Hassan* (Judgment) ICC-01/12-01/18, Trial Chamber X (26 June 2024) [712]–[715].

against Uyghurs and not other groups.[132] The fact that surveillance is justified by alleged interests of national security and counterterrorism by the Chinese government is has essentially the same effect as an explicit policy of banning religious or cultural practices like in the case of *Al Hassan*, as the threat of surveillance at all times prevents Uyghurs from exercising their culture and if caught, they may allegedly face punishments similar to criminal sanctions, including detention.[133] In the case of Xinjiang, it is likely that the acts of surveillance would be considered acts of persecution given their similarities in nature and effects to previous cases.

Second, in terms of the specific fundamental rights infringed upon, while there are numerous rights violated by the overall practice of the Chinese government against the Uyghurs, this section will only consider the rights violated through digital surveillance. These include the right to privacy,[134] the right to freedom of expression,[135] and the right to freedom of thought and religion.[136] Concerning the right to privacy, as mentioned in chapter six, section II.A in reference to gravity,[137] the use of digital surveillance methods on personal devices, inside the home, and in public spaces eradicates all sense of privacy. Further, this invasiveness leads to a 'chilling effect' on the targeted group members' freedom of expression, thought, and religion, as the knowledge that they are being watched forces them to suppress their cultural and religious practices in an effort to conform with the 'accepted' society.[138] Moreover, the reason Uyghurs are targeted is on the basis of their culture and religion – it has been reported that the digital surveillance used by the Chinese government is 'segregated', as it is specifically tailored towards the Uyghur Muslim population and generally ignores the majority Han Chinese, who make up approximately 36 per cent of Xinjiang's population.[139] Additionally, the policing system in Xinjiang, which relies heavily on a platform known as the Integrated Joint

[132] B Allen-Ebrahimian, 'Exposed: China's Operating Manuals for Mass Internment and Arrest by Algorithm' (International Consortium of Investigative Journalists, 24 November 2019) www.icij.org/investigations/china-cables/exposed-chinas-operating-manuals-for-mass-internment-and-ar-rest-by-algorithm/; C Buckley, P Mozur, and A Ramzy, 'How China Turned a City into a Prison' (New York Times, 4 April 2019) www.nytimes.com/interactive/2019/04/04/world/asia/xinjiang-china-surveillance-prison.html; Y Grauer, 'Revealed: Massive Chinese Police Database: Millions of Leaked Police Files Detail Suffocating Surveillance of China's Uyghur Minority' (The Intercept, 29 January 2021) theintercept.com/2021/01/29/china-uyghur-muslim-surveillance-police/; Human Rights Watch, '"Break Their Lineage, Break Their Roots": China's Crimes against Humanity Targeting Uyghurs and Other Turkic Muslims' (April 2021) www.hrw.org/report/2021/04/19/break-their-lineage-break-their-roots/chinas-crimes-against-humanity-targeting; Amnesty International (n 115).

[133] ibid.

[134] The right to privacy and family life is protected by international human rights law, including (but not limited to) Article 12 of the Universal Declaration on Human Rights (UDHR) and Article 17 of the International Covenant on Civil and Political Rights (ICCPR).

[135] The right to freedom of expression is enshrined in Article 19 of the UDHR and the ICCPR.

[136] The right to freedom of thought, conscience, and religion is enshrined in Article 18 of the UDHR and the ICCPR.

[137] See ch 6, s II.A of this book.

[138] See ch 6, s II.A of this book.

[139] C Buckley and P Mozur, 'How China Uses High-Tech Surveillance to Subdue Minorities' (New York Times, 22 May 2019) www.nytimes.com/20 19/05/22/world/asia/chinasurveillance-xinjiang.html.

Operations Platform (IJOP) that collects mass quantities of data, is based upon a grid system that breaks communities into geometric zones so that activities can be observed in a targeted way where Uyghurs reside.[140] Thus, as government officials implemented a policy of digital surveillance aimed at a particular group on the basis of their culture and religion, which in turn deprived them of their fundamental rights, it is possible that these elements of persecution are met.

However, under the Rome Statute, persecution must be committed in connection with another crime within the jurisdiction of the Court.[141] If, theoretically, the ICC did have jurisdiction in Xinjiang, the persecution through digital means could be linked with the crime against humanity of deportation, as Uyghurs have been allegedly forced across the border from other countries,[142] or additionally the crimes of deprivation of liberty and torture for the allegations pertaining to the internment camps.[143]

Concerning the mental element of persecution, in addition to the intent and knowledge to commit the offences as provided by Article 30, the perpetrator(s) must have purposefully targeted the victims on the basis of their group identity, and must have known that the conduct was committed as part of a widespread or systematic attack against a civilian population.[144] As argued earlier in this section, the targeted nature of the surveillance against the Uyghur population demonstrates that Chinese government officials implemented this policy with the intention to monitor and suppress the group, and would likely be aware of the broader context of a widespread or systematic attack against the population. Leaked documents from the Chinese government known as the 'Xinjiang Papers' have also demonstrated a clear intent to persecute the Uyghurs, framing the issue of eradicating their Islamic beliefs as a 'war on terrorism'.[145] Of the 400 pages of documents within the Xinjiang Papers, 161 pages constitute directives and reports on the surveillance of the Uyghur population, which highlights the importance of surveillance methods to the State's overall policy of repressing the Uyghur culture which the State views as 'terrorist' and 'criminal'.[146] For example, President Xi Jinping stated that a 'sweeping campaign of surveillance and intelligence gathering' would be required to 'root out resistance' in Uyghur society, and that 'new technology must be part of that solution' (in combination with traditional methods).[147] Further, in one of the documented speeches in the Xinjiang Papers, Xi Jinping argued that (in reference to Uyghurs) 'there must be effective educational remolding and transformation of

[140] S Feldstein, 'How Artificial Intelligence and Big Data are Transforming Repression' in S Feldstein, *The Rise of Digital Repression: How Technology is Reshaping Power, Politics, and Resistance* (OUP, 2021) 222.

[141] Rome Statute Elements of Crimes art 7(1)(h)(4).

[142] Amnesty International (n 115).

[143] ibid.

[144] Rome Statute Elements of Crimes arts 7(1)(h)(2) and (6).

[145] Ramzy and Buckley (n 113).

[146] ibid.

[147] ibid.

criminals'.[148] Within months of this statement, indoctrination sites began opening in the Xinjiang region that held 'sessions intended to pressure them into disavowing devotion to Islam and professing gratitude for the party'.[149] The clear negative sentiment of the Chinese government against the Uyghur population on the basis of their culture and religion, and the obvious awareness that surveillance methods are used to suppress the group and ultimately may lead to physical detention, both indicate that the mental elements for persecution would also be met for this case study.

ii. Apartheid

Another crime that could be considered for this case study is the crime against humanity of apartheid, which is prohibited by Article 7(1)(j) of the Rome Statute.[150] As the chapeau elements for crimes against humanity were considered in the previous section for persecution, the analysis will not be repeated for this section because it is very similar, as the apartheid would need to be connected to a widespread or systematic attack against a civilian population.

Apartheid refers to when the alleged perpetrator commits an inhumane act against one or more persons in the context of an institutionalised regime of systematic oppression and domination by one racial group over any other racial group.[151] Although it could be debated whether the Uyghur population constitutes a racial group, it has been argued that the definition of race is broader than only genetics or skin colour, and that the evolving definition of 'national, ethnic, racial or religious group' in genocide jurisprudence is relevant when interpreting the crime of apartheid.[152] Lingaas argues that race today, especially in reference to ICL, has evolved to mean the perception of a person's 'racial otherness', which is 'inevitably connected to a notion of prejudice and inferiorisation, by which the perpetrator justifies discriminatory treatment of a racially distinct group'.[153] Some scholars such as Hall and van den Herik take an even wider approach, arguing that the definition of race in ICL should be interpreted as broadly as the categories defined in the crime of persecution.[154] The Uyghur group is a Turkic ethnic group who speak a language written with an Arabic script, and are largely distinct from the majority Han Chinese population in appearance, and are therefore not only a

[148] ibid.
[149] ibid.
[150] Rome Statute art 7(1)(j).
[151] Rome Statute Elements of Crimes arts 7(1)(j)(1) and (4).
[152] C Baldwin, 'Human Rights Watch Responds: Reflections on Apartheid and Persecution in International Law' (Human Rights Watch, 9 July 2021) www.hrw.org/news/2021/07/09/human-rights-watch-responds-reflections-apartheid-and-persecution-international-law.
[153] C Lingaas, *The Concept of Race in International Criminal Law* (Routledge, 2020) 174–75.
[154] C Hall and L van den Herik, 'The Crime of Apartheid' in O Triffterer and K Ambos (eds), *The Rome Statute of the International Criminal Court: A Commentary* (3rd edn, Bloomsbury, 2016) 234.

different group based on their Muslim faith but also with regard to their language and appearance.[155] Thus, the Uyghurs could be said to constitute a different racial group as needed for the definition of apartheid.

Additionally, the Elements of Crimes provide that the 'inhumane act' must constitute either another crime against humanity under Article 7(1) or an act of similar character.[156] Considering exclusively the act of invasive mass digital surveillance (and not, for example, the alleged arbitrary detention or torture of Uyghurs), if this scenario took place where the ICC would have jurisdiction, the inhumane act could be the crime against humanity of persecution as explained in the previous section, or other inhumane acts (the definition of which was explained in section II.B.ii).[157] As analysed in relation to gravity, the digital surveillance used against the population both outside and inside their homes is inhumane, as they are stripped of all sense of privacy and prohibited from expressing their identities. This element would therefore also likely be met.

Further, the digital surveillance methods used by the Chinese government are arguably a key part of the systemic oppression of Uyghurs and aimed at maintaining such a regime, which are required elements of the crime of apartheid.[158] It has been reported that Chinese security agency scientists have been working to develop technologies that will be able to racially distinguish Han Chinese from Uyghurs and other minorities.[159] This is already the case for facial recognition cameras employed in Xinjiang, but multiple patents for new innovations have been filed by Chinese scientists, including for genetic tests that can determine whether an unidentified sample is Han Chinese or Uyghur.[160] This suggests a potential desire by the Chinese government to be able to separate out Uyghurs from the majority population and impose measures, including draconian levels of surveillance, to suppress the group. As stated by a witness quoted in a report by Amnesty International who noticed Uyghurs being subjected to more surveillance checks than others at a train station, the government official in the station affirmed that 'Uyghurs have to be treated differently because there are no Han terrorists'.[161] It is therefore plausible that both the actus reus and men rea elements of apartheid would be met if the ICC had jurisdiction, as mass digital surveillance is used to systemically oppress a racial group and to maintain that regime.

[155] B Crane, 'A Tale of Two Chinese Muslim Minorities' (The Diplomat, 22 August 2014) thediplomat.com/2014/08/a-tale-of-two-chinese-muslim-minorities/.

[156] Rome Statute Elements of Crimes art 7(1)(j)(2).

[157] See s II.B.ii of this chapter.

[158] Rome Statute Elements of Crimes arts 7(1)(j)(4) and (5).

[159] M Munsterhjelm, 'Scientists Are Aiding Apartheid in China' (Just Security, 18 June 2019) www.justsecurity.org/64605/scientists-are-aiding-apartheid-in-china/.

[160] ibid.

[161] Amnesty International (n 115).

B. Gravity

The gravity of the harm inflicted in this case example arguably meets the threshold for prosecution in terms of its nature, manner of commission, scale, and impact. However, before considering these elements, it is important to note that in this scenario and unlike the first case example which consisted of a single incident, gravity may be assessed for the cumulative effect of individual acts of surveillance. Although it could be argued that individual acts of surveillance (ie only cameras installed outside mosques for a time-limited period) may not be grave enough to constitute an international crime in terms of the severity of the harm in comparison with crimes traditionally recognised by ICL,[162] in this case study, the cumulative harm of all the digital surveillance measures is what creates the ever-present sense of invasiveness and chilling effects on freedom of expression, which I will argue does meet the gravity threshold. This method of assessing gravity of cumulative acts as opposed to individual acts is particularly important for the crime of persecution, for which as stated by the ICTY Trial Chamber in the *Kupreškić et al.* judgment:

> discriminatory acts charged as persecution must not be considered in isolation. Some of the acts mentioned above may not, in and of themselves, be so serious as to constitute a crime against humanity. For example, restrictions placed on a particular group to curtail their rights to participate in particular aspects of social life (such as visits to public parks, theatres or libraries) constitute discrimination, which is in itself a reprehensible act; however, they may not in and of themselves amount to persecution. These acts must not be considered in isolation but examined in their context and weighed for their cumulative effect.[163]

The ICTY Trial Chamber emphasises here that in the context of a crime like persecution, which is often comprised of multiple discriminatory acts or policies targeting a particular group, it flows logically that the assessment of gravity would be based on the collective effect of the acts.[164] This is also the case for other international crimes besides those perpetrated against a group – as argued by Lopez,

[162] See the discussion of the harms of genocide, crimes against humanity, and torture in ch 3.

[163] *Kupreškić et al* Trial Judgment (n 130) [615]. The Trial Chamber also cited to cases concerning the persecution of Jewish people, including the *Justice* case at Nuremberg Military Tribunal III, which found that 'the record contains innumerable acts of persecution of individual Poles and Jews, but to consider these cases as isolated and unrelated instances of perversion of justice would be to overlook the very essence of the offence charged in the indictment', and also the *Artukovic* case at the Zagreb District Court, which found that '"[t]he obligation of wearing a sign to signify Jewish origin . . . was not only inhuman behaviour [with regard] to the whole people, but also a revealing foreboding of death". It is not each individual act, but rather their cumulative effect that matters'; see *Kupreškić et al* Trial Judgment (n 130) fn 895.

[164] Of course, persecution may still be assessed based on one singular harmful act where appropriate, as long as there was still intention to discriminate on one of the listed grounds, see *Prosecutor v Vasiljević* (Judgment) IT-98-32-A, Appeals Chamber (25 February 2004) [113]; *Blaškic* Appeal Judgment (n 70) [135].

violations of international law may be deemed grave when the individual acts acutely harm a limited number of individuals, or when they are 'so widespread and systematic that the cumulative harm is severe'.[165] This is illustrated, for instance, by the requirement in the Rome Statute that crimes against humanity be part of a widespread or systematic attack against a civilian population,[166] which implies that potential crimes can be assessed cumulatively alongside other acts that render them part of the widespread or systematic attack. In addition, the Inter-American Commission on Rights (IACHR) has applied rules concerning 'grave' violations to 'both contexts of widespread and systematic violations' and 'to certain violations that, in particular circumstances of the case, are of a significant level of gravity'.[167] Further, in its Policy on the Crime of Gender Persecution, the ICC OTP explicitly noted that in regards to persecution, 'recognising the cumulative effect of such acts may inform the Office's evaluation of the gravity of a case'.[168] These examples help to illustrate that gravity may be assessed based on the cumulative effect of multiple acts, and moreover that such an assessment is actually encouraged with respect to systemic alleged crimes like persecution.

Moving on to the assessment of gravity in this example, as was considered in chapter four concerning the harms of mass surveillance, the nature of the harm in this case study is that of a severe invasion of privacy, the constant feeling of being watched, and a loss of dignity, all which can lead to chilling effects on freedom of expression.[169] These constitute serious psychological harms, and also lead to the suppression of the group's cultural and religious identity. Applying this to the situation in Xinjiang, in addition to psychological ailments that accompany the feeling of being watched,[170] the mass digital surveillance employed against the Uyghurs could (a) have a chilling effect that causes the group to abandon their cultural and religious practices, and freedom of expression,[171] and (b) have a conforming effect that results in Uyghurs adapting the mainstream Han culture, both of which would be detrimental to diversity and could ultimately lead to the extinction of the Uyghur culture. For instance, concerning chilling effects, as reported by the Subcommittee on International Human Rights at the House of Commons in Canada, the surveillance in Xinjiang has resulted in many Uyghurs avoiding family members, friends, and acquaintances in public spaces out of fear of exhibiting their cultural identity.[172] Further, in a brief submitted to the Subcommittee, a

[165] R Lopez, 'The Law of Gravity' (2020) 58 *Columbia Journal of Transnational Law* 567, 572.
[166] Rome Statute art 7(1).
[167] *Vera-Vera v Ecuador* (19 May 2011) 226 T 114; Lopez (n 165) 604–05.
[168] Office of the Prosecutor, Policy on the Crime of Gender Persecution (7 December 2022).
[169] See ch 4, s IV.A of this book, particularly the discussion of Foucault, Fanon, and Richards.
[170] For example, as noted in ch 4, s IV.A, surveillance increases anxiety, insomnia, fatigue, nightmares, and other forms of psychological distress; F Fanon, *Rencontre de la société et de la Psychiatrie: Notes de cours, Tunis 1959–60* (edited by Bensalem, Université d'Oran 1984); ME Kaminski and S Witnov, 'The Conforming Effect: First Amendment Implications of Surveillance, Beyond Chilling Speech' (2014) 49 *University of Richmond Law Review* 465.
[171] N Coca, 'The slow creep and chilling effect of China's censorship' (World Uyghur Congress, 22 August 2016) www.uyghurcongress.org/en/the-slow-creep-and-chilling-effect-of-chinas-censorship/.
[172] Canada House of Commons (n 124) 24.

witness stated that when he visited Xinjiang in 2018, none of his long-term Uyghur friends would meet with him out of a fear of being seen associating with foreigners, which is 'one of the criteria that made a Uyghur "untrustworthy"'.[173] Regarding the conforming effects, aside from the fact that many Uyghurs are forced to abandon their language and religion and assimilate into mainstream Chinese culture in re-education camps,[174] the knowledge that they are being monitored and could be marked suspicious for expressing their culture likely leaves little choice but to conform to the 'non-suspicious' majority way of life. These harms are similar in nature and gravity to those considered in chapters two and three in relation to the loss of 'cultural richness' as described by Arendt,[175] as the Uyghurs are pressured to suppress their cultural practices and to conform to the mainstream culture.

In the present case of Xinjiang, the digital element significantly exacerbates the harms of surveillance – prior to the availability of technologies such as cameras, facial recognition, and 'wifi-sniffers', surveillance was limited mainly to public spaces, however it is now ever-present, both inside and outside the home and at all hours of the day and authorities have the ability to quickly analyse the resultant data.[176] The manner of commission of the surveillance through digital means contributes to its extremely invasive nature. The Chinese government has reportedly required social media platforms such as WeChat (a dominant platform in China) to allow the State to monitor user activity, in addition to forcing users to provide voice recordings and facial scans to register for the platform along with their national IDs.[177] Platforms like WeChat (a messaging, social media, and mobile payment app) are vital for individuals to be able to communicate with friends and family and pay for goods and services, and so requiring users to agree to being monitored to use them essentially forces them to choose between accessing a necessary service to live in the digital age and retaining (at least some of) their privacy. In addition, the government has allegedly forced all residents of Xinjiang to download the app JingWang, which allows the State to monitor the data on personal devices, including the content a user views online (such as social media websites or banking information) and files stored on the device.[178]

[173] ibid.

[174] OHCHR, 'Assessment of human rights concerns in the Xinjiang Uyghur Autonomous Region, People's Republic of China' (31 August 2022) www.ohchr.org/sites/default/files/documents/countries/2022-08-31/22-08-31-final-assesment.pdf.

[175] See ch 2, s II and ch 3, s II of this book.

[176] However, although it may be exacerbated by the development of new technologies, mass surveillance by States is not new. For a historical overview, see D Lyon, 'Situating Surveillance: History, Technology, Culture' in K Boersma, R Van Brakel, C Fonio, and P Wagenaar (eds), *Histories of State Surveillance in Europe and Beyond* (Routledge, 2014) 32–46.

[177] R Smith, 'Corporate Violations of Human Rights: Addressing the Coordinated Surveillance and Persecution of the Uyghur People by the Chinese State and Chinese Corporations' (2021) 49 *Georgia Journal of International and Comparative Law* 641, 650; S McDonell, 'China social media: WeChat and the Surveillance State' (BBC News, 7 June 2019) www.bbc.co.uk/news/blogs-china-blog-48552907.

[178] Smith, ibid, 650–51; J Cox, 'Chinese Government Forces Residents To Install Surveillance App With Awful Security' (Vice, 9 April 2018) www.vice.com/en/article/ne94dg/jingwang-app-no-encryption-china-force-install-urumqi-xinjiang.

Further, as revealed in the leaked internal documents known as the 'China Cables', such mobile phone applications are also used to track Xinjiang Uyghurs living abroad.[179] Therefore, Uyghurs residing in the Xinjiang region and even outside of China know that virtually everything they do on their mobile phones, tablets, or computers is shared with the government.

Aside from surveillance online and on their personal devices, the Uyghur population is also subjected to monitoring both inside and outside the home. As reported by Human Rights Watch, networks of automated systems operate throughout the region, including iris scanners, surveillance cameras with facial recognition, automated licence plate recognition, and infrared capabilities, and security checkpoints and visitor monitoring systems.[180] Cameras are installed everywhere, including streets, doorways, shops, and mosques,[181] which also contribute to the scale and impact of the alleged crimes. Vehicles are also subject to mandatory location trackers, and even kitchen knives are required to be tracked using QR codes that include the owner's ID number, photo, ethnicity, and address.[182] As suggested in leaked police database documents, these technologies are used to help monitor civilians for signs of 'religious enthusiasm' (ie simply going to a mosque, praying, or eating traditional Uyghur cuisine) that are generally equated with extremism.[183] Therefore, after the surveillance data is collected, it is then processed and sorted in a discriminatory manner, designating certain individuals as suspicious or extremist.[184] Concerning this point, the Office of the United Nations High Commissioner (OHCHR) cautioned in its report on Xinjiang that associating 'extremism' with certain religious and cultural practices 'carries inherent risk of unnecessary, disproportionate, and discriminatory application to the ethnic and religious communities concerned'.[185]

The nature of this harm has been well characterised by Martinez-Aranda in the context of electronic monitoring used against migrants, namely that the digital component is used as a form of 'extended punishment'.[186] In this sense, the use of technology ensures that '[c]onfinement is no longer geographically and temporally specific', as immigrants 'carry the surveillance of detention with them wherever they go'.[187] Martinez-Aranda describes such monitoring technologies as 'tools of legal violence enacted by the State' and 'electronic leashes' that have serious psychological effects on individuals, including the constant fear of being watched and caught doing something 'wrong', the vulnerability to being detained or expelled on any occasion, and difficulties with maintaining self-respect and

[179] Allen-Ebrahimian (n 132).
[180] Human Rights Watch (n 132) 24.
[181] Buckley, Mozur, and Ramzy (n 132).
[182] ibid.
[183] Grauer (n 132).
[184] ibid.
[185] OHCHR (n 174) [35].
[186] MG Martinez-Aranda, 'Extended Punishment: Criminalising Immigrants through Surveillance Technology' (2022) 48 *Journal of Ethnic and Migration Studies* 74–91, 75.
[187] ibid.

dignity despite being labelled criminal or suspicious.[188] These harms are similar to those described in Citron and Solove's 'typology of privacy harms', which in addition to psychological and autonomy harms, includes physical, economic, reputation, relationship, and discrimination harms all associated with violations of privacy.[189]

These findings can be applied to the situation in Xinjiang where Uyghurs are allegedly monitored by the Chinese government in a way that seriously infringes upon their expression, autonomy, and privacy. In the digital age where it is essential to use the internet for basic necessities and communications, and where monitoring devices may be placed virtually anywhere, this threat of surveillance is arguably even more fear-inducing and likely results in severe psychological effects. For example, as stated by a young Uyghur woman under the pseudonym Maysem when interviewed about her experiences living in Xinjiang, her family was required to install a government camera in their living room.[190] Maysem said that this was 'devastating' for her and her mother, as '[t]he home was always the place where all of us could do whatever we wanted to do. A personal place, a place of privacy. I could read and talk and speak my mind'.[191] Following the installation of the camera, they 'didn't dare lay out their usual books or hold their candid discussions', and 'the absence of conversation was unbearable'.[192] This trauma followed Maysem even after she left Xinjiang to live in Turkey. She stated, '[w]hen I picked up my smartphone or opened my laptop, I flet like a machine was watching me, judging me, thinking about me', that 'she couldn't think or feel at all' anymore and that she would regularly check her home for cameras and surveillance devices.[193]

The knowledge that one could be monitored at any time or place, even inside the home, can instil a distressing sense of invasiveness and a loss of dignity, and in line with the literature and example mentioned above,[194] would likely deter individuals from expressing themselves in a way that the State does not approve of. This level of surveillance that is only possible through the use of digital technologies, likely combined with the alleged threat of physical detention in internment camps,[195] can result in chilling and conforming effects that infringe upon the Uyghurs' freedom of expression as a form of persecution. Further, as theorised

[188] ibid.

[189] D Citron and DJ Solove, 'Privacy Harms' (2022) 102 *Boston University Law Review* 793.

[190] G Cain, *The Perfect Police State: An Undercover Odyssey into China's Terrifying Surveillance Dystopia of the Future* (Hachette Book Group, 2021) 114.

[191] ibid 115.

[192] ibid.

[193] ibid 182.

[194] ibid; Martinez-Aranda (n 186); J Penney, 'Cybersecurity, Human Rights, and Empiricism: The Case of Digital Surveillance' in P Cornish (ed), *The Oxford Handbook of Cyber Security* (OUP, 2021) 411.

[195] Human Rights Watch (n 132); Amnesty International (n 115). It is also worth noting that the surveillance methods employed against the Uyghur population are not all digital – for example, as mentioned in the Human Rights Watch report (at 22), the Chinese government imposes a 'ten households, one unit' policy to encourage people to monitor each other, especially Muslims. However, as this book is focused on digital harm, only digital surveillance methods will be considered in this case study.

by Citron and Solove, the intense violation of privacy can result in discrimination harms, which manifest in feelings of 'shame and stigma as societal consequences of further entrenching disadvantages to marginalized groups'.[196] These feelings may result in grave psychological effects like those previously recognised in ICL jurisprudence for crimes like torture, outrages upon personal dignity, and genocide, where an individual knows that they are viewed as less than human and not worthy of respect.[197] As well summarised by Maya Wang, Associate Director of the Asia division at Human Rights Watch:

> Xinjiang really shows how privacy is a gateway right, where if you have no privacy, that's where you see that you have no freedoms as a human being at all. You don't have the right to practice your religion, you don't have the right to be who you are, you don't even have the right to think your own thoughts because your thoughts are being parsed out by these incessant visits and incessantly monitored by surveillance systems, whether they're human or artificial, and evaluated constantly for your level of loyalty to the government.[198]

IV. Analysis and Conclusion

While the two case studies considered above explored very different types of digital harms, there are some overarching themes that arise in reference to how they may be best accommodated by the ICL framework. First, it can be questioned how digital harms should be criminalised and prosecuted, and more specifically whether they should be included as acts of existing crimes or aggravating factors at sentencing, or warrant their own offences. Concerning the first case study, the act of filming and sharing footage of Foley's murder could be recognised as an aggravating factor during sentencing for the 'physical' crime of murder or an outrage upon personal dignity for the desecration of a corpse. This occurred in some similar domestic war crimes cases, for example in Germany, where a man was sentenced to 8.5 years in prison for recording footage of himself cutting off the ears and noses of already-dead Syrian soldiers in Aleppo, firing bullets into their heads, and kicking the heads until brain matter leaked out.[199] In this case, the footage was not shared on social media, but the defendant sent the video to contacts on his mobile phone.[200] The relatively higher sentence of 8.5 years reflects the fact that he was also convicted of membership in a terrorist organisation abroad, which had a penalty of six years under German law – the fact that the defendant recorded

[196] Citron and Solove (n 189).
[197] See ch 3 of this book.
[198] Grauer (n 132).
[199] Eurojust (n 58); *Prosecutor v Abdelkarim-El-B* (Judgment) 5-3 StE 4/16–4–3/16, Higher Regional Court, Frankfurt am Main (8 November 2016).
[200] ibid.

the gruesome and degrading footage and shared it aggravated the sentence by 2.5 years to eight years and six months.[201]

However, as argued throughout this book, the digital harm of sharing footage online is grave enough to constitute a standalone offence, and as demonstrated in section II.B,[202] can fulfil the necessary elements of war crimes and crimes against humanity. Moreover, for the first case study, there could be aggravating factors to consider in addition to the crime of sharing the footage online, including the nature of what was recorded and the audience of the website it was shared to. For instance, the Rules of Procedure and Evidence list multiple factors that could be considered aggravating, but the commission of the crime 'where the victim is particularly defenceless' and 'with particular cruelty' may be most relevant to this case.[203] This is because Foley was a prisoner of ISIS, and in the video is shown kneeling in an orange jumpsuit next to a man holding a knife, clearly being forced to address his family to the camera and unable to defend himself. Moreover, although committing and filming any method of murder would be cruel, beheadings are especially brutal and degrading.

In addition, posing the body and the public nature of the forum chosen to share the video could also be argued to exacerbate the cruelty of the offence, which is supported by domestic case law. For instance, the Frankfurt am Main Higher Regional Court in Germany referenced the level of privacy settings used on the social media account of the accused.[204] In that case, a man was sentenced to two years' imprisonment for war crimes for posing in three photographs with severed heads of enemy combatants impaled on metal rods.[205] The photographs were then shared to Facebook by a friend of the defendant to a 'page with limited privacy settings'.[206] In the judgment, the Court emphasised the fact that the accused clearly posed for the photos and the public nature of the Facebook page without privacy settings, both of which added to the degradation to the victim.[207] To apply this to the present case, it could be argued that the fact that the ISIS members shared the video to YouTube, a public website where anyone can access videos, should aggravate the sentence because it ensured a wider audience than uploading to a private web page. In addition, although the militant in the video did not pose with the body, the body was manipulated after death and posed with the head on the back, which instils a greater sense of dehumanisation and a loss of dignity than if the body were not pictured or posed. This could also therefore warrant a harsher punishment and aggravate the sentence.

[201] ibid.
[202] See s II.B of this chapter.
[203] ICC RPE Rule 145(2)(b).
[204] Eurojust (n 58); *Prosecutor v Aria Ladjedvardi* (Judgment) 5-3 StE 2/16-4-1/16, Higher Regional Court, Frankfurt am Main (12 July 2016).
[205] ibid.
[206] ibid.
[207] ibid.

Regarding the second case study, although I argue that the elements for persecution or apartheid may be met in an instance of digital mass surveillance weaponised against a minority group, it is worth considering that these offences may not capture the true nature of the harm in a way that would be meaningful for victims or for establishing a historical record of the crimes. This is because the terms 'persecution' and 'apartheid' do not illustrate on their own how the digital element drives the offence, which in addition to the issue of whether the harm perpetrated in the first case study should be criminalised as an 'add on' to existing crimes or prosecuted on its own, relates to the expressivist function of international criminal justice considered in chapter five.[208] In this respect, prosecuting digital harm as its own crime and modifying the law to include labels which reflect the true harm of the offence are both ways to express the seriousness and wrongfulness of digital harms and demonstrate that they are worthy of being treated similarly to traditional core ICL crimes. Although this chapter only explored the application of existing offences and their elements to the case examples, in the future, discussions should continue surrounding proposed new labels such as 'cultural genocide' or 'digital apartheid'.[209] This is important because in an increasingly digital world, offences perpetrated using technology will only continue to increase, and it will be critical that their gravity is recognised going forward in order to ensure tailored and meaningful justice for victims.

Further, while there will likely be obstacles that ICCTs will need to overcome to successfully adjudicate digital harms like the ones considered in the two case studies, such as through revamping their technological capacity and expertise or fostering better cooperation regimes with social media companies, it is important to remember that challenges exist for prosecuting any international crime and may be overcome. For instance, while it may be easy to dismiss criminalisation of digital harms under ICL because it would be too difficult to do so, progress made in other areas, such as movements to investigate and prosecute environmental harms,[210] demonstrates that ICL does have the capacity to progress in the modern age. In addition, although there were clear obstacles identified in each case study, such as issues with jurisdiction, most of those challenges did not stem from the fact that the harms in question were digital and would arise in cases of 'traditional' crimes as well. The two case studies combined thus illustrate the potential for ICL to accommodate a range of digital harms, while also revealing more clearly where the gaps lie.

[208] See ch 5, s II.C of this book.

[209] These terms are considered in detail in ch 5, s III.A of this book.

[210] See, eg Office of the Prosecutor, Policy on Addressing Environmental Harm Through the Rome Statute (December 2025).

8

Conclusion

In this book, I provide a novel analysis that answers the question of how digital harms may be criminalised and prosecuted under international criminal law (ICL). Drawing upon theories of harm and criminalisation, and considering the practical barriers to be faced by international criminal courts and tribunals (ICCTs) in a digital age, this book lays the groundwork for essential future conversations about how to achieve redress for victims of violence perpetrated using technology through ICL. Overall, I argue that digital harms warrant the attention of ICCTs and that until such harms are properly recognised by ICL, there will continue to be a gap in international justice and accountability.

To answer my first research sub-question of what digital harm is and how it is similar or different to the types of harm recognised by core international crimes, I have demonstrated that digital technologies have the capacity to enable a wide array of harms that are grave enough to warrant criminalisation under ICL. These harms are similar in their nature to those already addressed in ICL frameworks and in scholarship contextualised in harm and criminal law, as they can manifest at the individual, group, or collective levels and in both physical and non-physical ways.

Concerning my second research sub-question ('What are the reasons digital harm should be criminalised under ICL?'), I have drawn upon theories of criminalisation common to ICL and applied them to digital harms. In summary, I argue that the need for criminalising digital harms with a nexus to the perpetration of international crimes could be framed through harm prevention (via the harm principle), a need to punish and deter wrongdoing, or the expressivist idea that such criminalisation would send a message about the values of the international community. Each theory of criminalisation has its weaknesses, but overall it is clear that there are a variety of reasons for criminalising the digital harms considered in this book under ICL. To then address the third sub-question of *how* digital harm should be criminalised, the best way to go about the criminalisation of digital harm will vary depending on the ability of the harm to match the elements of existing international crimes. For instance, online hate speech that incites genocide can be understood as a traditional international crime simply being perpetrated using a new forum, as it does not stray much at its root from incitement via offline means. In addition, the harm associated with sharing footage of violent crimes to social media is similar in its degrading, humiliating nature to that of the war crime of outrages upon personal dignity. In these instances where the digital harm is similar (or even the same) as the 'traditional' harm associated with an international crime, I argue that ICL prosecutors and judges should be able to interpret these digital harms within the existing law given that the elements of crimes can be constituted. However, where the digital harm is particularly novel and does not fit as well within traditional offences, such as the use of technology to monitor and suppress the rights of a cultural group, existing frameworks may be insufficient to address the full scope of the harm and will need to be amended.

To answer my final research sub-question of what challenges may arise if digital harms are criminalised and adjudicated at ICCTs, I argue that although there will be challenges faced regarding criminalising and adjudicating digital harms at ICCTs, including (but not limited to) jurisdictional hurdles, meeting the gravity threshold, or obtaining information from relevant actors, these challenges are not impossible to overcome. Further, the existence of such challenges is not unique to digital harms and should not be any more difficult to resolve than issues that arose for previous novelties in ICL (for example, the introduction of expert witness testimony, or the prosecution of sexual and gender based crimes). For the international justice project to maintain its legitimacy and purpose, ICL must be able to adapt to the harms of the future, especially as new technologies (and the threats they pose) will only continue to develop.

There are some additional themes that arise throughout this book. For instance, I stress the need to improve cooperation between ICCTs and States, private companies, and civil society organisations, which will be critical for allowing ICL prosecutors to successfully investigate and prosecute digital harm. While cooperation from States remains essential, cooperation from non-State actors will have a bigger role to play in the digital age. For example, social media companies and digital archival organisations will possess information that could be used as evidence, and thus developing more comprehensive frameworks for cooperation to establish communications channels with the prosecution, defence, and legal representatives of victims will be important. Of course, ICL prosecutors should also endeavour to improve the technological expertise and capacity within their teams, which has already begun given recent developments like Project Harmony at the ICC.

Further, should digital harms be criminalised under ICL, careful attention should be paid to the balancing of rights. For instance, the criminalisation of online speech (including hate speech, disinformation, or footage of crimes) would need to be weighed against the freedom of expression of the uploader. This assessment may be clearer in some situations as opposed to others, such as direct calls for violence versus merely offensive speech, and will have to be done on a case-by-case basis. On this note, the book also emphasises throughout the importance of continuing to respect the rights of the accused and the interests of victims throughout all stages of ICL procedure, including those of privacy and protection from re-traumatisation, which will be especially relevant to some cases involving digital harms.

This book concludes that at present, there are gaps in ICL's ability to accommodate digital harms and in turn provide more tailored justice to victims. Yet, this also means there is an opportunity to develop the law to encompass those harms, either within existing definitions of crimes or as additions to ICL frameworks like the Rome Statute. This book provides the necessary foundation for discussions surrounding this development to assist the law in 'catching up' to modern times, which, as noted in chapter one, is essential for ICL to embrace the ideal of 'kaleidoscopic justice' that emphasises the 'varied, nuanced, ever-changing experience and understandings of justice' in the modern world.[1] Criminalising digital harms would serve the vital expressivist function of sending a message that crimes perpetrated through technology are wrong and will not be tolerated by the modern international community, and as digital technologies are used to inflict different forms of violence each day, it is of extreme importance that this issue continues to grow to the forefront of ICL.

[1] C McGlynn, 'Challenging Anti-carceral Feminism: Criminalisation, Justice and Continuum Thinking' (2022) 93 *Women's Studies International Forum* 102614.

INDEX

www.ingramcontent.com/pod-product-compliance
Ingram Content Group UK Ltd.
Pitfield, Milton Keynes, MK11 3LW, UK
UKHW021115011026
476157UK00003B/71

9 781509 997732